HEMINGWAY'S WARS
PUBLIC AND PRIVATE BATTLES

HEMINGWAY'S WARS
PUBLIC AND PRIVATE BATTLES

Linda Wagner-Martin

UNIVERSITY OF MISSOURI PRESS
COLUMBIA

ISBN: 978-0-8262-2125-4
Library of Congress Control Number: 2017930381
♾™ This paper meets the requirements of the
American National Standard for Permanence of Paper
for Printed Library Materials, Z39.48, 1984.
Typefaces: Caslon and Trajan

For Frederic Svoboda, Alex Vernon, James Meredith,
Kirk Curnutt, Susan Beegel, and Joe Haldeman

CONTENTS

ACKNOWLEDGMENTS

THROUGHOUT SEVERAL DECADES, I have been privileged to use the collections of Hemingway materials—manuscripts, correspondence, and photographs—at the Lilly Library, Indiana University Bloomington; the Harry Ransom Humanities Research Center, University of Texas at Austin; the Beinecke Rare Book & Manuscript Library, Yale University, New Haven, CT; the Firestone Library, Princeton University, Princeton, NJ; and the Ernest Hemingway Research Room at the John F. Kennedy Presidential Library and Museum, Boston, MA. My deep thanks to the staff members who so graciously helped me in these locations, and particular thanks to Megan Desnoyers and Stephen Plotkin, who not only helped with locating photographs of Hemingway but also helped me photograph items (such as the pieces of shrapnel taken from Hemingway's war wound) in the upper-level storage/museum area in the John F. Kennedy Library.

At this point in the twenty-first century, a number of materials previously found only in the manuscript collections are now available in print, but this book also draws from still-unpublished archival texts. For permission to use those words, I am grateful to the sources listed above.

My thanks, too, go to fellow Hemingway scholars Michael Reynolds, Paul Smith, Scott Donaldson, Frederic Svoboda, Alex Vernon, Paul Hendrickson, Bernice Kert, Rose Marie Burwell, Susan Beegel, William White, Gail Sinclair, Allen Joseph, Sarah Wood Anderson, H. R. Stoneback, Amy Strong, Joseph Waldmeir, Jackson Benson, Lawrence Broer, Jim Meredith, Robert Trogdon, Milt Cohen, Kirk Curnutt, Larry Grimes, Jim Plath, Joe Flora, Jennifer Haytock, Valerie Hemingway, Shari Benstock, Debra Moddelmog, Carlos Baker, Bud Rovit, Jim Nagel, Sandy Spanier, Rena Sanderson, and Miriam Mandel. In some respects, this book has become a cooperative effort.

ILLUSTRATIONS

All photographs are used by permission of the Ernest Hemingway Collection, John F. Kennedy Presidential Library and Museum, Boston, MA.

ABBREVIATIONS

The Works of Ernest Hemingway (based on the Cambridge Edition of *The Letters of Ernest Hemingway*)

ARIT	*Across the River and into the Trees*
BL	*By-Line Ernest Hemingway: Selected Articles and Dispatches of Four Decades*
CP	*Complete Poems*
CSS	*The Complete Short Stories of Ernest Hemingway: The Finca Vigía Edition*
DIA	*Death in the Afternoon*
DLT	*Ernest Hemingway, Dateline: Toronto: The Complete "Toronto Star"' Dispatches, 1920–1924*
FC	*"The Fifth Column" and Four Stories of the Spanish Civil War*
FTA	*A Farewell to Arms*
FTA 2012	*A Farewell to Arms*, Hemingway Library Edition, 2012
FWBT	*For Whom the Bell Tolls*
GHOA	*Green Hills of Africa*
HOW	*Hemingway on War*
IIS	*Islands in the Stream*
IOT	*In Our Time*

MAW   *Men at War*

MF   *A Moveable Feast*

MF
restored   *A Moveable Feast* restored edition

OMATS   *The Old Man and the Sea*

SAR   *The Sun Also Rises*

SL   *Ernest Hemingway: Selected Letters, 1917–1961*

THAHN   *To Have and Have Not*

HEMINGWAY'S WARS
PUBLIC AND PRIVATE BATTLES

Wars and Their Omnipresence

IT HAD NOTHING to do with Ernest Miller Hemingway, the pervasive presence of cataclysmic wars during his comparatively short life. Born July 21, 1899, Hemingway was a boy fascinated with the tragedies that accompanied all wars, and from the start of World War I in the spring of 1914, he was a conscientiously thorough student of the science of war. History books were filled with that material: many of the world's great historians were themselves masters of the strategies of warfare. Learning his history battle by battle, Hemingway saw the stuff of war as the reality of people's lives, particularly of men's lives, and he also came to appreciate what historian Paul Fussell terms the "myth" of war. Fussell writes in his study of World War I that the import of the brutal conflicts, and the real meaning of the thousands and thousands of lives lost, lies in "the way the dynamics and iconography of the Great War have proved crucial political, rhetorical, and artistic determinants on subsequent life. At the same time the war was relying on inherited myth, it was generating new myth, and that myth is part of the fibers of our own lives."[1]

Hemingway's son Patrick added his personal comment to the discussion: "How much did his [Hemingway's] going to the wars affect his health and shorten his life? In my opinion, a great deal. As a fortunate American he *chose* to go to war rather than, as an unlucky Spaniard or an even unluckier Pole, have it inevitably come to him."[2] Never drafted yet never avoiding service, Ernest Hemingway showed both his fascination with war and his individual patriotism through his voluntary involvement in much of the military action of the twentieth century.

Focusing on World War I from another perspective, historian James H. Meredith emphasizes the reality of all war—"indiscriminate killing and destruction"—and agrees with the larger assessment of Kirk Curnutt, whom he quotes:

> Of the many displacements experienced by Hemingway's generation, none affected them as intensely as "the Great War," as World War I was called before the rise of Adolf Hitler guaranteed its gruesome sequel. . . . Perhaps the greatest casualty was the idea that war was a noble endeavor fought for patriotism, the honor and glory of sacrifice, and the valiant defense of one's principles and convictions.[3]

As a corollary, Frederick J. Hoffman explains, "The war had itself been so violent a departure from custom, from 'the rules,' that it was almost impossible to return to them. One either went away or tried to change the rules."[4]

In a more expansive sense, historian Wendy Steiner observes,

> The nineteenth-century dream of progress expressed in the plot of social ascent had suffered a death blow. . . . The dislocation brought on by World War I, the fact that even the winners came home to a world they could not live in, provoked a profound analysis of the phenomenon of victimization. Woodrow Wilson's argument for neutrality had been based on the need to avoid the dynamic of physical battle, on the grounds that the difference between winner and loser was too slight.[5]

Elaine Scarry translates these somewhat abstract comments into her self-defined language of pain: "The activity of war is injuring the enemy." She continues that the structure of war "requires both the reciprocal infliction of massive injury and the eventual disowning of the injury so that its attributes can be transferred elsewhere, as they can if they are permitted to cling to the original site of the wound."[6]

The work of Eric Leed focuses on the trauma that returning soldiers experienced. Noting that the incidence of "shell shock" increased *after* the war ended, Leed describes the "profound, deeply internalized disruption of self [that accrued] from this mechanized warfare first experienced in World War I."[7]

Hemingway came of age as the United States finally entered the conflict, graduating from high school in his hometown of Oak Park, Illinois, in the same spring, 1917. It was his insistent pushing to join the war that allowed him to sign up with the American Red Cross the following year and travel to Italy. His choice was a personal effort, one never sanctioned by his middle-class, conservative parents. Given that Hemingway suspected that his damaged left eye would keep him out of service once the United States was officially participating, the choices he made before he sailed to Europe seem prescient.

In high school, Hemingway played at football, swimming, and tennis, wrote for all the school publications (serving as editor of the weekly paper his senior year), participated in musical and dramatic activities, hunted, hiked, camped out, and read voraciously. Because he later so valued relationships with other men who had shared his experiences, his comparative lack of close friendships during his school years may reflect the tight control of his traditional family. Biographer Carlos Baker sees his social patterns as normal, whereas Michael Reynolds notes that a few of Hemingway's classmates remembered him "as a sometime bully . . . or as conceited, bumptious and boastful."[8] From his friend Lewis Clarahan's oral history in Denis Brian's *True Gen*, we know that Hemingway "spent more time with me [Clarahan] than with other friends because we lived on the prairie, and he liked to get out there and shoot and hunt with me. . . . He didn't want to be beaten at anything, always wanted to be number one."[9] As Hemingway matured, he learned to keep his usual competitiveness somewhat disguised.

After graduating from Oak Park High School, Hemingway spent that last summer (as he had the previous summers) living at the family cottage, Windemere, on Walloon Lake in Upper Michigan. There he formed some of the closest friendships he would ever know, with Jim Dilworth and the townspeople, including Native Americans, and with other summer people, such as Carl Edgar and siblings Bill and Katy Smith; he learned to love the immense Michigan forests, the rivers and lakes filled with all varieties of fish, the untouched beauty that taught him a deep understanding of nature.

As summer ended, Hemingway went to Kansas City, where his uncle had arranged that he begin working for the imposing—and highly regarded—*Kansas City Star*. The rookie Hemingway progressed quickly, from his novice standing to being considered a talented, if young, reporter. As he would throughout his life, Hemingway learned from *immersion*: from listening to professional reporters, from hanging out with other beginning writers, from reading, reading, reading the work that others on staff wrote. If anything, Hemingway was a practicing journalist when he ended his seven months in Kansas City. But as he left the *Star*, he did not intend to stay a writer: his aim was to become a soldier, and he showed his wily inventiveness in finding a way to join the European war so that he could absorb as much knowledge of and experience about war as possible.

Ernest Hemingway was one of the bluntest of America's modern writers. As he told Lillian Ross in 1949, in material published in her long-famous *New Yorker* portrait of him, "I am interested in the goddam sad science of war." As he then bragged about his novel in progress, which would become *Across the River and into the Trees*, he told her that this book would "beat" his 1929 *A Farewell to Arms* because "it hasn't got the youth and the ignorance."[10]

No critic has ever accused Hemingway of being a single-themed writer, and even though his first best-seller (and the first of his novels made into a Hollywood film) was the World War I love story *A Farewell to Arms*, he was not typed as a war writer. Yet, retrospectively, he seemed to categorize himself in that way. To Ross he confided that he had spent years working through his experiences in the First World War: "I can remember feeling so awful about the first war that I couldn't write about it for ten years. . . . The wound combat makes in you, as a writer, is a very slow-healing one. I wrote three stories about it in the old days—'In Another Country,' 'A Way You'll Never Be,' and 'Now I Lay Me.'"[11] Not to contradict Hemingway, but it is clear that a number of his early poems, as well as his first novel with Scribner's—*The Sun Also Rises*—also relate to the memories, and the actualities, of that war. His file of early journalistic writing is weighted toward the coverage of European wars that followed World War I; the later writings include his North American Newspaper Alliance (NANA) and *Ken* magazine columns written from and about the Spanish Civil War and his *Collier's* articles about World War II.

It was as a practiced student of war that Hemingway later wrote the introduction to his collection of writings about warfare, *Men at War*, published in 1942 by Crown. *Men at War* was bought avidly by readers who once again faced America's participation in a great European war—this time under a military draft that conscripted men regardless of their class or education. Hemingway announced in that introduction, "This book will not tell you how to die. This book will tell you, though, how all men from the earliest times we know, have fought and died. . . . There are no worse things to be gone through than men have been through before" (*MAW* 5).

The collection was based on the principles he had learned from studying Karl von Clausewitz's *On War*. Hemingway covered many plausible approaches to the study of war—from tactical problems to psychological ones. He drew excerpts for the book from texts written by T. E. Lawrence and Winston Churchill, Richard HilLary, Victor Hugo, Richard Aldington, William Faulkner, and others. In this work, war was Hemingway's subject just as bullfighting was in his 1932 book *Death in the Afternoon*. Hemingway as writer had developed the practice of collecting materials (photographs as well as writings, both by others and by himself) and then, in a different kind of writing process, creating a work more pastiche than narrative, bringing the assembled segments of what he had collected into something new.[12]

Hemingway saw himself as a diligent scholar of whatever subject he chose; for instance, bullfighting was an exotic and genuinely rare field of study in the 1920s, and Hemingway loved it with real passion.[13] But the field of study that he considered his primary province, from his eighteenth year on, was the international science of war. Reminiscing in his *Men at War* introduction, Hemingway recalled that his first involvement—as a volunteer in the Red Cross Ambulance Corps—was based primarily on his sheltered, unrealistic innocence:

> When you go to war as a boy you have a great illusion of immortality. Other people got killed; not you. It can happen to other people; but not to you. Then when you are badly wounded the first time you lose that illusion and you know it can happen to you. After being severely wounded two weeks before my nineteenth birthday I had a bad time until I figured out that nothing could happen to me that had not happened to all men before me. Whatever I had to do men had always done. If they had done it then I would do it too and the best thing was not to worry about it.
>
> I was very ignorant at nineteen and had read little. *(MAW 6)*

As that last sentence suggests, Hemingway's "instruction" about topics always stemmed partly from his reading. Just a cursory glimpse of the books he both owned and borrowed from Sylvia Beach's Shakespeare and Company bookshop in Paris in the 1920s shows that he had read—perhaps more than once—Stendhal's *Charterhouse of Parma, Abbess of Castro*, and *The Red and the Black*; Isaac Babel's *Red Cavalry*; George Moore's *Hail and Farewell*; Leo Tolstoy's *War and Peace*; Henri Barbusse's *Under Fire* and *We Others: Stories of Fate, Love and Pity*; Blasco Ibanez's *Four Horsemen of the Apocalypse*; Victor Hugo's *Les Miserables* and *Ninety-Three* (stories); Ivan Turgenev's *Fathers and Sons, Sportsman's Sketches*, and his poems in prose; Richard Hillary's *Falling through Space*; Marquis James's *They Had Their Hour*; Byron Kennerly's *Eagles Roar!*; Colonel John W. Thomason Jr.'s *Lone Star Preacher*; and others.[14]

Prominent as well in the listings are English-language writings about World War I, such as Mildred Aldrich's *A Hilltop on the Marne*, John Dos Passos's *Three Soldiers*, Alden Brooks's *Fighting Men*, Private 19022's *Her Privates We*, Richard Aldington's *Roads to Glory*, Ford Madox Ford's *Good Soldier*, Charles Nordhoff and James Norman Hall's *Falcons of France*, Winston Churchill's *A Roving Commission*, T. E. Lawrence's *Seven Pillars of Wisdom*, James Hilton's *War Years*, e. e. cummings's *Enormous Room*, William Faulkner's *Dr. Martino* (stories) and *Soldiers' Pay*, Thomas Boyd's *Through the Wheat*, Willa Cather's *One of Ours*, Virginia Woolf's *Jacob's Room* and *Mrs. Dalloway*,

Thomas Beer's *Fair Rewards*, and James Boyd's *Long Hunt*. Hemingway also owned numerous volumes of Rudyard Kipling's writings. Today's reader needs to understand that Hemingway was seldom candid about the ways in which his reading provided information that he used in his own writings. He avoided specifics about practices that he seemed to consider private, even secret. He later admitted, in *Green Hills of Africa*, how central, even crucial, his knowledge of war was to *all* his writing:

> I thought . . . about what a great advantage an experience of war was to a writer. It was one of the major subjects and certainly one of the hardest to write truly of and those writers who had not seen it were always very jealous and tried to make it seem unimportant, or abnormal, or a disease as a subject, while, really, it was just something quite irreplaceable that they had missed. (*GHOA* 70)

Carlos Baker recounted numerous times that Hemingway talked about the importance of writing about war. "War, he said, was the best subject of all. It offered maximum material combined with maximum action. Everything was speeded up and the writer who had participated in a war gained such a mass of experience as he would normally have to wait a lifetime to get."[15]

The 1942 printing of Hemingway's *Men at War* also included the whole text of Stephen Crane's 1895 novella *The Red Badge of Courage*. When Hemingway's book was reedited for its 1950s publication, the Crane selection was omitted because Hemingway wanted to add a number of World War II selections, some of which had not yet been published in 1942. But in his introduction to that reissue of *Men at War*, he praised Crane lavishly, saying that he could not excerpt a selection from *The Red Badge of Courage* because "it is all as much of one piece as a great poem is" (*MAW* 10).[16]

As Hemingway's introduction made clear, he was consistently interested in the physical and mental condition of men who had fought, who had lived through the brutality, the inhumanity, of warfare. Dedicated, as the later issue of the collection also was, to his three sons—Jack, the oldest, himself about to fight in World War II; and Patrick and Gregory, who were schoolboys throughout the conflict that took both their older half-brother and their father into harm's way—Hemingway saw *Men at War* as a manual of conduct, a way of explaining the code of bravery that warfare mandated. He wrote,

> Worrying does no good. . . . A good soldier does not worry. He knows that nothing happens until it actually happens and you live your life up until then. Danger only exists at the moment of danger. To live properly in war, the individual

eliminates all such things as potential danger. . . . Cowardice, as distinguished from panic, is almost always simply a lack of ability to suspend the functioning of the imagination. Learning to suspend your imagination and live completely in the very second of the present minute with no before and no after is the greatest gift a soldier can acquire. (*MAW* 17)

In 1940, Hemingway wrote a preface to Gustav Regler's novel about the Spanish Civil War, *The Great Crusade*. In that set of remarks, he described the humanity of soldiers in battle, even when they thought they would win. His emphasis in this preface falls on statements like this: "There is no man alive today who has not cried at a war if he was at it long enough. Sometimes it is after a battle; sometimes it is when someone that you love is killed; sometimes it is from a great injustice to another; sometimes it is at the disbanding of a corps or a unit that has endured and accomplished together and now will never be together again. But all men at war cry sometimes, from Napoleon, the greatest butcher, down."[17]

In his description of the narrative, Hemingway told readers that Regler's story is about "the golden age of the International Brigades when all their gold was iron." He dwelt on the greatness of both the Eleventh and the Twelfth Brigades, saying of the latter that it was "where my heart was. . . . The period of fighting when we thought that the Republic could win the Spanish civil war was the happiest period of our lives. We were truly happy then for when people died it seemed as though their death was justified and unimportant. For they died for something that they believed in and that was going to happen."[18]

He also described Regler's severe wounding ("a hole in the small of his back which uncovered the kidneys and exposed the spinal cord and that was so big, where the pound and a half piece of steel drove through Gustav's body from side to side, that the doctor pushed his whole gloved hand through in cleaning it") and ended the preface with a plea for giving asylum to the veterans of the Spanish conflict, regardless of their nationality. When the novel appeared, Regler was stranded with other veterans at Ellis Island. Hemingway became active in collecting funds to provide legal aid for the forgotten veterans.

Hemingway made a similar plea in a signed mimeographed letter that was widely distributed and appeared in his foreword to Joseph North's 1939 *Men in the Ranks*. There he insisted that honoring the dead in Spain mandated "seeing that no man who fought in Spain should lack proper medical care and the opportunity to earn his living." Regler's case was difficult because he was German, though he was anti-Nazi.

From the characteristics of individual men, braving their natural fear to accomplish the greater good of a battle's outcome, to a recognition of the empathetic humanity that all such warriors know, to the men's camaraderie, as Hemingway described these things in his fiction during the last several decades of his writing, the author assumed the accomplished, mature voice of a veteran. He first employed this tone in his three-part preface to a collection of works by artist Luis Quintanilla, *All the Brave, Paintings by Luis Quintanilla*, where he mourned the loss of Quintanilla's lifetime of work during the Spanish Civil War and its wide-reaching destruction in general. Hemingway commented there that he hated war, that he had never liked it, but that he had "a small talent for it." In recounting the international character of the men assembled to try to keep Spain free from fascism, Hemingway commented that the difference between wartime and his earlier years in Madrid, when he wrote and Quintanilla painted—the two meeting for drinks in the evening once their work was done—was that "seeing a signboard saying 350 kilometers to such and such a town, you knew that if you followed that road you would get to that town. While now you know that if you follow that road you will get killed."[19]

Hemingway spoke specifically about his friend Quintanilla's role in the military, saying he

> led the attack on the Montana Barracks that saved Madrid for the government. Later, studying military books at night while he commanded troops in the daytime, he fought in the pines and the gray rocks of the Guadarrama; on the yellow plain of the Tagus; in the streets of Toledo, and back to the suburbs of Madrid where men with rifles, hand grenades, and bundled sticks of dynamite faced tanks, artillery, and planes, and died so that their country might be free.[20]

He used the occasion as well to promote the writer's obligation to write only the truth, saying he would like to write about the Spanish conflict as "cleanly and as truly as Luis Quintanilla draws and etches. War is a hateful thing. It is unexcusable [*sic*] except in self-defense. In writing of it, a writer should be absolutely truthful because, of all things, it has the least truth written about it. . . . To write about it truly you have to know a great deal about cowardice and heroism. For there is much of both, and of simple human endurance, and it is a long time since anyone has balanced them truly."[21]

Hemingway's animosity toward war peppers his articles written about the Spanish civil conflict. From the first of these—published through NANA in mid-March, 1937—the unelaborated detail brings home the catastrophic message. "A trimotor bomber had just come over, with two pursuit planes as escort, and had dropped its load of bombs on the town, killing seven and wounding thirty-four. Only by a half-hour had we missed flying into the dog-fight in which the Insurgent planes were driven off by Government pursuit ships" (*BL* 257). His April 11, 1937, NANA column, "Shelling of Madrid," describes the bombing casualties, after "the shells came with the sudden flash that a short circuit makes and then the roaring crash of granite-dust. During the morning, twenty-two shells came into Madrid. They killed an old woman returning home from market, dropping her in a huddled black heap of cloth-ing, with one leg, suddenly detached, whirling against the wall of an adjoining house" (*BL* 259).

In Hemingway's May 22, 1937, NANA dispatch, he described the results of a shelling secondhand: his chauffeur, David, came to him after going to get gas for the auto.

> "Come and look at the car," he said. "It's full of blood. It's a terrible thing." He was pretty shaky. He had a dark face and his lips trembled.
> "What was it?"
> "A shell hit a line of women waiting to buy food. It killed seven. I took three to the hospital."
> "Good boy."
> "But you can't imagine it," he said. "It's terrible. I did not know there were such things." *(BL 271)*

Several of Hemingway's Spanish Civil War articles are themselves examples of the most masterful reportage: "The Fall of Teruel," December 13, 1937, involved Hemingway not only as observer but as participant. He survived the outright warfare, along with his correspondent friends Herbert L. Matthews and Tom Delmer, and walked through the carnage into the town that had once been "that great rebel strong point." As they neared the town, they found "in the road a dead officer who had led a company in the final assault. . . . We lifted him, still limp and warm, to the side of the road and left him with his serious waxen face where tanks would not bother him now nor anything else and went on into town" (*BL* 280).

Amid Hemingway's relentlessly powerful dispatches was his *Ken* article "A Program for U.S. Realism," which opens,

> Question: What is War?
> Answer: War is an act of violence intended to compel our opponent to fulfill our will.

Question: What is the primary aim of war?

Answer: The primary aim of war is to disarm the enemy.

Question: What are the necessary steps to achieve this?

Answer: First; the military power must be destroyed, that is, reduced to such a state that it will not be able to carry on the war. Second; the country must be conquered. For out of the country a new military force may be formed. Third; the will of the enemy must be subdued.

Question: Are there any ways of imposing our will on the enemy without fulfilling these three conditions?

Answer: Yes. There is invasion, that is the occupation of the enemy's territory, not with a view to keeping it, but in order to levy contributions on it, or to devastate it.

Later in the lengthy discourse, Hemingway dropped his scholarly tone and pointed out, "There has been war in Spain, now, for two years. There has been war in China for a year." Then he returned to the scholarly voice, with new emphasis: "Now what is war again? We say war is murder, that it is inexcusable, that it is indefensible, that no objective can justify an offensive war" (*BL* 290–91).

Hemingway's tone of lament came through clearly again in his foreword to the 1946 collection *Treasury for the Free World*. Here he looked hard at the dynamics of World War II, the war he had come to know better than he knew either World War I or the Spanish Civil War.

We have waged war in the most ferocious and ruthless way that it has ever been waged. We waged it against fierce and ruthless enemies that it was necessary to destroy. Now we have destroyed one of our enemies and forced the capitulation of the other. For the moment we are the strongest power in the world. It is very important that we do not become the most hated. . . .

We need to study and understand certain basic problems of our world as they were before Hiroshima to be able to continue, intelligently, to discover how some of them have changed and how they can be settled justly now that a new weapon [the atomic bomb] has become a property of part of the world.

We must study them more carefully than ever now and remember that no weapon has ever settled a moral problem.[22]

The whole essay used as a foreword was, in fact, focused on a continuing peace. Hemingway's aim was "finding a way for all men to live together on this earth." He told his readers that the postwar time was "more difficult" than the war itself because it was then "man's duty to understand his world rather than simply fight for it."[23]

Hemingway was not finished writing about war: in 1950 appeared his late novel, *Across the River and into the Trees*; in 1952, *The Old Man and the Sea*; and in the remaining handful of years before his suicide, other, shorter pieces about warfare, both actual and metaphoric. War continued to be the preoccupation of Hemingway's writing life. By that time, Kurt Vonnegut was not alone in saying of Hemingway that "he was a reporter of war, and truly one of the best the world has ever known"; Charles Whiting echoed that "war was his special subject." In the later words of Thomas Strychacz, "Hemingway wrote compellingly and movingly about the experience of war—its logic, its madness, its brutal consequences, its effects on women and, in particular, on men."[24]

Early in the twenty-first century, Sean Hemingway—Ernest Hemingway's novelist grandson—selected and edited a major collection of his grandfather's writings about war. Titled *Hemingway on War*, the Scribner's-produced book not only sold well, but it helped readers see the cohesion that existed throughout Hemingway's work in journalism and fiction. In his lengthy introduction, the editor emphasizes the fact that Hemingway's writing shows him to have been a true scholar of military conflicts:

> His accounts, both fictional and journalistic, represent an extraordinarily rich depiction of war as it evolved into the modern era, through the development of machine warfare to the first deployment of the atomic bomb. Hemingway was a military expert, a student of war in its totality, from machine gun emplacements, tactics, and maneuvers to civilian morale and industrial organization. . . . One of his greatest accomplishments as a writer . . . is his portrayal of the physical and psychological impact of war and its aftermath.[25]

To illustrate the truth of his assessment, Sean Hemingway chose excerpts from Hemingway's fiction (not only the war-related short stories but selected passages from *A Farewell to Arms*, *For Whom the Bell Tolls*, and *Across the River and into the Trees*) and also from his journalism about battle, beginning with the early 1920s articles for the *Toronto Star* and continuing through his reportage for *Collier's*, the North American Newspaper Alliance, *Ken*, *Esquire*, *PM*, and other commercial venues. Sean Hemingway thereby proved through his careful selection that what some critics have seen as two separate streams of Hemingway's writing—fiction and nonfiction—instead make up one steady stream of information. And much of that stream deals with the mechanics of war and battle.

Sean Hemingway included a previously unpublished short story that was written in 1919. In "The Mercenaries," Hemingway worked largely through dialogue among veterans—one American, one French—talking in a Chicago bar. The two have been hired to fight for two hundred dollars, gold, per month in the conflict between Peru and Chile. They offer a similar position to the story's American narrator, but he is not an artillery officer so the narrative moves to a story about an Italian nobleman's bravery, or non-bravery, when he found the American mercenary in his wife's bedroom. Terse, idiomatic, ironic, the dialogue shows a kind of battlefield camaraderie few civilians could have drawn. It also describes the national rivalry/ribaldry that the American's making love to the Italian's wife created.

More to the point, perhaps, was Sean Hemingway's inclusion of an excerpt titled "Black Ass at the Cross Roads," based on a sketch of his grandfather's from World War II. Published posthumously, the account shows the author's involvement with the accurate logistics of killing the enemy. This is the opening:

> We were set up for the simple job of assassination astride an escape route. We were not astride, technically, because we did not have enough people to set up on both sides of the road and we were not technically prepared to cope with armored vehicles. But each trap had two German *Panzerfausten*. They were much more powerful and simpler than the general-issue American bazooka, having a bigger warhead and you could throw away the launching tube; but lately, many that we had found in the German retreat had been booby-trapped.

After several thousand words of clear description—during which the few Americans are able to divert and destroy several German vehicles—the narrative slows, pays a kind of homage to the ingenuity of the outnumbered Americans, and focuses on the concluding episode of two German soldiers riding bicycles into what they have not yet discovered are perilous circumstances:

> "I'll try one with the M-1," I said . . . [waiting] till he was past the half-track . . . and then had the sight on him, swung with him and missed. . . . I tried it again swinging further ahead. The German fell in the same disconcerting heartbreaking way and lay in the road with the *velo* [bicycle] upside down and a wheel still spinning.

The narrative continues, with Claude, the narrator's friend, trying to make the German comfortable as he dies. Claude says only, "This dirty whore of a war," and then the narrator states, "Claude had the black ass bad too" (*HOW* 213–14). Hemingway's account was shaped to remind the reader that even victors hate killing, no matter how necessary it might be.

Lest a reader, because of this story, label the collection "sentimental," a charge that sometimes gets applied to descriptions of genuine emotion, Sean Hemingway included a number of Hemingway's varied descriptions of war. From *Across the River and into the Trees*, a segment the editor calls "The Dead" describes the catastrophic number of casualties the 22nd Infantry Regiment experienced in the Hürtgen Forest. Colonel Cantwell dulls his memory by thinking of those horrors only in the abstract: "It was a place where it was extremely difficult for a man to stay alive even if all he did was be there" (*HOW* 231). Scripted around key images, the aging colonel mourns those losses still:

> Cantwell recalled the soldier driving a truck who stopped to tell them, "Sir, there is a dead G I in the middle of the road up ahead, and any time a vehicle goes through they have to run over him, and I'm afraid it is making a bad impression on the troops."
> "We'll get him off the road."
> So we got him off the road.
> And I can remember just how he felt, lifting him, and how he had been flattened and the strangeness of his flatness. (*HOW* 232)

Here, the terse understatement prompts the reader to do the all-important envisioning of that ruined body on personal imaginative terms.

Nearly one-third of *Hemingway on War* is made up of Hemingway's journalism—about war and politics—dating from 1920 through 1944. Given that both *By-Line: Ernest Hemingway* and *Ernest Hemingway, Dateline: Toronto*, collections edited by William White, reprinted much of his syndicated journalism, what accrues from placing more than two dozen of these articles in this collection is that Hemingway's achievement as he spoke in his taut journalistic voice can be correlated with his more familiar fiction.

Though his fiction shows more versatility, there are keen differences as well within his war-related articles. The predictive but seldom insulting early reportage as he covered the growing power of Benito Mussolini; the nostalgia as he talked with the barmaid in Schio—"'I was here during the war,' I ventured.

'So were many others,' she said under her breath, bitterly"; the cut-and-dried facticity as he followed what happened to the Christian population of Eastern Thrace during the Greco-Turkish War—all the excerpts selected show his careful word choice.

Compared with Hemingway's World War II coverage, these early articles seem limited, almost light. By 1944, he was writing for *Collier's* about troops— "wax-gray with seasickness"—looking for their attack point at Fox Green beach. Lengthy, punctuated with dialogue among the troops, Hemingway's World War II essays are a combination of narrative, complete with suspense, and pithy scenes of horror. The article "Voyage to Victory" states, "We had six craft missing, finally, out of the twenty-four LCV(P)s that went in. . . . No boat was lost through bad seamanship. All that were lost were lost by enemy action." In his understated reportorial voice, Hemingway closed, "There is much that I have not written. You could write for a week and not give everyone credit for what he did on a front of 1,135 yards. Real war is never like paper war, nor do accounts of it read much the way it looks" (*HOW* 326). As he had in his composition of *A Farewell to Arms*, Hemingway consistently relied on numbers and facts drawn from verifiable data, giving his readers the means to draw their own useful, and hopefully accurate, conclusions.

One of the most interesting choices Sean Hemingway made as he created his compilation *Hemingway on War* was to use as a preface to the journalistic segment of the book a middle paragraph from Ernest Hemingway's letter to his family written on August 18, 1918—just a few weeks after his near-fatal wounding. This is the only excerpt reproduced from Hemingway's plentiful cache of letters, but it provides focus and a kind of context for one key issue about Hemingway's compelling need to write about war:

> You know they say there isn't anything funny about this war and there isn't. I wouldn't say it was hell, because that's been a bit overworked since Gen. Sherman's time, but there have been about 8 times when I would have welcomed Hell. . . . For example, in the trenches during an attack when a shell makes a direct hit in a group where you are standing. Shells aren't bad except direct hits. You must take chances on the fragments of the bursts. But when there is a direct hit your pals get spattered all over you. Spattered is literal. (*SL* 14)

A point to be made with Sean Hemingway's inclusion of this letter that reports on physical wounds is that Hemingway's experience with war was never simply biographical. Yes, he had himself been brutally wounded. But the 227 shrapnel wounds were not in themselves the reason for his confidence that he could portray war more realistically than could most other writers. These wounds—and their scars that remained throughout his life—were as talismanic as they were physical. His readers remembered that Ernest Hemingway, two weeks before his nineteenth birthday, was nearly blown to bits by an exploding shell, the shell that killed outright the soldier standing beside him.

Hemingway's wounding marked the moment he found himself a would-be writer with a *topic*, something to write about—a gift that becomes a necessity for all young and generally inexperienced writers. In this case, too, what Hemingway knew of a near-death experience gave him insight into a number of states of trauma—whether those states resulted from physical injuries or emotional ones—so that the then-teenaged boy could write so as to convey a mature understanding of character, one far beyond his own chronological age.

As fellow novelist Ella Winter said of Hemingway after his death, in a February 10, 1962, letter to biographer Carlos Baker, "I of course knew Hemingway as the big-broad-shouldered, dark-haired, most handsome 'boy' who walked in that peculiar way not exactly limping but lurching, and who *talked writing* and *ate and drank and dreamed and thought writing.* . . . You felt in him such a clean, clear strength."[26]

Adrienne Monnier's recollections of Hemingway's early Paris years include her statement that "the young Hemingway [was] the 'real' Hemingway." The exuberant young American took Monnier and Sylvia Beach to the six-day bicycle races and to boxing matches and spent hours and hours with them in Beach's Shakespeare and Company bookshop.[27]

As Margaret Anderson recalled, after she had accepted several of Hemingway's early stories for her *Little Review*, "Hemingway is so different from his legend that there may be no use trying to show him as he is . . . so soft-hearted that it must be as much as he can bear to beat a punching bag." What stands out about him is "his huge enjoyment in living."[28]

In the words of his longtime friend Archibald MacLeish,

Hemingway was a *participant*. He could never go to a war—and he went to *every* war available to him—without engaging in it. He went to the First World War as an ambulance driver and got his knee smashed by a shell in a front-line trench where no one had sent him. He went to the war in Spain to write a scenario for a movie and learned how you washed the powder burns off your hands without water. He went to the last World War as a correspondent—and worried the high command by turning up with other tools than typewriters—mementos he called them. And between wars there were lions and elephants. And between elephants and lions there were marlin. Also bear.

A strange life for a writer and a difficult life to judge at the end. Indeed, a difficult life to judge before the end.[29]

CHAPTER ONE

The Writer Writes

I ate the end of my piece of cheese and took a swallow of wine. Through the other noise I heard a cough, then came the chuh-chuh-chuh-chuh—then there was a flash, as when a blast-furnace door is swung open, and a roar that started white and went red and on and on in a rushing wind. I tried to breathe but my breath would not come and I felt myself rush bodily out of myself and out and out and out and all the time bodily in the wind. I went out swiftly, all of myself, and I knew I was dead and that it had all been a mistake to think you just died. Then I floated, and instead of going on I felt myself slide back. I breathed and I was back. The ground was torn up and in front of my head there was a splintered beam of wood. In the jolt of my head I heard somebody crying. I thought somebody was screaming. I tried to move but I could not move. (*FTA* 54–55)[1]

WOUNDED BY A trench mortar shell on July 8, 1918, Hemingway did not write about his out-of-body experience for nearly ten years. Rather than being obsessed with his writerly aim of describing such wounding, he buried the experience in his subconscious and instead practiced, rigorously, the craft of writing.

Hemingway's physical healing took much of the next two years of his life. Moved from the battlefield site to the newly opened American Red Cross hospital in Milan, Hemingway underwent surgeries (the last on August 10, 1918) as well as extensive physical therapy. He fell in love with the American nurse Agnes von Kurowsky, who was in attendance until she was transferred to Florence. She returned to Milan for several weeks and then was sent to Treviso. After Hemingway visited her there for one day, he considered them engaged. He returned to action but became badly jaundiced and so was hospitalized again. Then the war ended, and he spent the rest of his time in Italy visiting his Red Cross supervisor, James Gamble, in Taormina, Sicily.

Hemingway was discharged from the Red Cross on January 4, 1919, and sailed for New York via Gibraltar, crossing the Atlantic on the *Giuseppe Verdi*. When he arrived in New York on January 21, he returned home to Oak Park and began convalescing, giving talks, wearing his unofficial "Italian" uniform, hiding alcohol in his bedroom so that he could continue the drinking that had gotten him through his Italian convalescence, writing letters to Agnes, and writing fiction.[2]

When Agnes sent him a "Dear John" letter in March, explaining that she was too old for him,[3] Hemingway became deeply depressed. He went to the Michigan cottage several months before his family came, and he planned to spend the next fall and winter writing there, supported by a small monthly stipend from his Travelers Insurance policy. Part of his anxiety at living at home probably stemmed from his parents' urging him to go to college. As he wrote in an April 30, 1919, letter, "My family . . . are wolfing at me to go to college. They want me to settle down for a while and the place that they are pulling for very strongly is Wisconsin" (*SL* 24).

Because most of his writing from these months was never published, exact dates cannot be recovered. But there is enough evidence—given in the biographies about Hemingway's war and postwar years, particularly those by Peter Griffin, Michael Reynolds, and Charles Fenton—to show that his progress as a competent fiction writer was slow. All three critics excerpt from work that remains in manuscript or was among the writing lost in 1922 when first wife Hadley Hemingway traveled to Schruns with a suitcase filled with Hemingway's writings—including carbons—and the case was stolen.[4] All that remained then of Hemingway's early writing were several stories already mailed to magazines or carried in his personal luggage to share with other journalists, such as "My Old Man."

There were stories (and partial stories) about living in Michigan, about the war, and about characters that appear to be drawn from some imaginary small town (perhaps modeled on Sherwood Anderson's *Winesburg, Ohio* "grotesques"),[5] as well as poems, or perhaps the kind of "poems" he would later collect in both *in our time* and *In Our Time*. His word for the brief prose poem he was practicing—and its terse language—was "cablese," as he told Lincoln Steffens: "Just read the cablese, only the cablese. Isn't it a great language?"[6]

Figure 1. Hemingway recuperating at a hospital in Milan during World War I after both of his legs were wounded by a trench mortar shell on July 8, 1918.

Of his early successful short fictions, grouped into a collection Hemingway called *Crossroads—An Anthology*, among the strongest are those that rely on a concluding irony. "Ed Paige" recounts the townspeople's disbelief that Paige, a lumber worker, was able to stay in the ring with professional boxer Stanley Ketchel for the allotted time. Paige won the advertised $100 and then (emotionally) retired on his laurels. Later, the townspeople began to question that "wonderful slashing, tearing-in battle."[7]

Hemingway used the same kind of scenic structure in "Old Man Hurd—and Mrs. Hurd" as the younger wife laments to the narrator's mother that she could have married better, "I was a right likely-looking girl then." But after her father's death, she could not run the small farm alone. Old Man Hurd would appear every evening and tell her, "Sarah, you'd better marry me." Like Anderson's *Winesburg* characters, Mrs. Hurd had no real choices, so she ended her days married to the man who "has a face that looks indecent. He hasn't any whiskers, and his chin kind of slinks in and his eyes are red rimmed and watery, and the edges of his nostrils are always red and raw."[8]

Sorrow links the vignettes. The often-quoted "Pauline Snow" describes the title character as "the only beautiful girl we ever had out at the Bay . . . like an Easter Lily coming up straight and lithe and beautiful out of a dung heap." But her friendliness with her only suitor, the rough Art Simons, leads the townspeople to condemn her: "They sent Pauline away to the correction school down at Coldwater. Art was away for awhile, and then came back and married one of the Jenkins girls."[9]

If not jarringly dismissive about the collective consciousness of a community, Hemingway's sketches tried to give insight into men who had served in the military abroad. "Bob White," which uses another play on significant naming, as in "Snow" and "Hurd," plays his village for a group of fools, telling them lies about his war (and about French women and their families). His giving listeners "news right direct" is a shameful travesty. Unlike Bob White, "Billy Gilbert," who joined the Scots Black Watch for a chance to see real action, performed bravely, to the honor of his Ojibway tribe near Susan Lake. But his wearing the required kilt and bonnet makes him the object of his neighbors' ridicule—his wife has left him, his farm is in disrepair, and "his eyes looked a long way through the dark."[10]

Through these stories, Hemingway attempted to write about his war, but his efforts—whether in short pieces or longer—illustrate what critic Jennifer Haytock describes as "problematic." She notes that the art of writing is, in itself, "a sign of civilization; when a soldier writes about war, he attempts to

Figure 2. Some of the shrapnel pieces removed from Hemingway's legs.

process a civilization-destroying activity into something that can be understood *by* civilization."[11]

Foreshadowing the kind of results Hemingway would achieve a few years later, as he honed and polished the vignettes that formed the frame of *in our time*, these early stories caught the essential character not only of the person named in each title but of the culture and of the community, represented collectively.

There are also poems, free-form poems with unrhymed lines that stagger a bit as they try to mimic idiomatic speech, their line divisions creating a semblance of modernist literary finesse. Some of the best are his "Michigan" poems, such as "Along with Youth," which opens

> A porcupine skin
> Stiff with bad tanning,
> It must have ended somewhere.

> Stuffed horned owl
> Pompous
> Yellow eyed . . . (*CP* 26)

and some scattered single lines, such as "The grass has gone brown in the summer" (*CP* 19). These strong lines counteract a sense of quasi-humorous irony that spoils many other of Hemingway's poems. Among his more accomplished are those about war. Though fewer, they borrow the terse attention to detail so apparent in his journalism. Later published in *Poetry,* "Riparto d'Assalto" begins with a description of soldiers riding in a cold truck—their physical discomfort and pain, their sexual reveries, and then the ride itself,

> Damned cold, bitter, rotten ride,
> Winding road up the Grappa side . . .

In keeping with the shock of the war's deaths for the soldiers, this poem evokes the reader's parallel shock. Hemingway ends the description of the soldiers' ride with a single line, naming the place "where the truck-load died" (*CP* 27). With such other war poems as "Ultimately," "The Age Demanded," "Shock Troops," "Arsiero, Asiago," "All armies are the same," "Poem, 1928," "Captives," the haunting "Killed, Piave 8th July, 1918," and "Champs d'Honneur," the best of Hemingway's poetry connects "the young Chicago poet," as the biographical note in *Poetry* calls him, with war in its various dimensions. In "Champs d'Honneur," for example, Hemingway's irony works toward the powerful final couplet, partly because of effective word repetition. The poem opens,

> Soldiers never do die well;
> Crosses mark the places—
> Wooden crosses where they fell . . .

From the pastoral scene of marked graves, the poem takes the reader to the throes of death itself, as "soldiers pitch and cough and twitch."[12] That they have smothered because of an enemy gas attack comes almost as an afterthought at the poem's end.

In "To Good Guys Dead," Hemingway warns against the use of abstract words:

> Patriotism
> Democracy

Honor—
Words and phrases
They either bitched or killed us.[13]

One of Hemingway's most poignant war poems signals its autobiographical intent. "Killed, Piave 8th July, 1918" aligns the author's severe wounding with the mysticism of both pain ("gentle hurtings") and death, with the threatening presence of the latter described in the poem's conclusion as

A dull, cold, rigid bayonet
On my hot-swollen, throbbing soul.[14]

At the heart of Hemingway's early writing apprenticeship, however, lay the fiction. He saw in the crafting of every phrase, every sentence, the clear difference between the effects he tried for in his journalism and the work that would make his name as writer. In addition to the *Crossroads* sketches, Hemingway had early written "The Mercenaries," about the French and American veterans going off to Peru; a now-lost story titled "Wolves and Doughnuts," rejected by George Horace Lorimer, editor of the *Saturday Evening Post*; and "Portrait of the Idealist in Love—A Story," clearly autobiographical and clearly aimed at ladies' magazines, as was the more complex "The Current—A Story." There was the more sophisticated "The Ash Heel's Tendon—A Story," which brought what Hemingway thought of as his knowledge of boxing and detective work into a plotline, somewhat parallel to that in "The Woppian Way," a title that biographer Jeffrey Meyers terms a "bad pun on Appian Way. This tale described an Italian boxer, fighting under an Irish name, who gives up a championship fight, joins the *Arditi* on the Italian front, achieves victory in battle but then cannot return to his tame career in the ring."[15] This last story became a Hemingway staple, titled at times "The Passing of Pickles McCarty." One might speculate that his long-unpublished story "Up in Michigan,"[16] the sexual-predator narrative that used the real names of Jim Dilworth and Liz Coates, drew from both the more realistic early stories such as "The Mercenaries" and the poetic *Crossroads* sketches. "My Old Man" could be described as realistic as well, with the somewhat cluttered geographic and emotional sections of that story leaving little space for a reader's intuition.

These fictions also benefited from Hemingway's becoming a freelancer for the *Toronto Star* and the *Toronto Star Weekly*. By a remarkable twist of fate, Ernest Hemingway, the young, wounded ambulance driver, spending the winter of 1920 in his family's cottage on Walloon Lake near Petoskey, Michigan, while he wrote stories and poems that no literary journal or magazine would buy, was invited to live with Ralph and Harriet Connable's family in Toronto. Paid to be a mentor and caregiver to the Connables' teenaged son, he was told he would have ample writing time. True to that promise, Ralph Connable, head of the Canadian F. W. Woolworth chain of stores, gave him the promised free time and paid him a salary of twenty dollars a week.

Ralph Connable was originally from Chicago, where he and Dr. Clarence Hemingway were friends. His summer home on Walloon Lake was near the Hemingways', and he had known Ernest his entire life. There are alternate stories about this invitation to Toronto: one insists that Harriet Connable was in the audience when Hemingway, wearing his Italian cape and boots, spoke about the war and his wounding. After the talk, she invited him to come live in their guest house, to be a companion to their disabled son. However the invitation came about, it was timely: Hemingway had written a friend that he was down to his last twenty dollars and had been promised a job soon at the local pump factory.[17] Another benefit to his going to Canada was the fact that the Connables were friends of both Gregory Clark and J. Herbert Cranston, the features editors of the *Toronto Star Weekly*.

Hemingway thought of himself as an experienced journalist. Biographer Charles Fenton agreed that he understood a good bit about journalism after his seven diligent months at the *Kansas City Star*.[18] But what the *Toronto Star Weekly* (the weekend paper) wanted was not reporting: they wanted human interest stories. Hemingway's first byline for the *Star Weekly* came as early as February 14, 1920, with a story about local women who paid artists a fee for the use of original paintings for six months. Titled "Circulating Pictures," the article provided useful information concisely. It was followed March 6 with "A Free Shave," describing the services of the local barber college, replete with humor and extensive dialogue. The list of Hemingway's articles is long, averaging one every weekend. Irony, as in "Popular in Peace—Slacker in War" and a tongue-in-cheek "Store Thieves' Tricks," was plentiful. Some of the articles were based in nature (several were about trout fishing, others camping). Many were based on local news situations, as in the case of "Fox Farming." Others stemmed from abuses during, first, the war and, then, Prohibition, and what Hemingway called "Canuck whiskey."

The *Star Weekly* provided Hemingway a showcase for his many topics (and their differing treatments). With hardly a break after he left Toronto and returned to Michigan for the summer of 1920, the articles continued, though their topics were less often about Toronto. As Fenton pointed out in his assessment of Hemingway's skillful adaptation to human interest journalism, "The American and Canadian papers . . . were of such diverse natures that had his relationship with them been reversed—had he gone to Toronto in 1917 and to Kansas City in 1920—the entire pattern of his apprenticeship would have been seriously altered and damaged."[19]

Comparatively little of Hemingway's *Star Weekly* journalism was included in William White's first collection, *By-Line: Ernest Hemingway* (1967). White instead drew from the quantity of articles only those that suggested some of the writer's later fiction—e.g., "Plain and Fancy Killings, $400 Up" (December 11, 1920), which related to Hemingway's story "The Killers," and "American Bohemians in Paris" (March 25, 1922), which tied to his novel *The Sun Also Rises*. White also concentrated on Hemingway's coverage of politics and war, running up through 1944 rather than ending the articles with his 1924 departure from the Toronto papers. The full run of the *Star Weekly* articles, however, appeared in White's 1985 collection, *Ernest Hemingway, Dateline: Toronto, The Complete "Toronto Star" Dispatches, 1920–1924*. It was the *Dateline: Toronto* collection that proved the range of the still-young journalist. If there was something to be written about, Hemingway would find a way to write the story effectively.

Critics who know journalism agree that Hemingway had a knack, a finesse, a calling. Scott Donaldson notes that Hemingway's articles for the Toronto papers were praised for "their freshness and wit and liveliness. These newspaper pieces . . . were remarkably personal for a profession which lays claim to objectivity." Donaldson gave much of the praise for Hemingway's training to the famous *Star* journalist Lionel Moise, who, according to Hemingway, "could carry four stories in his head and go to the telephone and take a fifth and then write all five at full speed to catch an edition. There would be something alive about each one."[20] For Robert Stephens, Hemingway's journalism was one part of his generally effective nonfiction, which included the many essays and articles later published in magazines. As Stephens points out accurately, nearly one-third of Hemingway's lifetime of writing was nonfiction. Choosing to isolate Hemingway's war reports, Stephens calls attention to their "showing him as adviser on military actions, both strategic and tactical. . . . The major period of his war writing, 1937 to 1944, was also the time when he was most self-consciously the *knower*. It was a propitious time for showing his expertise: his lifelong interest in military history and campaigns came into practical focus, and the world was ready to recognize his special understanding."[21]

Returning to Michigan after his months with the Connables in Toronto, Hemingway planned to spend another good summer with friends. He included Bill Horne, the Red Cross buddy to whom he had turned after he received Agnes's "Dear John" letter, and Ted Brumback, the *Kansas City Star* colleague who had joined the Red Cross with him. Along with them, Carl Edgar, Bill and Katy Smith, some younger Michigan friends of his siblings, and his old friends would make up an active, happy group for a summer filled with swimming, rowing, fishing, flirting, and doing the usual family chores. But unexpectedly, some kind of anger swept through Hemingway's parents: even as his father wrote from Oak Park that he hoped they could "chum" during the summer, he indicated that Hemingway's behavior around the family cottage had become offensive. Strangely, as his mother planned a party for Hemingway's twenty-first birthday (July 21, 1920), inviting Brumback and Horne as well as local friends, she decided to write him a letter that not only surprised him but tore into his heart—and left him with a pain comparable to that which Agnes von Kurowsky's rejection had created.

The interaction between Grace and Clarence, both upset over what they considered their son's irresponsible behavior (Why is he not earning money, now that he has come home? How can writing, even for publication, be considered "working"?), is best described—in thorough detail—by critic Max Westbrook. Whereas most biographers credit Grace with the sobering "kick-out" letter, Westbrook thinks the real anger came from Clarence. He quotes from two letters Clarence wrote to Grace in mid-July, both saying that he had been urging Ernest to get work: "I have advised him to go with Ted down Traverse City way and work at good wages and at least cut down his living expenses. . . . I wanted him to get busy and be more self supporting and respectful and leave the Bay."[22]

The letter that Clarence—still in Oak Park—had sent to Grace—in Michigan—in draft form was evidently presented to Hemingway, not on his birthday but perhaps on July 26; there is much correspondence between Clarence and Grace about the letter and its date. But the letter does insist that Hemingway and Ted Brumback leave the Hemingway cottage and not return until they are *invited*. In Grace's reply to Clarence, she says of her son, "He is distinctly a menace to youth. . . . Of course Ernest called me every name he could think of, and said everything vile about me. . . . He insulted me every minute; said 'all I read was moron literature,' that Dr. Frank Crane who writes such glorious helpful articles in the *American* was the 'Moron's Maeterlinck' and asked me if I read the *Atlantic Monthly* just so some one would see me doing it."[23]

Elaine Scarry explains that any person in pain loses access to normal language, that "physical pain is not only resistant to language but also actively destroys language, deconstructing it into the pre-language of cries and groans. To hear those cries is to witness the shattering of language."[24] Rather than apply this diagnosis to Hemingway only after his 1918 physical wounding and convalescence, one could well use the axiom also to describe what seems to have been his shock at receiving the "kick-out" letter. In fact, during Hemingway's first years after graduating from high school, all three sets of unexpected experiences were indescribably painful—the mortar-shell explosion (and the necessarily long recovery), the rejection letter from Agnes von Kurowsky, and the scolding and hostile letter from his parents. Even though Hemingway was in his beloved Michigan when the latter ax fell, and even though Hemingway attributed the harmful behavior to only his mother, he once again turned to his friends in order to survive. It was exactly that, a matter of survival. And now, along with searching for language and a narrative to describe the war that he had so hated, he found himself in the position of having to use his writer's strategies to describe the behavior of the family he had believed would be his support forever.

It may be appropriate to use the word *trauma* to describe all three experiences. In the words of Evelyn Jaffe Schreiber, "trauma, whether initiated by physical abuse, dehumanization, discrimination, exclusion, or abandonment, becomes embedded in both psychic and bodily circuits. Psychoanalytic theory and neurobiological studies explore the difficulty of the recovery process, given the psychological structures and bodily components."[25] Psychiatrist Judith Herman, too, sees any traumatic state as staining a broad swath through a human being's consciousness. All people, says Herman, depend on their belief that certain human beings can be trusted. In Hemingway's case, just as he had trusted Agnes, the woman he intended to marry, he even more emphatically trusted his parents. To find that innocence betrayed and his unconditional acceptance revoked was a near-physical blow. Herman discusses the need to rebuild trust, to validate both the consciousness that unexpectedly was wounded and the psyche that was forced to learn new patterns of behavior.

After trauma, one common psychological reaction is dissociation. Self-protective, a person so wounded—whether emotionally or physically—cannot fixate on the injury. At least part of that person's reaction must be avoidance. Herman insists on the need for dissociation, noting that "traumatic experience can produce lasting alterations to the endocrine, autonomic, and central nervous system. . . . [In compensation, the wounded person creates a mechanism] by which intense sensory and emotional experience are disconnected from the social domain of language and memory."[26]

Traumatic events, Herman notes, "shatter the construction of the self that is formed and sustained in relation to others" and "cast the victim into a state of existential crisis." There is a long-lasting process of grieving, not only for the immediate loss but also for "what was never theirs to lose." Anyone so traumatized by loss may experience "recurrent and intrusive recollections . . . or recurrent distressing dreams."[27]

For Cathy Caruth, *trauma* is a broad descriptor for "an overwhelming experience of sudden or catastrophic events in which the response to the event occurs in the often delayed, uncontrolled repetitive appearance of . . . intrusive phenomena." Perhaps more permanently, Caruth sees that "trauma is a shock that appears to work very much like a bodily threat but is in fact a break in the mind's experience of time."[28]

For psychiatrist Kali Tal, the kernel event is much less important, in itself, than the way the victim of trauma rebuilds his or her psyche. Tal calls this process "mythologization," finding a way to reduce the traumatic event "to a set of standardizing narratives," which then become "the 'story' of the trauma." Such a story is, then, "a contained and predictable narrative."[29] Each of Hemingway's biographers, in response to his growing anger at his mother's behavior, worked hard to explain the way the young writer's stories about his mother *darkened*. This self-creation (Grace Hemingway as evil) has usually been viewed as enigmatic, even mysterious. But it may be understood as a part of Hemingway's responsive myth-building. Considering the three life-altering events—the wounding in war, Agnes's rejection, and being told to leave the family summer home—Hemingway saw that he was powerless in the first two instances. It was only in his reaction to the "kick-out" letter that he could visualize some personal control over any of these traumatic events. (In Hemingway's consciousness, all three of the events were the result of war. Had he not gone to war, he would not have been wounded. Had he not been recuperating in the Milan hospital, he would not have met and come to love Agnes. Had he not been forced to take so many months recuperating from the wounding, he would have by the summer of 1920 become a significant journalist, if not an important writer: his parents' worrying about whether or not he would ever make a living, then, also stems from the conditions of war.)

These considerations support Paul Hendrickson's 2011 commentary about Hemingway's character and his psyche. Hendrickson observes, "I also believe there was so much more fear inside Hemingway than he ever let on, that it was almost always present, by day and more so by night, and that his living with it for so long was ennobling. The thought of self-destruction trailed Hemingway for nearly his entire life, like the tiny wakes a child's hand will make when it is trailed behind a rowboat in calm water—say, up in Michigan." This biographer also finds one root of Hemingway's repressed psychological development in the often brutal punishments given to all the Hemingway children by their father, the educated doctor who seemed to be eager to wield his razor strap. Hendrickson assesses these punishments—both in severity and unpredictability—as illustrations of the doctor's "incipient bi-polarism."[30] Some meaningful detail can be gathered from the now-classic *Prisoners of Childhood*, the book in which German psychiatrist Alice Miller describes the devastation of any child who learns that parents are *not* supportive but, rather, that parental "love" is given to a child who excels, rather than to a child who exists. She comments that for any child so stunted by parental abuse, the only remedy is to "cut off . . . the childhood roots."[31]

Like Schreiber's and Caruth's, Tal's definition of trauma is so broad that the three "wounds" Hemingway experienced fit within a triangle of overlapping pain: "An individual is traumatized by a life-threatening event that displaces his or her preconceived notions about the world. Trauma is enacted in a liminal state, outside of the bounds of 'normal' human experience, and the subject is radically ungrounded." The path to recovery is often unpredictable. Tal discusses what she calls "the theory of a literature of trauma" and the way creating that literature is the basis of "the reintegrative process." Given Hemingway's self-definition of "Ernest Hemingway as writer," his constant and continuing attempts to write about his world should provide ample evidence of this process of reintegration. But as Tal points out, the process is never simple, nor is it necessarily chronological. There may be "several separate chronologies that must be maintained." In Hemingway's case, there is the visible trauma of war. But there is also the sometimes-hidden trauma of lost love, and that lost love bifurcates into both a lost romantic partner and lost parentage. Tal emphasizes, "Retellings appear at different stages, and it is essential to consider each retelling as a part of the larger process of revision."[32]

Herman adds that post-traumatic recovery must entail the "empowerment of the survivor and the creation of new connections." She points out that contact with "a single, caring, comforting person may be a lifeline. . . . The reward of mourning is realized as the survivor sheds his [her] stigmatized . . .

identity."[33] Phrased somewhat differently, Caruth also deliberates about the question of prior identity: "In extreme trauma one's sense of self is radically altered. And there is a traumatized self that is created. Of course, it's not a totally new self, it's what one brought into the trauma as affected significantly and painfully, confusedly, but in a very primal way, by that trauma. And recovery from post-traumatic effects, or from survivor conflicts, cannot really occur until the traumatized self is integrated."[34]

Recovering his equilibrium after the devastation of his parents' asking him to leave "home," Hemingway worked and lived with Ted Brumback during the rest of the summer. He then went to Chicago after Katy and Bill Smith's older brother, Y.K., got him an interview with an advertising agency. In Chicago he shared an apartment with Bill Horne until Horne lost his job; then Hemingway took a room with Y.K. and his wife, Doodles Smith. In October of 1920, Katy Smith invited her school friend from St. Louis, Hadley Richardson, for a visit. The immense attraction between Hadley and Hemingway encouraged the St. Louis woman to extend her stay.

Nearly eight years older than Hemingway, Hadley was a beautiful, calm woman—trained as a pianist, courted by musicians and others in St. Louis, she had cared for her mother as she aged and died. (Her father had committed suicide when she was thirteen; it was her older sister and her brother-in-law who then provided a home for Hadley.) During her several-week stay in Chicago, Hadley spent ample time with Hemingway—whose job with the *Cooperative Commonwealth* had not yet begun. They saw all of Chicago, including Hemingway's beloved Field Museum and the Chicago Art Institute; they drank, smoked, and danced (behaviors which neither of their families had allowed); they talked and talked about art and their practice of it. (At that time, Hadley was a more advanced student of the piano than Hemingway was of literature.)

Returning to St. Louis, Hadley wrote almost as many letters to Hemingway as he sent to her. In November, there were already clear indications of intimacy—in one letter Hadley wrote that she was wearing Doodles's blue silk kimono, which she promised to return "when I can wrench myself apart from it." In another letter she closed by asking Hemingway to kiss her—"any way at all." In a January letter of seven pages, she closed with "I want you here my dear. I know just ezzactly what I would do for you—but I can't do it so I won't tell you—did do it once."[35]

Hadley returned to Chicago after the holidays; Hemingway visited St. Louis in March of 1921 and again in May. They became engaged, with a wedding planned for late summer. They wrote countless letters about what they were reading—and through Hadley, who loved Dorothy Richardson, Henry James, Charles Dickens, and the full range of British novelists, Hemingway read a new kind of novel, though he had found early Conrad on his own. Together they read Hugh Walpole and Strindberg's play *Married*, Floyd Dell's *Moon Calf*, Sinclair Lewis's *Main Street*, the shocking *Trilby*, F. Scott Fitzgerald, the Brownings. Hemingway, who had read William James and the turn-of-the-century sexuality books (Havelock Ellis's *Erotic Symbolism* and Freud's *Psychology of Sex*), mentioned that kind of reading to Hadley.

There was little time for his own writing. His creative energies were being poured into the letters to his beloved and the plans he was making with Hadley. In midsummer, she moved out of her sister and brother-in-law's house and returned to Chicago for a week with Hemingway. Then she spent a month at a Wisconsin camp before arriving in Michigan for the September 3, 1921, wedding. Hemingway continued working in Chicago—as well as writing articles for the *Toronto Star Weekly*—until a week before the wedding. He then went on a three-day fishing trip with his Michigan and Red Cross friends, returning in time for dinner the night before the wedding.

Relief was the chief emotion Hemingway's parents experienced: for the honeymoon, Grace gave Ernest and Hadley the use of the Horton Bay cottage, Windemere. Then the Hemingway family returned to Oak Park, and Hadley and Hemingway moved to a fifth-floor walk-up in Chicago. On December 8, they sailed to France on the *Leopoldina*. Docking at Havre, they took the train to Paris and stayed at Hotel Jacob until they rented the small Left Bank apartment at 74 rue Cardinal Lemoine.

Because Hemingway had met and become a friend of Sherwood Anderson's during the past Chicago winter, he knew about finding Paris housing and he knew about making contacts—Anderson had given him letters of introduction to Ezra Pound as well as to Gertrude Stein, a particular favorite of Sherwood's. He had also helped Hemingway learn to understand modernism.

According to the leading critical views of Hemingway's short stories, most of the stories now considered his classic works were written during his and Hadley's sojourn in Paris—but not immediately. There would be countless hours spent with both Pound and Stein, with Hemingway absorbing different kinds of information from the two (they did not overlap; in fact, they disliked each other). From Pound, Hemingway learned the strategies of modernist, free-form poems. He was introduced, often literally, to H.D., William Carlos

Williams, T. S. Eliot, D. H. Lawrence, Ford Madox Ford, F. S. Flint, and the Pound of the early *Cantos* as well as the Pound of the Chinese-influenced shorter poems. But it was from Gertrude Stein, who did not do the line editing that Pound was famous for, that Hemingway learned the most about finding his way to a successful, and highly personal, creative process. As John Peale Bishop quoted years later, Hemingway had told him, "Ezra was right half the time, and when he was wrong, he was so wrong you were never in any doubt about it. Gertrude was always right."[36]

Hemingway continued working freelance for the *Toronto Star* and *Star Weekly* while in France, which kept him very busy. The job never paid well, but it allowed for days and weeks of travel all over Europe. When Dr. Hemingway complained that he sometimes could not find his son's articles in the weekend *Star Weekly*, Hemingway had to point out that much of his journalism, from his current home base in Paris, appeared in the daily *Star*. That was true more and more frequently. After his arrival in France, Hemingway averaged more than one article a week—for the next two years. Whereas the story "Paris Is Full of Russians" would appear in the *Star*, as would "Poincare's Election Promises," other articles, such as "Living on $1,000 a Year in Paris" and "The Luge of Switzerland," were published in the *Star Weekly*. Gradually, Hemingway became the European correspondent for the Toronto paper. He was sent, alone, to cover the Greco-Turkish war from Constantinople as well as the World Economic Conference in Genoa; he was also asked to report on other, less specific political news.[37] Even as he made his living from journalism, however, Hemingway felt it was inferior to the kind of fiction he wanted to write. As he said in the *Men at War* introduction, his life's business was to tell the truth, "truer than anything factual can be" (*MAW* xi).

Working on his fiction in relatively close proximity to Stein, Hemingway believed he should follow her well-intentioned advice that he give up journalism. Stein had been a student of William James's while she did undergraduate work at the Harvard Annex; she had taken his year-long graduate seminar "Consciousness, Knowledge, the Ego, the Relation of Mind and Body" even though she was only an undergraduate. She had continued to research the mind and its psychology while she was in medical school at Johns Hopkins, and she had spent a year after leaving the medical program there doing research on the brain with Chicago forensic philosopher Llewellys Barker. (Barker's now-classic 1899 book *The Nervous System and Its Constituent Neurones* includes several references to "the work of Miss Gertrude Stein.") Stein was not only a trained philosopher and a physician, she had long been immersed in studying the anatomy of the brain.

In her own writing, and in the prose she valued, Stein veered far from the factual. One of her reasons for warning Hemingway about his immersion in journalism was that she knew how inimical fact-based writing could be. Although he might never have found as much internal coherence as Stein believed he possessed, the young American was willing to investigate his emotional and subjective life in ways she found interesting. As Stein was later to write in *The Autobiography of Alice B. Toklas*, "What a book . . . would be the real story of Hemingway, not those he writes but the confessions of the real Ernest Hemingway."[38]

From both Pound and Stein, Hemingway heard mention of not only William James but Henri Bergson. One segment from Bergson's *Introduction to Metaphysics* connects his theories of timelessness with the kind of opening of consciousness that Stein found so valuable: "The image has at least this advantage, that it keeps us in the concrete. . . . Many diverse images, borrowed from different orders of things, may, by the convergence of their action, direct consciousness to the precise point where there is a certain *intuition* to be seized."[39]

Whereas Pound lectured Hemingway about the image, the heart of any modernist poem, and the structural arrangement of words and lines that would lead to true *vers libre*, Stein prodded the young journalist more gently. She led him to see, perhaps through studying paintings that captured that luminous opening provided by "intuition," that he could not completely control the activities of his mind, nor should he aim for such control. Being truly creative was more than crossing off items from a "To Do" list: Hemingway's busy life as a journalist had given him a frantic agenda. Following that pragmatic list would not allow him to open his mind, a process necessary to his discovering what he could unearth, and then try to portray, as a writer.

Hemingway believed Stein. He saw that she wrote according to her own mysterious schedule. The day was cleared for whatever she needed to experience, and writing was an integral part of her experience. If only for half an hour in the morning, or an hour after a late lunch—the imperious Stein took what time she needed, and her companion, Alice Toklas, smoothed the rough edges so that Stein's absence was not disruptive. What occurred, in fact, was that both Stein and Toklas led their lives so as to enable Stein's writing.

When Stein had been enrolled in William James's graduate seminar (and laboratory), James had paired her with the brilliant California graduate student Leon Solomons. Stein and Solomons performed a lengthy experiment to test a normal person's ability to perform various acts without consciously "thinking" of doing so. The team concluded that "real automatism, that is, dropping out of consciousness" comes only for very short periods of time—and only when "the attention is sufficiently distracted." This is the kind of work Gertrude Stein was trying to do for Hemingway, to separate him from the factual overload his journalism demanded of him, both in content and in travel, so that he could experience those "distracted" moments where he might reach into his interior consciousness.[40]

A decade later, as he tried to make his nonfiction book *Green Hills of Africa* as much about aesthetics as about big-game hunting, Hemingway brought together William James, Henri Bergson, P. D. Ouspensky, Edward Carpenter, and John Dewey (with Stein providing the foundational tone of voice). In his fictional dialogue with Kandisky that closes the first chapter, the Hemingway character explains that his writing is "worth doing—as an end in itself." He understands "the kind of writing that can be done. How far prose can be carried if any one is serious enough and has luck. There is a fourth and fifth dimension that can be gotten."[41] Kandisky asks what happens when a writer gets this dimension. "Then nothing else matters. It is more important than anything he can do. The chances are, of course, that he will fail. But there is a chance that he succeeds." Kandisky assumes it is poetry. Hemingway says,

> No. It is much more difficult than poetry. It is a prose that has never been written. But it can be written, without tricks and without cheating. With nothing that will go bad afterwards. . . . There must be the conception of what it can be and an absolute conscience as unchanging as the standard meter in Paris, to prevent faking. Then the writer must be intelligent and disinterested and above all he must survive. Try to get all these in one person and have him come through all the influences that press on a writer. The hardest thing, because time is so short, is for him to survive and get his work done. (*GHOA* 26–27)

CHAPTER TWO

in our time, In Our Time and Dimensionality

T_HE PROGRESSION OF_ Hemingway's fiction-writing skills between Robert McAlmon's Contact edition of *Three Stories and Ten Poems* in 1923 and the Boni & Liveright publication two years later of *In Our Time* was incredibly slow. The 1925 *In Our Time* includes two of the three stories from *Three Stories and Ten Poems*, but in place of the poems, Hemingway used the eighteen prose poems (brief snatches of fiction written in paragraph form) that had appeared, arranged differently, in a 1924 booklet titled *in our time*. Published by Bill Bird at Three Mountains Press, this lowercase *in our time* conveyed its author's ironic view of his war-torn culture. The slim collection of Hemingway's vignettes was barely noticed, even though Edmund Wilson reviewed Hemingway's first two books because the young author personally sent copies to him. In Wilson's *Dial* review ("Mr. Hemingway's Dry-Points"), which appeared in October of 1924, he praises the young author for his "strikingly original" vignettes, declaring that *in our time* presented "a harrowing record of barbarities." In his endeavor, Wilson notes, Hemingway "is showing you what life is, too proud an artist to simplify. And I am inclined to think that his little book has more artistic dignity than any other that has been written by an American about the period of the war."[1]

An unknown writer could coast for a decade on such high praise, and from it grew a wave of American approval—Wilson being F. Scott Fitzgerald's good Princeton friend, Maxwell Perkins at Scribner's being Fitzgerald's editor. And in the words of critic Milton Cohen, the pamphlet-like *in our time* proved to be "a laboratory" for Hemingway. As he worked through materials from what Cohen lists as "war, crime, politics, and the bullfight," Hemingway saw the tactile differences between factual representations, stripped to stark outlines, and the "quiet" close-up narratives he was writing as stories: "the stories (in their civilian settings, comparatively slower, more gradual development, and understated emotion) muffle the explosive chapters."[2]

Without self-consciousness, Hemingway wrote the following account of those early years of his development as a writer in his notes toward "the Paris book," the segments that his fourth wife, Mary Hemingway, would posthumously order and then title *A Moveable Feast*. Unpublished until the appearance in 2009 of what Scribner's calls the "restored" edition of *A Moveable Feast*, this is Hemingway's far-from-complete description of the way he became a writer:

> In the early days writing in Paris I would invent not only from my own experience but from the experiences and knowledge of my friends and all the people I had known. . . . I was very lucky always that my best friends were not writers and to have known many intelligent people who were articulate. In Italy when I was at the war there, for one thing that I had seen or that had happened to me, I knew many hundreds of things that had happened to other people who had been in the war in all of its phases. My own small experience gave me a touchstone by which I could tell whether stories were true or false and being wounded was a password. (*MF* restored 180–81)

War as touchstone, war as continuing theme, appears here in retrospect with no apology. Yet the context in which Hemingway drew on his (and others') war experiences was itself a multilayered process, making clear that the assessments of both Judith Herman and Kali Tal, discussed in the previous chapter—that a person traumatized by whatever emotional chaos had surrounded years of his life needs to *re-create* an existence, an experience that is itself mythologized—seem, in this case, valid. That the war vignettes are told impersonally, as if Hemingway the writer were *only* an observer, speaks to the trauma victim's need to dissociate *his* experiences from those he has fictionalized.

There was also the much-publicized allure of being a writer who knew the war, who could write with authority about it. As John Dos Passos remembered,

> War was the theme of the time. I was in a passion to put down everything, immediately as it happened, exactly as I saw it. . . . The chance of death sharpened the senses. The sweetness of the white roses, the shape and striping of a snail shell, the taste of an omelet, the most casual sight or sound appeared desperately intense against the background of the great massacres.[3]

As John Aldridge sees it in a larger context, many of the new modernist writers were young, and accepting them, and approving of their work, became a standard cultural position.

> One reason . . . for this preoccupation with youth is that World War I had the effect of seeming to annihilate past history and the old styles of history. Hence, the generation that had fought in the war felt urgently the need to establish new premises, to redefine the terms of existence. . . . Only the young were sensitive and adjustable enough to be able to determine whether a given emotion or experience conformed to the new standards of authenticity produced, at least in large part, by the war. Besides, they were the ones who had "been there," been initiated, had heard all the big words and learned that those words did not describe how they felt or what they had been through.[4]

There was a wide difference between knowing about wartime emotions, wounds, and survival, and knowing how to *write* about those difficult subjects. In Alex Vernon's view, Hemingway absorbed some of his knowledge about writing from Stephen Crane's *Red Badge of Courage*: "[Hemingway] learned from Crane to trust his imagination in locating his war stories outside his personal history. . . . He wrote what he knew but also what he did not know." Vernon's description of this method is "stirring together of experience and innovation."[5]

Even at this very early stage of scrutinizing Hemingway's writing, the observer must ask, could the existence of his trauma of loss be the consistent starting point for his creative process? Was the memory—and the embodiment—of his shell-torn body a more significant point of origin than his long-lived emotional losses (of both Agnes and then, in the following year, of his parents)? It makes sense that self-protection would have looked appealing. As a means of disguise, the tough factual extension of experience drew for Hemingway's readers a picture of the author as *survivor*: no character as vulnerable as the person Ernest Hemingway was in real life would appear in his writing for decades.

Part of Hemingway's consistent narrative strategy was aimed at forming this miasma of toughness. Just as Herman wrote about a damaged psyche in search of a lifeline, so Hemingway's seemingly quick proposal to Hadley Richardson created that legal and emotional tether for him. Hadley's innate goodness, her comparatively mature appearance, and her willingness to put Hemingway's writing before all their other considerations as a couple proved her devoted love for him. She also freely contributed her inheritance to their dream of living abroad. Hadley, who was happy to be pregnant, insisted that their child be born in Canada rather than in France out of concern for the baby's health and safety during delivery. Other than in this circumstance, Hadley was the spirit of self-abnegation.

In his fiction, Hemingway seldom wrote about Hadley. We see a close-mouthed, almost diffident woman character in such of the early stories as "Out of Season," "Hills Like White Elephants," and "Cat in the Rain." Ironically, Hemingway gave us Hadley as the image of the perfect wife decades after she had stopped being Mrs. Ernest Hemingway. When he memorialized Hadley in the notes to *A Moveable Feast*, he wrote about the two of them as a couple: "Our pleasures, which were those of being in love, were as simple and still as mysterious and complicated as a simple mathematical formula that can mean all happiness or can mean the end of the world." He noted that after he gave up writing for the Toronto papers, he and Hadley vowed to keep "our own tribal rules . . . standards, secrets, taboos and delights" (*MF* restored 184).[6]

Critical reactions to both Hemingway's 1924 *in our time* and the better-known 1925 *In Our Time* (where short stories, some about young love, also appear) seldom mention women characters. Rather, Hemingway created male characters isolated from the women who might comfort them; but more emphatically we see the stark prose about war and bullfighting. Painted with the bright blacks and reds of both the most famous Stendhal novel and the omnipresent gore of the bullfight, Hemingway's portraits of contemporary, postwar life were vividly evocative of sustained despair. As Asian American novelist Chang-rae Lee said admiringly in 2011, when he had re-read Hemingway's *In Our Time*, the reader's attention is so focused that "there is a dropping away of everything else."[7]

*   *   *   *   *

While the bombardment was knocking the trench to pieces at Fossalta, he lay very flat and sweated and prayed oh jesus christ get me out of here. Dear jesus please get me out. Christ please please please christ. If you'll only keep me from getting killed I'll do anything you say. I believe in you and I'll tell every one in the world that you are the only one that matters. Please please dear jesus. The shelling moved further up the line. We went to work on the trench and in the morning the sun came up and the day was hot and muggy and cheerful and quiet. The next night back at Mestre he did not tell the girl he went upstairs with at the Villa Rossa about Jesus. And he never told anybody. (*IOT* 67)

Placed at the exact midpoint of Hemingway's collection *In Our Time*, which includes fourteen stories and more vignettes like this one, this particular vignette, "Chapter VII," comes after the more familiar "Nick sat against the wall of the church," in which that character and his friend Rinaldi lie wounded. Between these two prose poems Hemingway placed "A Very Short Story," an account of a soldier who loses the love he had found during the war. After this grouping is "Soldier's Home," the searingly poignant description of Harold Krebs's return to a midwestern family he could no longer understand. The book appears to be shaped directly from Hemingway's re-creation of war and its effects. (*In Our Time* closes with the two-part "recovery" story "Big Two-Hearted River," in which the war is never mentioned. And in that story the Nick Adams character, who will continue to be Hemingway's first choice of alter ego throughout his career, cannot bear *any* human companionship.)

One of Hemingway's vignettes illustrates how effective the content, and the structure, of *In Our Time* was and is. We know that Hemingway argued against achieving the fifth dimension *in poetry*. As his writings about modernism show, he was looking for a means to create that as-yet-mysterious dimension in *prose*. His early work illustrates that what accrued from his intense scrutiny, and polishing, of his war memories comes close to creating a poem—what readers have responded to as a *vignette*, an *interchapter*, a *glimpse*, a *technique* that almost erases the need for divisions by literary genre. Ezra Pound later praised Hemingway's brief prose vignettes, referring to them as his best work.[8] As far as changing the way readers absorbed modernist writing, Hemingway's prose poems, which appeared in both *in our time* and *In Our Time*, were instrumental in teaching people how to read a few well-chosen words as if they replaced whole paragraphs. Hemingway later described these vignettes, which he referred to as "unwritten stories," as coming from a period when he was, in fact, aiming "to write paragraphs that would be the distillation of what made a novel" (*MF* 75).

Most of Hemingway's commentary about writing came decades after these first books, but some of what he said—for instance, in the 1958 *Paris Review* interview—applied retrospectively. There, he answered George Plimpton's questions with respect, but he also let the interviewer, himself a writer, understand that many of his assumptions were wrong. In describing how a paragraph of fiction works, for example, Hemingway said,

Sometimes you know the story. Sometimes you make it up as you go along and have no idea how it will come out. Everything changes as it moves. That is what makes the movement which makes the story. Sometimes the movement is so slow it does not seem to be moving. But there is always change and always movement.[9]

Trying to get the interviewer to see how amorphous, how tenuous, the writer's control over his work must necessarily be so that unconscious knowledge can intrude into the simply factual, Hemingway segued into his most famous pronouncement about his fiction. This statement followed his emphasis on a writer's need to *observe*:

> If a writer stops observing he is finished. But he does not have to observe consciously nor think how it will be useful. Perhaps that would be true at the beginning. But later everything he sees goes into the great reserve of things he knows or has seen. If it is any use to know it, I always try to write on the principle of the iceberg. There is seven eighths of it under water for every part that shows. Anything you know you can eliminate and it only strengthens your iceberg. It is the part that doesn't show. If a writer omits something because he does not know it then there is a hole in the story.[10]

Reading Hemingway's vignettes juxtaposed with short stories throughout *In Our Time* gives the reader the task of plunging his or her own consciousness into the author's most intimate "great reserve." It is a reciprocal process: the writer describes, the writer draws from his storehouse (his "reserve," to use Hemingway's language), and in his presentation of those artifacts of memory and language, leaves open pathways, entrances—sometimes unexpectedly—for a reader to re-create, to assimilate, the depiction. The organization of *In Our Time* provides a plan of action for the ideal relationship between author and reader that most modernists envied.

In his October 18, 1924, letter to Edmund Wilson, Hemingway gave the best set of instructions possible about the process of reading *In Our Time*. He was thanking Wilson, already an influential critic, for his earlier review of *Three Stories and Ten Poems* as well as of *in our time*, and then explaining the processes a reader should employ in reading his forthcoming book, *In Our Time*:

> Finished the book of fourteen stories with a chapter on [of] *in our time* between each story—that is the way they were meant to go—, to give the picture of the whole between examining it in detail. Like looking with your eyes at something,

say, a passing coast line, then looking at it with 15X binoculars. Or rather, maybe, looking at it and then going in and living in it—and then coming out and looking at it again.

He continued, with a modesty that was surely feigned, "It has a pretty good unity. In some of the stories since the *in our time* I've gotten across both the people and the scene. It makes you feel good when you can do it. It feels now as though I had gotten on top of it" (*SL* 128).

Making a number of the same structural choices as the authors of the long poems of the early 1920s—T. S. Eliot's *Waste Land* and Ezra Pound's *Hugh Selwyn Mauberley*, among others—Hemingway constructed the enigmatic *In Our Time* both to help initiate and to reflect what was becoming common practice for modernist American writing. He also used "My Old Man" and "Out of Season," as well as the rest of his recent fiction, beginning with "Indian Camp" and "The Doctor and the Doctor's Wife"—his stories of the boy and his family—and including the truly magnificent war stories "Soldier's Home" and "Big Two-Hearted River."

It was clear that Hemingway was reading everything that came through the doors of Sylvia Beach's bookstore, Shakespeare and Company; he was talking to everyone he met in Paris about both the paintings and the writing of his time; he was mining the interest in him of both Ezra Pound and Gertrude Stein for their sense of why France had become the home of American modernism as well as for their advice about his writing. But when Pound left Paris to live in Italy, Hemingway became more and more involved with Stein's sense of the creative self. It was in 1923 that she gave Hemingway "the run of the studio." If he came while she was gone, the maid brought him refreshments and he stayed until she returned. (It was during 1923 that he wrote "Out of Season," "A Very Short Story," "The Revolutionist," "Indian Camp," "Cat in the Rain," and perhaps some beginnings of the 1924 stories "The End of Something," "The Three-Day Blow," "The Doctor and the Doctor's Wife," "Soldier's Home," "Mr. and Mrs. Elliot," "Cross-Country Snow," and "Big Two-Hearted River.")[11] He wrote most of the 1924 stories during that spring. They seem to be continuations of the steady stream of excellent fiction that he had begun writing in mid-1923.

Because Stein seldom wrote to Hemingway (after all, they both lived in Paris much of the time), the record of what she instructed him to do to change and to develop his writing can only be inferred. There are, however, friends' recordings of her critiques of him and his work. According to Alix Du Poy

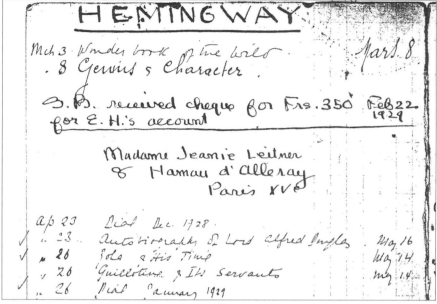

Figure 3. Hemingway's 1925–1929 borrowing list from Sylvia Beach's Shakespeare and Company bookshop in Paris (detail).

Daniel, Samuel Barlow, and others, Stein once said during a salon evening, "I've been trying to persuade Hem to omit that fishing episode he's used twice already, but he maintains that he has no imagination and must use what happened to him. . . . If only Hem would give up that show-off soldiering, that bogus bull fighting, the lowdown on his friends and forget that phoney [*sic*] grace under pressure and just *be himself* he'd turn out a real book."[12]

Less often concerned about his subject matter, Stein encouraged Hemingway to find those rarely explored avenues to a central scene that would open into full expression—but never journalistically. To supplement this re-creation of what Hemingway's time at 27 rue de Fleurus might have given him, consider this description from painter and poet Marsden Hartley's 1921 book *Adventures in the Arts*, where he explained, "We have our best esthetics over the coffee." For Hartley, Stein's salon embodied the way painting and writing merge, conflate, and share essential qualities:

> The studio of Gertrude Stein, that quiet yet always lively place in the rue de
> Fleurus, is the only room I have ever been in where this spirit [existed] . . .
> for here you had the sense of the real importance of painting, as it used to be

thought of in the days of Pissarro, Manet, Degas, and the others, and you have much, in all human ways, out of an evening there, and, most of all, you had a fund of good humour thrust at you, and the conversation took on, not the quality of poetic prose . . . a kind of William James intimacy, which . . . is style bringing the universe of ideas to your door in terms of your own sensations.[13]

To create an atmosphere so open that all minds could find expression, since the genesis of the truly creative is individual—"your own sensations"—is far different from a lecture-class kind of strategy, which was the manner Pound often chose.

Hemingway's *In Our Time* became both the treasure *of* modernists and the instruction manual *for* modernist fiction. Given that he had continued to write for the *Toronto Star* and the *Star Weekly* through 1924, the accumulation of his good journalism far outweighed his good creative work. Wise enough to see the value in his vignettes and stories—some very short, others extremely long—Hemingway had found the essential spring, a source that Stein had been pointing him toward. He had taken a plunge into his by now opened consciousness: *In Our Time* was the reward for that exploration.

Shortly after Scribner's published the book, long after Hemingway had shown his innate shyness in somewhat fearfully meeting and befriending F. Scott Fitzgerald, whose *Great Gatsby* so impressed the literary world in early 1925 (although selling fewer copies than either of his first two novels, *This Side of Paradise* and *The Beautiful and Damned*), Hemingway wrote a tongue-in-cheek letter to Fitzgerald, the man who had left Princeton to enlist but never left the States during his time in the military. Dated December 15, 1925, Hemingway wrote,

> The reason you are so sore you missed the war is because war is the best subject of all. It groups the maximum of material and speeds up the action and brings out all sorts of stuff that normally you have to wait a lifetime to get. What made *Three Soldiers* a swell book was the war.[14] What made *Streets of Night* a lousy book was Boston. One was as well written as the other. . . . Love is also a good subject as you might be said to have discovered. . . .
>
> And don't for Christ sake feel bad about missing the war because I didn't see or get anything worth a damn out [of it] as a whole show, . . . because I was too young. Dos [Dos Passos], fortunately, went to the war twice and grew up in between. His first book was lousy. (*SL* 176–77)

Living as he was, still hampered by the effects of his myriad war injuries, Hemingway was here being disingenuous about what he had learned or not learned: as the oeuvre of his writing would show, he had seen incredible carnage (some of the worst, not on the battlefield but as he did his work for the ambulance service, clearing away the charred bodies—many of them women's bodies—after a munitions factory exploded outside of Munich); he had learned a great deal about the wounded and their painful recuperation during his months in the Milan hospital; he had continued to learn what happened to veterans—both in the States and in France—once a war ended and few people cared about those military men's survival. He found that for one who has not been there, the experiences of war cannot be imagined.

Being in France, and being in close contact with professional journalists who had themselves experienced the war, Hemingway kept learning about the First World War. As Alex Vernon points out, "America suffered fewer than 400,000 wartime casualties. . . . [In contrast,] at the Battle of the Somme alone, where Catherine's fiancé was killed [in *A Farewell to Arms*], the British suffered 419,654 casualties, the French 194,451 and the Germans around 600,000." Had Hemingway continued to live in the States, he would have been much more isolated. Vernon, himself a tank commander during the First Gulf War, also notes about the effects of Hemingway's war wounding: "Like Nick (and in part proven by the existence of Nick), the emotional trauma of the war continually reasserted itself through Hemingway's life. In addition, his legs provided a consistent physical reminder; over thirty years afterward, extreme pain sent him to the doctor, whose x-ray showed seven shell fragments and bits of bullet casings in his calves."[15]

British critic David Seed echoes Vernon's emphasis on the role of Nick Adams, noting that this character "exemplifies the sights and experiences of war. He is both seen and seeing; object and subject."[16] Obviously, Hemingway's personal experience gave him these avenues of perception. He had not only been "at war" and then, for a much longer period, "in convalescence," he had also later covered wars and peace negotiations throughout Europe. His subjective vision was forced to merge with the objectivity necessary for journalism; and throughout the process of his learning about war and its effects, he was reading—not only accounts of World War I but memoirs, fiction, battlefield stories, and maps. Hemingway was creating himself as *maestro of the battlefield*. Neither Ezra Pound nor Sherwood Anderson could mentor him in these subjects, but Stein's having driven a supply Ford for the Red Cross throughout France qualified her to be a kind of observer, although Hemingway would later deny any influence on her part.

Less competitive than becoming a writer of war was Hemingway's developing identity as writer of the bullfight. By the time of his publishing his 1932 *Death in the Afternoon*, a companion volume to the bullfight, Hemingway had thoroughly explored the lore and traditions of the religious ritual; he knew many of the premier bullfighters, and he valued his friendships with them. His exacting vignettes in *in our time* and *In Our Time* introduced the world of readers in English to the serious religious ceremony of the Spanish bullfight and to the risks matadors faced as they entered every ring.

As the manuscript collections of Hemingway materials (at the Lilly Library at Indiana University, the Harry Ransom Center at the University of Texas, and the John F. Kennedy Presidential Library) show, Hemingway kept stacks of materials about both bullfighting and war—fragments, essays, news clippings, maps, photographs, and manuscript drafts. These materials were his storehouse of valuables, and he had come to them almost from the start of his writing career. As Frederic Svoboda comments, "He was lucky to find his essential concerns rather early in life and even luckier that these concerns proved to be widely shared by the reading public." Svoboda notes that the central Hemingway themes were love and war, wilderness and loss; and that war undergirded his treatment of both loss and love.[17]

Part of Hemingway's strategy as he carefully wrote and arranged the vignettes that composed all of *in our time* and became interchapters within and between the short stories that created the longer book, *In Our Time*, was to disguise the centrality of the themes of both war and the bullfight. An avid reader of contemporary book reviews, Hemingway knew that he could not appear to be monolithic: he did not want to be the "returning wounded soldier" who wrote repeatedly about himself and his wounds.[18] He wanted to be the vibrant, even brilliant, young writer who knew how to create a story with very few well-chosen (and probably unexpected) words. He wanted the emphasis in the reviews of *In Our Time* to be on *craft*.

Partly for that reason, and also to bring the world of readers into the seriousness of the postwar decision-making period, Hemingway chose to use as his title a phrase from the English *Book of Common Prayer*. Not only did the sonority of *In Our Time* echo a religious passage in itself; it made the book appealing to readers who respected the new, even the avant garde, couched in the envelope of formal religious ceremony. Hemingway's 1925 book, then, echoed the tone of T. S. Eliot's *Waste Land* and perhaps suggested James Joyce's *Ulysses*. Modern writing was, without question, serious business. Although some of the vignettes are about crime in the United States, and many of the stories are about courtship, marriage, and male friendships, the dominant tone of the book comes from the war vignettes and stories. It is a tone of powerful seriousness. The exotic quality, the sense of romantic travel and unknown cultures, comes from the vignettes based on bullfighting—although at the heart of the bullfighting vignettes is the recognition of omnipresent death. Hemingway had learned during those months of trying to sell his fiction to popular magazines that he could not write candidly about his small midwestern town—nor could he be satiric about it.[19] What Hemingway had in his writer's kit was less a knowledge of comedy; it was instead truly remarkable material—the war, deaths of friends, his own wounding (told eventually in his 1929 novel *A Farewell to Arms* as an out-of-body experience, which his character Frederic Henry survives), the deaths of matadors as well as bulls, and stories of great love, as well as memories of European travel.

The centrally placed stories and vignettes in *In Our Time* are about war. The excitement of enlistment shapes some of the early vignettes, but most of the war pieces are somber, as are the evocative stories. These share the trauma of a damaged man's experience in returning home. Classically accurate in describing Harold Krebs's post-traumatic stress disorder, "Soldier's Home" draws the troubled veteran, alienated from all family members except his sister, trying to place himself in relation to the social norms he had once understood. Equating Krebs's mother with a superfluity of religious zeal, Hemingway chastises her for her utter ignorance about war and, more pointedly, her ignorance about what has damaged her son. (The mother's comments about her understanding what her father had endured during the Civil War are often ridiculed, as well as chosen to show the depths of the irony at play in the various dialogue scenes between Harold and his mother.)

All the "war" details in the story are blurred, caught as if in an aging photo, to indicate that Harold's reactions, too, are blurred. He is treading water/ treading life as he tries to avoid irreparably hurting his family, especially his mother, and probably as a result is irreparably hurting himself. What irony does exist spins outward from the story's title: "Soldier's Home" effectively misleads the reader to believe that the man has been institutionalized in some impersonal veterans' "home." But the more despairing realization for a reader is that Harold might have made a better recovery if he *had* been somewhere besides his own home. Subsequently, the initial, positive reading of *home* in the title is changed to one of despair, if not anger. As the bacon fat hardens on Harold's plate, and the reader envisions his taking someone who knows nothing about his experiences on a date in that prestigious family car, the sorrow the story has created etches only gloom for the reader.

"Big Two-Hearted River" gives the returning veteran a second kind of scrutiny. Going off alone, leaving that coercive family behind, the Nick Adams figure here conveys his decisions in meticulous detail—whether or not to carry the cans of food, whether to bait the hook with this or with that. Life-giving choices obscure the fact that the character has little "self" left to employ in making any choices. The protagonist of this story has no mentors—no family, no parents or grandparents, no lover—and his psychological health does not allow for anything but very limited, and careful, concentration. To get through an hour, a day, a week—that is the task for the troubled young veteran. The unusually long story, divided into two parts, leads the reader to empathize with this tense concentration: this man cannot do more than he is already accomplishing. One of the most diligent sections of Hemingway's objective description closes the story as, laboring over this prose poem, he worked to take the reader step by step through the end of the day spent fishing:

> Nick cleaned them [the trout], slitting them from the vent to the tip of the jaw. All the insides and the gills and tongue came out in one piece. They were both males; long gray-white strips of milt, smooth and clean. . . . He washed the trout in the stream. When he held them back up in the water they looked like live fish. Their color was not gone yet. He washed his hands and dried them on the log. Then he laid the trout on the sack spread out on the log, rolled them up in it, tied the bundle and put it in the landing net. (*IOT* 155)

Does Nick think his reverent care will, in fact, bring the dead back to life? How long does the appearance of life remain in a body already dead? The kinds of implied questions the description suggests create a metaphoric battle scene, set as it is—ironically—in the tranquility of Nick's beloved natural setting. And when he finishes his duties, having completed every part of those tasks with great seriousness, he comes to the goal he has set for himself, the creation of an elusive calm. The story closes with Nick's realization that "there were plenty of days coming when he could fish the swamp" (*IOT* 155–56).

Praised for its innovative structure, as well as the fact that a great deal of the emotional impact of both the separate stories and the vignettes is never directly expressed, Hemingway's *In Our Time* may be the first example of his reticence to tell his own story. James Meredith discusses the fact that it could be conscious—it could be that Hemingway was creating a "language of loss" that would serve to "project the disjointedness of the postwar, modern period."[20] Echoed by Ulrich Baer, this statement of theoretical causality might encompass forty years of modernist history: "The traumas of modernism are characterized by the way in which they disrupt established and conventional ways of human remembrance and forgetting, and in which this disruption can itself be traumatic. Modernist writing does not suspend reference but leaves undecided whether the imposition of meaning is overwhelming . . . or whether the words on the page bear no relation any longer to comprehensible reality."[21]

Any reading of *In Our Time* adds specificity and force to the sense of the permanence of war for its survivors. Hemingway opens the book with "On the Quai at Smyrna," a chilling account of an evacuation during the Greco-Turkish war during which the pack animals are dumped into the sea with their forelegs broken so that they will drown and cannot be used by the other army. More horrifying is the description of pregnant women giving birth under blankets on the chaotic pier. War writ large has no room for sympathy or pity.

"Chapter I" is the recruits' first mission: "Everybody was drunk." "Chapter II" returns to that Smyrna evacuation. "Chapter III" shows the deaths of German soldiers as they climb over a wall in France: "We shot them. They all came just like that" (*IOT* 29). (All the vignettes in the first group are war-related; the bullfight vignettes do not begin until "Chapter VIII.") Placed between the pairs of vignettes are the stories, arranged chronologically: "Indian Camp," with its Indian mother giving birth while the white doctor has forgotten to bring his anesthetic; "The Doctor and the Doctor's Wife," with the genteel doctor stealing lumber and accusing the Indian laborer of trying to cheat him; "The End of Something," as Hemingway's callous young man—no longer a child, as he was in the first stories—breaks up with his girlfriend. "Three-Day Blow" is a self-indulgent conversation between the same characters, Nick and Bill, who planned Nick's previous breakup.

There is another relatively positive vignette, "Chapter IV," in that the Allied Forces seem to be doing the killing. Then, in "Chapter V," six cabinet members are executed—some of them facing death less bravely than others. Treated with more emotion, in "Chapter VI" two soldiers are gravely wounded—or dead, in the case of Rinaldi. In "Chapter VII," which began this section above, the soldier's thoughts reveal his petrifying fear.

The stories that alternate with these vignettes also grow more and more troubled. In "The Battler," Nick comes to understand the damaged fighter as a man crushed in the crucible of a kind of fame—needing now to be cared for by his African American companion. The story of postwar lost love, "A Very Short Story," followed by "Soldier's Home," lends particulars to the somber vignettes about the conscious or unconscious maiming of war.

Following "Soldier's Home" comes "Chapter VIII," the police brutality there illustrating American racial prejudice and legal profiling. The United States cannot be considered superior to less educated countries so long as these practices continue. Then the bullfighting vignettes begin. These passages are not just an afterthought. They are integral, both in *in our time* as well as in *In Our Time*, to the description of, the continued presence of, the act of dying. If the tone of *In Our Time* is the somber plateau between living and dying, initiated perhaps by Hemingway's own stark realization of death's presence within life itself, then the embroidery of death onto life occurs as well in the bullfighting scenes.

Placing the specifics of bullfighters and their aim to participate courageously in the ritualized bullfights after the vignettes that chart criminal behavior in the United States is not accidental. Hemingway often praised the Spanish culture, its religious beliefs, and its adherence to tradition. As Malcolm Cowley wrote early, Hemingway's reverence for Spain had long been a part of his personal "preoccupation with death"; his kinship with the Spanish, said Cowley, was based on the fact that they "retain a primitive dignity in giving and accepting death."[22] With full recognition of the limitations of his highly focused and stylized vignettes, Hemingway barely introduced the Spanish culture here, but he would return to that country and to the highly significant ritual of bullfighting as soon as he attempted to write his early novel.

Hemingway's concerns in the fictions included in *In Our Time* were less geographical and political than they were familial. An important cluster of his stories portrays a young married couple, with "Cat in the Rain" paired with "Out of Season," in which the wife will not fish illegally and the husband feels sympathy for the drunken guide; the tone in both stories is *dissonance*. When Hemingway followed that pair with "Cross-Country Snow," the idyll about two men skiing in untracked Alpine snow takes on an even darker cast: because of his young wife's pregnancy, her spouse fears that his skiing days—like his masculine friendship—may be over.

The last two stories are "My Old Man," in which the bereaved son listens to the gossip about his father's perhaps criminal past and loses his sense of the man's value, and the two-part "Big Two-Hearted River." Between those two stories, the last of the bullfighting vignettes, "Chapter XIV," describes the death of Maera. (This is the first account in the book of actual death, and, ironically, that death occurs in the bullring and not on a battlefield.) The last "chapter," placed between the two halves of the concluding story, is the somber account (again set in the States) of the hanging of Sam Cardinella, a white man who is executed along with several African Americans. Working ironically, while the Nick Adams character survives to grow stronger back in the Michigan woods, Hemingway's narratives are punctuated with the deaths of a Spanish expert bullfighter and an American urban criminal.

Most of the vignettes and stories are about men. As Hemingway places "Indian Camp" and "The Doctor and the Doctor's Wife" at the beginning of the fictions, the reader is jarred into understanding the failure of one father in the eyes of his son, a motif that recurs at the end with "My Old Man." Contextualizing these fictions with the war vignettes leaves the reader to wonder, "Where do the sons of successful men learn to be successful?" Perhaps a larger question has to do with masculinity itself—when the husband in "Cat in the Rain" chooses not to hear his homesick wife, telling her abruptly to "shut up and get something to read," his behavior is far from sympathetic (*IOT* 94). Most of Hemingway's stories about young married couples seem to be fictions of *renunciation*, as if the author could never reclaim the joy he had felt hunting and fishing with his Michigan pals, or could never communicate with a woman in the same way he did with his Michigan, or his ambulance corps, or his journalism buddies. The tonal key is set in "The End of Something," but it recurs throughout the short-story oeuvre, most startlingly perhaps in Hemingway's "Hills Like White Elephants."[23]

Never focused on a single theme, even the briefest of these stories takes on interrelated, reemphasized narratives. The whole of *In Our Time* forces readers to find patterns that might exist tangentially, provoked only through a single metaphor; the places where connections might exist are left blank. *In Our Time* is a book of often surprising white spaces.

Just as Hemingway shaped "Indian Camp" to close with the son's reassurance from his father that nobody he loves will ever die, the childhood innocence of living in a well-ordered society runs again and again against harsh truth, *killing* truth. The book gains its surprising dimensionality through the combination of recurrence and emphasis, and it is aptly named. *In Our Time* is never simply or exclusively about war. It is much more encompassing as it shows the reader what postwar culture has become, after the governmental lies and the slaughter, the evacuations and the destruction. Throughout the Western world, dreams cannot exist again until the nightmares of war have been forgotten. The continuum that Hemingway had charted in his 1920s journalism—the European military conflicts, followed by the posturing at peace conferences, the posturing that substituted for genuinely intent peacemaking—helped to keep him realistically involved in world affairs. Even as a young American, Ernest Hemingway was never so politically naïve as either Ezra Pound or Gertrude Stein—or as Grace and Clarence Hemingway.

CHAPTER THREE

When the *Sun* Rose

IT WAS OFTEN considered a roman à clef. Hemingway's first real novel, *The Sun Also Rises*, appeared from Scribner's in 1926 and immediately propelled Hemingway into an elite kind of literary fame. Hadley said years later, with her usual candor, that she remembered every event in the book:

> I lived right through *The Sun Also Rises* and can remember almost the whole thing. The dialogue and situations are very true to what I recall happened. It was a very upset summer for me; I don't know why, because Ernest and I had not started to fall apart at that time. But everybody was drinking all the time, and everybody was having affairs all the time. . . . Harold Loeb had a glorious affair with Duff Twysden, a wonderfully attractive Englishwoman, a woman of the world with no sexual inhibitions.[1]

Flush with the success of *In Our Time*, Hemingway knew he had to give the readers of his world a novel. It was a long stretch from the prose poems of *In Our Time* to a full-length work of fiction. Perhaps taking his vignettes about bullfighting as a guide, he saw the summer visit to Pamplona, Spain, as his road map: the exoticism of the ritual and the gravitas of the Spanish people would be intensified when set against the roaming, and usually hedonistic, Americans and British. For in all respects, *The Sun Also Rises* was a postwar novel. Lured by the favorable exchange rate, travelers from both the United States and England were (literally) feasting in France, Italy, and Spain. Surely there was a compelling story resting within that apparent insistence on adventure.

When Hemingway started to write his novel, on his July 21st birthday in 1925, he had little idea where it would end. Recounting the process years later to George Plimpton, he admitted, "Everybody my age had written a novel and I was still having a difficult time writing a paragraph."[2] When he showed the manuscript to a friend, six weeks after that beginning, and the friend advised him to cut out some of the travel, Hemingway saw that those "travel" passages were the heart of the book: he realized that he needed to "keep in the travel (that was the part about the fishing trip and Pamplona)." Whereas the bull-fighting setting and scenes were comparatively new to him, Hemingway felt confident that he could do justice to the fishing adventures. These sections allowed him to return to his favorite memories about a Michigan that he pretended not to miss, but as his December 6, 1924, letter to Bill Smith makes clear, he knew that his summers in that state, along with his boyhood friends, could never be replaced.

> I know how damn good all our old stuff was Bird because everything, almost everything worth a damn I've written has been about that country [Michigan]. It was the whole damn business inside me and when I think about any country or doing anything it's always that old stuff, the Bay [Little Traverse], the farm, reinstein [*sic*] fishing, the swell times we used to have with Auntie [Mrs. Charles] at the farm, the first swell trips out to the Black and the Sturgeon and the wonderful times we had with the men and the storms in the fall and potato digging and the whole damn thing. And we've got them all and we're not going to lose them—and the only way we could ever lose them would be trying to go back and do them all over—but we can go on and get some new ones and some damn fine ones. Like over here and Spain and Austria up in the mts. in the winter time. (*SL* 136–37)

Since Hemingway's experiences with his boyhood friends were foundational for him, it seems to have been fairly easy for him to transfer those male friendships to his Spanish story.

In some respects, Hemingway had already won the substantial acclaim of modernist *readers*, and other modernist *writers*, with the publication of his first three small books. There was little need for him to practice those same moves with this European-American novel. Apprenticeship served, Hemingway could move much more casually through the worlds of his Paris modernist friends and New York publishers: he realized that what he had learned during the early years of the 1920s had provided him with deeply grounded prowess.

The mistake that Hemingway did *not* make in writing *The Sun Also Rises* was to invest the entire novel in the character of war-wounded Jacob Barnes: as the novel was read, Jake Barnes was a terse newspaperman, a modest American observer of the more British-dominated panoply of postwar survivors. Even as Hemingway seemed to think his story would encapsulate the beautifully tragic Lady Brett Ashley, who had survived both an abusive spouse and working as a Voluntary Aid Detachment (VAD) nurse in British hospitals, changes in his original manuscript lessened that character's importance. As Frederic Svoboda's important 1983 analysis of the novel's manuscripts makes clear, Hemingway's long introductory section about Brett—which originally began the book—was slashed and nearly deleted, leaving the character of Princeton boxer Robert Cohn to provide the book's opening.[3] By having Cohn, in tandem with Jake Barnes, provide a bifurcated narrative perspective, Hemingway changed the story from a glamorous postwar saga to a masculine tour de force. That fiction was able to include the wounded but wise Count Mippipopolous as well as long passages of dialogue with the British fisherman Wilson-Harris. It is this character who takes readers back to the war years when he thanks Jake and Bill for fishing with him: "Really you don't know how much it means. I've not had such fun since the war" (*SAR* 129). The dialogues among Wilson-Harris, Jake, and Bill are extensive (as are the dialogue scenes between Jake and Bill throughout the novel), as if to emphasize the importance of the community of men, happy to be existing together, separate and apart from either the bullfights or Brett. The novel accordingly became a more accessible story, particularly given the temper of the modernist times: readers had survived World War I, or they were visibly damaged by it, or they had made bad—or good—choices about drinking and working and loving on the basis of their war experiences.

Reading further back in the handwritten manuscripts of *The Sun Also Rises*, however, one finds an even earlier version of the novel's opening. In manuscript #197 of the Ernest Hemingway Collection at the John F. Kennedy Library, Hemingway's novel begins with a description of the Spanish "boy," a figure of European/Spanish innocence who has become a rising matador:

The Sun Also Rises

A Novel

It was half past 3 in the afternoon in the dark bedroom in the Hotel Montoya in Pamplona, Spain. It was a cheap room because the boy who lived in it had not yet learned to appreciate luxury. He stood under the electric light in the center of the room and he seemed quite alone altho there were five people in the bedroom.

He was 20 years old and very straight and handsome and unsmiling. Each afternoon that he killed bulls he made seven thousand five hundred pesetas which is a little over a thousand dollars. This year if nothing happened he would make seventy thousand dollars. Montoya, the owner of the hotel, made a little speech telling the boy what great lovers of bullfighting the Americans were. Pedro Romero listened very seriously.

In #197A, the revision of this beginning, the prose quickens; the figure $60,000 instead of $70,000 is used to suggest Romero's annual money-earning possibilities, and the text moves quickly to describe Brett's attraction to the bullfighter. But the sense of real innocence, which this short text creates through the repetition of "boy," is consistent.[4]

Judging from the number of (unfinished) starts that the Hemingway Collection contains, one of Hemingway's favorite places to turn for new fictions was to the male friendships that had marked his boyhood in Michigan, his first war experience in Italy, and the Paris of his first marriage. These friendships would, literally, have been among very young men—"boys"—and so his connecting himself as author here with Pedro Romero, the startlingly young matador (despite the character's being named as if he were the famous matador of Spanish history), created an unusually revealing dimension.

The personal dimensions in *The Sun Also Rises* were carefully fictionalized. Set in Paris and Pamplona, the novel attributes contemporary living to the characters' postwar malaise. Lives are in disarray. Brett, who worked during the war as a VAD, has seen plenty of sorrow; Jake Barnes is unrelievedly the wounded survivor. (One of the book's most memorable images is of Jake's inspecting his body: "Undressing, I looked at myself in the mirror of the big armoire beside the bed." The scene continues with comments about the way French rooms are furnished. Jake then thinks to himself, "Of all the ways to be wounded, I suppose it was funny" [*SAR* 303]). His wound seemingly discounted, Jake and his crippling become central to the novel's tone. When Miriam Marty Clark describes Hemingway's 1920s writing as presenting a map of "collective suffering," she assesses that suffering as stemming from "the deeply embedded violence of marriage, the outright violence of life among men, the brutal violence of war."[5]

Rather than focusing on one or two characters, or one or two romances, Hemingway here drew from a wealth of relationships. The men compete not just for Brett's affections but for each other's friendship:[6] at the center of the male wrangling stands Jake, withdrawn from most actual conflict. The women compete for the love of the young matador. The Spanish bullfights are depicted as arenas for conflict, buttressed by the religion underpinning the battles, "sport" a more appealing matrix than the carnage of war.

Figure 4. Hemingway with other American expatriates at dinner in Pamplona, Spain, 1925. *Above left*, Gerald and Sara Murphy; *above right*, Pauline Pfeiffer, Hemingway, and Hadley Hemingway.

Running throughout the book, whether Hemingway was drawing fishing scenes or bullfights, bedroom scenes or bar conversations, is a steady set of classical analogies: Jake Barnes as surrogate for the long-suffering biblical Jacob, with overtones of Roland, the great French warrior immortalized in *La Chanson de Roland* in the eleventh century. The Rinaldi who appeared both in the key *In Our Time* vignettes and in Hemingway's 1929 *A Farewell to Arms* is the second-in-command for Roland in this epic. The primary historical battle occurred at Roncesvalles, the site of Bill and Jake's pilgrimage with their new friend Wilson-Harris, and it is there that Jake finds, and begins to absorb, peace. There are analogies between Brett and Circe. Throughout the religious scenes, Jake is comfortable, but Brett prefers to visit the gypsy camps (at one point, she is turned away from a Catholic church because she wears no hat: she cannot even try to go to confession).

Much of the heart of this novel takes place in Spain, so that the highly ritualized celebration of the Catholic religion absorbs the reader. As some critics point out, Hemingway saw the bullfight as an analogue for the writer's art: "Bullfighting was Hemingway's metaphor or model for the artist's way. He was first attracted to the bullfight because only there, after the war, could he observe violent death, one of the 'simplest things' and therefore one of the most important for a writer to study."[7] As Carlos Baker argues, Hemingway's use of the first chapter of Ecclesiastes ("All is vanity and vexation of spirit") gives the novel an unexpectedly moral tone. In Baker's words, "The moral norm of the book is a healthy and almost boyish innocence of spirit, and it is carried by Jake Barnes, Bill Gorton, and Pedro Romero." Set against these innocents is the more sophisticated trio of "Ashley-Campbell-Cohn." "Something tarnished is opposed to something bright; vanity is challenged by sanity."[8]

Part of the innocent effect Baker stresses here came from the presence of Bill Gorton, Jake's old friend, with whom he creates an American alliance. Hemingway showed the depth of their friendship through much of the humor that exists in the novel, and as James Hinkle and Scott Donaldson point out, Bill's humor is both wise and contagious. Bill, modeled on Hemingway's friend Donald Ogden Stewart, "directs jibes at ideas and institutions, not human beings," Donaldson says. "In this way, Gorton provides a model of behavior that—unlike the code of the intrepid Romero—it is possible to emulate." As Jake reflects in one of his monologues, "I did not care what it was all about. All I wanted to know was how to live in it" (*SAR* 148). Bill seems to have discovered how: without Jake's sarcasm, without Mike's and Brett's disingenuous self-deprecation. As Donaldson notes, "The lengthy dialogue passages between Bill and Jake also reinforce the Americanness of their attitudes as well as of their language."[9]

In the assessment of Zvonimir Radeljkovic, maintaining the sense of Americans' ingenuous attitudes was crucial. He points out that four of Hemingway's seven novels (those published in his lifetime) take place in Europe:

> Italy, France and Spain, perhaps not in that order, were all at some time, his second countries, lands where culture, civilization and characteristic world-view helped him at least to appreciate his own. War, to be sure, was perhaps the main European ingredient which Hemingway saw in 1919 [1918]. War revealed itself to the still idealistic Midwestern boy who dreamed of heroism and saw the enemy as the visiting football team through Paris bombarded by the Big Bertha; through Milan where the munition factory had exploded on the day of his arrival and where he helped carry parts of dead female bodies; and finally through his wound near Fossalta.[10]

John Aldridge takes this commentary a step further when he links Hemingway's fiction with "instruction manuals or how to respond to and behave in the testing situations of life now that the rules have changed and the world has become, in effect, an unknown foreign country." Attributing these kinds of changes to the war, Aldridge notes that place—always one of Hemingway's primary concerns—became more fluid during circumstances that existed postwar.[11]

The finesse Hemingway achieved in his organization of the narrative about Jake, Brett, Bill, Robert, Pedro, Mike, and the rest of the cast of characters takes several readings to appreciate. *The Sun Also Rises* was assembled from the juxtaposition of scenes, as well as kinds of stories, and its effect as pastiche makes its relationship to modernist writing clear. Embedded in those long dialogue passages, highlighted by the increasingly bitter conflicts among the characters that turn *fiesta* into minor-league war, is the Jake-Brett plotline. Despite his resolve, Jake cannot abandon some vestigial hope that he will, somehow, succeed in winning Brett. In the boil of the fast-paced narrative, the reader hopes for a romantic resolution. Instead, Hemingway created the famous brief closing (often quoted to illustrate what irony meant to modernism). "Oh, Jake. . . . We could have had such a damned good time together," says Brett. But even before his answer, the reader knows from the contextualizing that Hemingway provided that this pairing is not going to work.

What happens in the brief book 3 is Jake's return to a kind of sanity he earlier experienced. He has spent time alone in France, at San Sebastian, envying the professional bicycle riders, swimming, being on his own. His tranquil state of mind allows him to answer Brett—sadly, without malice—"Yes. . . . Isn't it pretty to think so?" (*SAR* 147).[12] Because this closing follows Jake's peaceful time alone, his state of mind tends to elevate the book's closing scene.[13]

Any sense of how different *The Sun Also Rises* would have been if Hemingway had kept the Pedro Romero opening makes this concept of Jake Barnes as *American* speaker, *American* patriot, indelible. In the published novel, Pedro Romero is not introduced till page 163, and then Montoya presents him—with almost no physical description and no details about his room or his wages—to Jake as if *only* Jake deserves to meet the young matador. By making his reader aware of both Robert Cohn's and Jake Barnes's privileged American life, and by setting that life against the British existences that seem equally privileged (of Brett and her friends), Hemingway drew *any* Spanish life, even that of a relatively famous matador, into a more moral, even religious, landscape, which most of the "foreigners" have difficulty appreciating.

Because the structure of the novel allows Jake to find answers eventually, *The Sun Also Rises* was a kind of answer to T. S. Eliot's *Waste Land*. Whereas F. Scott Fitzgerald's *Great Gatsby* may have answered Eliot mockingly, especially if readers were taught to train their sights on the word *great*, *The Sun Also Rises* brought those same attentive readers into the full sun of optimism about the outcome of war-damaged characters. A few years later, in his *Death in the Afternoon*, Hemingway wrote about the Spanish reverence for the sun, and his explanation can enlighten readers on the title of his first book:

> The sun is very important. The theory, practice and spectacle of bullfighting have all been built on the assumption of the presence of the sun and when it does not shine over a third of the bullfight is missing. The Spanish say, "El Sol es el mejor torero." The sun is the best bullfighter, and without the sun the best bullfighter is not there. He is like a man without a shadow. (*DIA* 15)

Considering the 1926 *The Sun Also Rises* in comparison to Hemingway's 1932 nonfiction study of the bullfight shows the continuing thread between the postwar malaise he drew in the earlier novel and his often somber thoughts in the second book about the ritual of Spanish bullfighting, a serious endeavor that (even as he talked about it as being corrupted) endured in the country's culture, regardless of tourism and its necessary abuses.

It was in *Death in the Afternoon* that Hemingway wrote about his personal wounding from an abstract perspective, saying "a man who has been wounded knows that the pain of a wound does not commence until about a half an hour after it has been received and there is no proportional relation in pain to the horrible aspect of the wound" (*DIA* 9). It was here also that he wrote about his great respect for the matador and his willingness to live with the threat of death:

> The matador, from living every day with death, becomes very detached, the measure of his detachment of course is the measure of his imagination and always on the day of the fight and finally during the whole end of the season, there is a detached something in their minds that you can almost see. What is there is death and you cannot deal in it each day and know each day there is a chance of receiving it without having it make a very plain mark. (*DIA* 56)

Famous for its pithy definitions of bullfighting (such as "The bullfight . . . is a tragedy; the death of the bull, which is played, more or less well, by the bull and the man involved . . ." [*DIA* 16]), the book contains some of Hemingway's most brutal descriptions—not only of the ritualized bullfights but of war and its wounding.

One early scene in *Death in the Afternoon*, for instance, describes a young brother and sister who are seeking revenge on the bull that gored and killed their older brother. When the aging bull is slated for slaughter in Valencia, the brother asks that he be allowed to kill the animal (the siblings had tracked the bull for several years). Hemingway described the boy's actions, digging out both of the bull's eyes

> while the bull was in his cage, and spitting carefully into the sockets, then after killing him by severing the spinal marrow between the neck vertebrae with a dagger, he experienced some difficulty in this, he asked permission to cut off the bull's testicles, which, being granted, he and his sister built a small fire at the edge of the dusty street outside the slaughter-house and roasted the two glands on sticks and when they were done, ate them. (*DIA* 25)

Emphasizing the youth of the siblings, Hemingway created an image of revenge that seemingly justified the youngsters' acts and revealed the toll taken by their immense bereavement.

There are also scenes in the book of death in the bullring, or the memory of such wounding. Several times, Hemingway created a visualization that is scarifying.

> Waking in the night I tried to remember what it was that seemed just out of my remembering and that was the thing that I had really seen and, finally, remembering all around it, I got it. When he stood up, his face white and dirty and the silk of his breeches opened from waist to knee, it was the dirtiness of his slit underwear and the clean, clean, unbearably clean whiteness of the thigh bone that I had seen, and it was that which was important. (*DIA* 20)

Hemingway added this revealing caveat, "For myself, not being a bullfighter, and being much interested in suicides, the problem was one of depiction" (*DIA* 20).

In retrospect, in *In Our Time*, Hemingway described Maera's death in much detail. He devoted two of the *In Our Time* vignettes to this bullfighter, concluding the second one, "Chapter XIV," with his impressionistic whirl into the matador's final loss of consciousness.[24] That segment begins, "Maera lay still, his head on his arms, his face in the sand. He felt warm and sticky from the bleeding. Each time he felt the horn coming. Sometimes the bull only bumped him with his head. Once the horn went all the way through him and he felt it go into the sand" (*IOT* 131). Of the unnamed matadors who are gored in the first two segments of the bullfight described in "Chapter IX," less description is given; the emphasis lies instead on "the kid," the youngest bullfighter, who faces having to fight five bulls rather than three.

In contrast, there are no descriptions of the bulls killed in *The Sun Also Rises*. Hemingway's attention in the novel remained on Jake's instruction of Brett about what she was seeing, particularly about the skill with which Pedro Romero killed his bulls. The only goring described is a pre-bullfight casualty, a slow-moving steer. Hemingway wrote about that death in an interesting imagistic way. Given that most of the men in the novel are vying for Brett, the symbolism of the wounded steer's becoming a pariah seems applicable to her competitive suitors: "The steer who had been gored had gotten to his feet and stood against the stone wall. None of the bulls came near him, and he did not attempt to join the herd" (*SAR* 140). There is also the goring and death of Vicente Girones, the bystander whose funeral is given a reflective space as if to echo the waiter's lament, "All for fun. Just for fun" (*SAR* 197). Almost as a replacement for the actual deaths of matadors and bulls, Hemingway chose to include a somber description of the tawdry properties of the bullfight itself.

The sword-handlers and bull-ring servants came down the callejon carrying on their shoulders the wicker baskets of fighting capes and muletas. They were bloodstained and compactly folded and packed in the baskets. The sword-handlers opened the heavy leather sword-cases so the red wrapped hilts of the sheaf of swords showed as the leather case leaned against the fence. They unfolded the dark-stained red flannel of the muletas and fixed batons in them to spread the stuff and give the matador something to hold. (*SAR* 211)

This use of the imagistic technique of expressing emotion through the factual—or, in the phrase coined by William Carlos Williams, "no ideas but in things"—showed Hemingway's constant push to shape a reader's consciousness through various layers of narrative. Whoever read *The Sun Also Rises* would have a similar sense of disappointment, of sorrow, as the characters that experience the bullfights.

Several times in *Death in the Afternoon*, Hemingway meditated on what it took to become a matador. "The usual bullfighter is a very brave man, the most common degree of bravery being the ability temporarily to ignore possible consequences. A more pronounced degree of bravery, which comes with exhilaration, is the ability *NOT* to give a damn for possible consequences; not only to ignore them but to despise them" (*DIA* 58). In a later passage, Hemingway clarified this definition through a description of the killing: "The whole end of the bullfight was the final sword thrust, the actual encounter between the man and the animal, what the Spanish call the *moment of truth*, and every move in the fight was to prepare the bull for that killing" (*DIA* 68). His positive view of the killing required in a successful bullfight came through in a different discussion, as he pointed out, "If the people of Spain have one common trait it is pride and if they have another it is common sense and if they have a third it is impracticality. Because they have pride they do not mind killing. . . . As they have common sense they are interested in death and do not spend their lives avoiding the thought of it and hoping it does not exist only to discover it when they come to die" (*DIA* 264).

Critics of Hemingway's work, from John Killinger, who in 1960 named the American author an existentialist because of his interest in death and dying,[15] back through Ivan Kashkeen[16] and Malcolm Cowley in the 1930s, to his current biographers and such recent critics as Mark Cirino, Trevor Dodman, James Plath, and David Richter, share the belief that much about Hemingway's fascination with death stemmed from his early European experiences, both those of war and those of the bullfight. For Richter, Hemingway, like French philosopher Georges Bataille, "experienced Spanish culture first-hand and . . . [was] captivated by the invigorating force of death and its implications for artistic expression. Hemingway, for example, maintains that through an understanding of death one can further appreciate and experience an enhanced life. Indeed, his works related to Spanish culture and bullfighting exhibit a profound consideration of death and the graceful artistry that gives rise to an aesthetic rooted in deathly tones."[17] In this regard, Hemingway seems closest in spirit to the Spanish poet Federico Garcia Lorca, with his professed love for the duende. Lorca, too, found ranges of character in the matadors' bravery within the bullring.

For critic Mark Cirino, Hemingway remains "a writer so notoriously fascinated with death" that all his works must be read through that perspective, an activity this critic calls "a rich, rare phenomenological experience."[18] John Killinger summarizes Hemingway's philosophy, calling it a vision of

> violence in the blinding flash of a shell, in the icy-burning impact of a bullet, in the dangerous vicinity of a wounded lion, in the sudden contact of a bull's horn, in that ill-defined twilight between life and immanent death where time and place are irrelevant questions [and] man faces his freedom. Nothing has any

meaning at that instant except survival and existence. The superfluities of culture, race, tradition, even religion, all disappear in the face of one overpowering fact—the necessity to exist on an individual basis. This is the "separate peace," the only peace which can be won in our time.[19]

For Richard Ruland and Malcolm Bradbury, the fact that Hemingway's best writing occurred in some of his stories and in *A Farewell to Arms* (works that dealt with "his own serious wounding, his initiation into modern exposure . . . his fundamental loss and his conviction that modern war and violence emptied the great heroic abstractions") shows the power of his "acquaintance with a new historical condition and so leads onward into a world of trauma, sleeplessness, an awareness of *nada*, of all meaning lost except that which can be arduously reconstructed."[20]

Most of Hemingway's own writing would never present such an abstract assessment—at least not without a hint of personal anger. But implicit in much of his fiction, as well as in passages from *Death in the Afternoon*, is the pervasive concern not only about death but also about its presence within many of life's encounters. Perhaps Hemingway tried to relieve the effects of some of his vivid detail in *Death in the Afternoon*. As he was reading the proofs for the book, he added the supposedly humorous character of the obtuse "old lady." One of the dialogues between the narrator and this figure is useful (others, however, are not). For example, the narrator explains to this woman about the inevitability of death,

> Madame, all stories, if continued far enough, end in death, and he is no true-story teller who would keep that from you. Especially do all stories of monogamy end in death, and your man who is monogamous while he often lives most happily, dies in the most lonely fashion. There is no lonelier man in death, except the suicide, than that man who has lived many years with a good wife and then outlived her. If two people love each other there can be no happy end to it. (*DIA* 122)[21]

Among other sections of dialogue between Hemingway's narrator and the old lady are two somewhat inexplicable inclusions for a book ostensibly about bullfighting. The second is a dialogue overheard by a newspaperman and related to the narrator, a homosexual tryst, with the younger and, one assumes, more naïve man crying out, "I didn't know it was that. Oh, I didn't know it was that! I won't! I won't!" followed by what the newspaperman describes as "a despairing scream" (*DIA* 181).

More troublesome in some ways was Hemingway's placing what he later admitted is a short story at the center of *Death in the Afternoon*. "A Natural History of the Dead" is not about bullfighting; rather, it recounts the terrors of the narrator's picking up bodies and body parts after the 1918 munition factory explosion. Reeking with a complacent irony, the narrator uses this selection to calm the old lady listener, who is disappointed in his stories. The narrator pacifies her with the statement that this story was written "in popular style and is designed to be the Whittier's *Snow Bound* of our time," adding, "It's not about wild animals nor bulls" (*DIA* 133). Tangentially, if the old lady feared those topics, what she is about to hear is far beyond any of the bullfighting details included in the book: "A Natural History of the Dead" is both gruesome and relentless.

Pretending to draw from the best scientific methodology, given his title for the story, the narrator opens the piece matter-of-factly: "It has always seemed to me that the war has been omitted as a field for the observations of the naturalist." Accolades then accrue to the uses of scientific method, with emotion either distilled or omitted. The narrator's staged language conveys his adherence to the scientific method. He notes, for example,

> In war the dead are usually the male of the human species although this does not hold true with animals, and I have frequently seen dead mares among the horses. An interesting aspect of war, too, is that it is only there that the naturalist has an opportunity to observe the dead of mules. (*DIA* 134)

When the old lady interrupts, telling the speaker that he has written about dead mules before (in "On the Quai at Smyrna"), the reader's attention moves to these preliminary pages of stilted exposition. Then the narrator begins the story proper, using a segue from the fact that *male* bodies are the usual subjects of discussions about the dead. His manner is forthright:

> The sight of a dead woman is quite shocking. I first saw inversion of the usual sex of the dead after the explosion of a munition factory. . . . We drove to the scene of the disaster in trucks along poplar-shaded roads, bordered with ditches containing much minute animal life, which I could not clearly observe because of the great clouds of dust raised by the trucks. Arriving where the munition plant had been, some of us were put to patrolling about those large stocks of munitions which for some reason had not exploded, while others were put at extinguishing a fire. . . . We were ordered to search the immediate vicinity and surrounding fields

for bodies. We found and carried to an improvised mortuary a good number of these, and, I must admit, frankly, the shock it was to find that these dead were women rather than men. . . . [Then] we collected fragments. Many of these were detached from a heavy, barbed-wire fence which had surrounded the position of the factory and from the still existent portions of which we picked many of these detached bits. . . . The picking up of the fragments had been an extraordinary business; it being amazing that the human body should be blown into pieces which exploded along no anatomical lines, but rather divided as capriciously as the fragmentation in the burst of a high explosive shell. (*DIA* 135–37)

Continuing in his pseudoscientific tone, the narrator then discusses the fact that there were no wounded at all. The explosion had killed everyone.

The next site of observation was the Austrian military offensive of June 1918. Having observed the bodies of both Italians and Austrians, he notes archly that the bodies deteriorated every day: "The color change in Caucasian races is from white to yellow, to yellow-green, to black. If left long enough in the heat the flesh comes to resemble coal-tar . . . and it has quite a visible tarlike iridescence. The dead grow larger each day until sometimes they become quite too big for their uniforms, filling these until they seem blown tight enough to burst" (*DIA* 137).

Such repulsive description continues, again, as if in "scientific" writing. After his description of the Spanish influenza that killed millions during World War I, the narrator closes the story with an account of a powerful medical doctor who played God within his field station.

The doctor could not save the wounded, but neither could he kill them. To an objection from an artillery officer (who thought killing the wounded would be more merciful than letting them suffer), the doctor "tossed the saucer full of iodine in his face," blinding him. Then "the lieutenant fumbled for his pistol. The doctor skipped quickly behind him, tripped him and, as he fell to the floor, kicked him several times and picked up the pistol in his rubber gloves. The lieutenant sat on the floor holding his good hand to his eyes."

"I'll kill you!" he said. "I'll kill you as soon as I can see."
"I am the boss," said the doctor. "All is forgiven since you know I am the boss. You cannot kill me because I have your pistol." (*DIA* 143)

In the narrator's earlier fusion of animal and human, male and female, careful detail and gruesome coloration, all polite categories of response have been lost. Only as the seemingly well-intentioned doctor abandons his façade of civility does the truth about warfare emerge.[22] The brutalization of everyone connected with its shameless destruction marks the end of Hemingway's story.

Death in the Afternoon ends with many pages of photographs from the bullfights, along with a substantial glossary of terms and chronologies of dates for the bullfights. It was much worked over in the proof stage, as Hemingway told John Dos Passos: "Have gone over book 7 times and cut out all you objected to (seemed like the best to me God damn you if it really was)" (*SL* 360).

A letter to Max Perkins, his editor at Scribner's, at about the same time shows that Hemingway was frustrated in 1932 by the advance publicity for this book, which was admittedly not fiction (for the most part). He was feeling that his writerly judgment was being questioned by not only Perkins but all the literary world. Accordingly, Hemingway wrote Perkins an unusually outspoken letter. His chief complaint was that the typesetter had headed every other galley page with the rubric "Hemingway's Death." In his words, "You know I am superstitious and it is a hell of a damn dirty business to stare at that a thousand times even to having it (in this last filthy batch) written in with red and purple ink. If I would have passed out would have said your goddamned lot put the curse on me" (*SL* 361).[23]

As famous and established as the literary world thought Hemingway had become, his private letters show that his investment in whatever he wrote, and the way that writing was perceived, remained the most important consideration of his existence.

CHAPTER FOUR

To the War

HEMINGWAY REFLECTED THAT he had written only three stories about World War I before he attempted his novel *A Farewell to Arms*. He listed "In Another Country," "Now I Lay Me," and "A Way You'll Never Be," clearly thinking of the other apparent stories of the war—"Soldier's Home" and "Big Two-Hearted River"—as somehow integral to *In Our Time* and so discounting them in this listing. As he arranged his finished stories for the publication of his second collection of short stories, *Men Without Women*, scheduled to appear in 1927, he chose to open the book with "The Undefeated," the bullfighting story that had been published twice before. He followed that story, however, with "In Another Country." Rich as this collection is, including such short stories as "The Killers" and "Hills Like White Elephants" (the two stories that follow "In Another Country"), Hemingway inferred that readers would understand the strong relationships among these first two stories—or, perhaps, the first four stories—and the fiction he chose to close the book, "Now I Lay Me." He carefully, then, chose to keep *Men Without Women* focused on the death and loss that resulted from both war and the surrogate warfare of the bullring, of love, and of crime.

Remembering Hemingway's desire *not* to be the single-theme writer, identified as the returning veteran writing about his wounding and his troubled return to civilization, many readers responded accurately to the arrangement of both of the collections that followed *In Our Time* (*Men Without Women* in 1927; *Winner Take Nothing* in 1933). Besides emphasizing the bleakness of isolation and loss, the title *Men Without Women* signaled an unexpected theme: less about war than relationships, the 1927 collection included only two war stories, which Hemingway had written, together, during the autumn of 1926. He described "In Another Country" as a strong story. And when—during the same month—he began to write "Now I Lay Me," he titled it "In Another Country—II." This strategy of connection had worked for him when he published the two parts of "Big Two-Hearted River," placing them together at the close of *In Our Time*. For "In Another Country" and "Now I Lay Me," however, Hemingway's tactic was to place them at opposite ends of the collection. Critic Paul Smith notes that because "In Another Country" was "too revealing, too obviously autobiographical," Hemingway did not try to publish it in journals.[1]

Smith's indispensable *Reader's Guide to the Short Stories of Ernest Hemingway* discusses all his published stories in the order of their *composition*, not as Hemingway arranged them within books. Smith's emphasis shows that Hemingway realized the power in these war stories, as well as the importance of their placement within the collections. He chose to, in effect, open *Men Without Women* with "In Another Country," bringing the reader's attention to its power as a construct of *language*.

The first story in the book is "The Undefeated," probably to attract readers who already knew *The Sun Also Rises*. That story, however, was several years old and had been published previously. Hemingway was much more interested in readers' responses to "In Another Country." In this somber story, Hemingway drew from the successful mood he had created to etch Jake Barnes in *The Sun Also Rises*. Reticent, even taciturn, Barnes became a prototype for the returning—and wounded—veteran. There are some glimpses of action, but here the war is presented through tone, not act. As Hemingway often replied when questioned about his writing, he liked to use repetition, placing a word in the text "consciously over and over the way Mr. Johann Sebastian Bach used a note in music when he was emitting counterpoint."[2] Accordingly, "In Another Country" opens,

> In the fall the war was always there, but we did not go to it any more. It was cold in the fall in Milan and the dark came very early. Then the electric lights came on, and it was pleasant along the streets looking in the windows. There was much game hanging outside the shops, and the snow powdered in the fur of the foxes and the wind blew their tails. The deer hung stiff and heavy and empty, and small birds blew in the wind and the wind turned their feathers. (*CSS* 206)

Here, the resonating words are *fall, cold, and* (used as more than a conjunction), and *wind*. The word *war* appears only once. All repeated words are accented in their respective sentences, and their position in the sentence gives them more prominence than does their literal meaning, cushioned as they are among descriptive prepositional phrases. The paragraph itself seems to be extended because Hemingway made use of delayed sentences ("In the fall," "It was," "it was pleasant," "There was much game"); of carefully staged, step-by-step description; and of a hollowness at the center of the story. That the story is about the broken and wounded older character, dying not from his withered hand but from the unexpected loss of his young wife, carries out what is already a typical Hemingway pattern of reticence. The wounds are not those of the war so much as they are the wounds of a loving life.

Like a fugue, the ending sentence of this opening paragraph provides an effective refrain:

> It was a *cold fall and* the *wind* came down from the mountains.[3]

Miriam Marty Clark points out that stories that do not belong to the (understood) Nick Adams character (such as "In Another Country") differ appreciably from the more autobiographical "Now I Lay Me," in which it is Nick's insomnia, the testament to his war wounding, that governs the action.[4] In that story, Hemingway set up a striking contrast between the stoic Nick and his younger, optimistic aide-de-camp, John. In effect, the author pitted the understanding of war against the pious platitudes of a non-war society. When John tells his superior officer that marriage would solve his traumatic symptoms, the reader has only to revert to the title of the collection. That same reader might take a detour to the third story, "Hills Like White Elephants," and then move on to the cluster of "marriage" stories ("A Canary for One," "An Alpine Idyll," and the memories of Nick's parents' studied cruelty to each other, described in "Now I Lay Me") to see the futility of the younger man's suggestion.

Despite its title, the tone of "Now I Lay Me" is far from prayer. It is rather of a prayer frustrated, so that the childlike innocence of the story's opening keeps the reader focused on the war-ravaged man's childhood—and, then, accordingly, on his parents. There is no religious comfort here, only the stifling silence of the intrusive natural world:

> That night we lay on the floor in the room and I listened to the silk-worms eating. The silk-worms fed in racks of mulberry leaves and all night you could hear them eating and a dropping sound in the leaves. I myself did not want to sleep because I had been living for a long time with the knowledge that if I ever shut

my eyes in the dark and let myself go, my soul would go out of the body. I had
been that way for a long time, ever since I had been blown up at night and felt it
go out of me and go off and then come back. (*CSS* 276)[5]

For all his reliance on repetition, Nick does *not* repeat the story of his
wounding; what he turns to regularly in the story is the sound of the silk-
worms, doing what they are required to do by nature, just as he later tells John
that he *will* recover: "I'll get all right. It just takes a while" (*CSS* 281). As Clark
observes, most of Hemingway's story collections stemmed from "Nick's own
story. . . . It takes many stories to tell *a* story of suffering. . . . *Woundedness*
calls for metaphor, reiterations, silences—more than Nick's story alone will
bear. . . . At the same time, Nick's injuries provide a metaphor for the suffer-
ings of the world. The crouched, the dying, the traumatized become knowable
by us through our engagement with Nick, not only in his narrative account
but also in the emotional demands a story like 'Now I Lay Me' makes on us."[6]

We have seen that Hemingway included one story from his third collection, *Winner Take Nothing*, among the "war stories" that he said came before
the "war" novel, *A Farewell to Arms*. (According to Smith, that story, "A Way
You'll Never Be," was written in 1932, so Hemingway's memory failed him
about its chronology.) In looking at this story—focused on war-induced mental breakdown—the reader might benefit from a consideration of the second
story in that collection, "A Clean, Well-Lighted Place." ("A Way You'll Never
Be" is the fifth story in the book.) Again borrowing the image of a child's
prayer, Hemingway converted the words of all religious terms to the single
Spanish word *nada* in his bleak narrative of the old man who has lost hope.

For the survivor who takes what comfort he can in "A Clean, Well-Lighted
Place," the alcohol that helps erase memory, like the light that enables him to
see, merges with the support of other sympathetic men. It is the "unhurried"
waiter who argues with the impatient one, trying to allow the old man (described as "a very old man walking steadily but with dignity") more time in the
clean café. This man goes to his own bed to face his own brand of insomnia.
"Many must have it," this waiter tells himself consolingly as the story closes.

This character translates "The Lord's Prayer" into the *nada* version that
made the story famous. Unexpectedly, given his empathy with the customer
who has earlier tried to hang himself, he dreads the return to his own lonely
home: "What did he fear? It was not fear or dread. It was a nothing that he
knew too well. It was all a nothing and a man was nothing too. It was only
that and light was all it needed and a certain cleanness and order. Some lived

in it and never felt it but he knew it all was *nada y pues nada y nada y pues nada*. Our *nada* who art in *nada*, *nada* be thy name thy kingdom *nada* thy will be *nada . . .*" (*CSS* 291).

Aligning "A Way You'll Never Be" with "A Clean, Well-Lighted Place," perhaps Hemingway's most powerful story of relinquishment, the reader understands the full damage of the scene that opens the former. As Nick replays the battle through visualizing the positions of dead soldiers in the field, he sees that among the scattered debris are "mass prayer books, group postcards showing the machine-gun unit standing in ranked and ruddy cheerfulness as in a football picture for a college annual." The prayer books are as silently ineffectual as the photo of the men ("now they were humped and swollen in the grass"). Nick continues punishing himself by processing what he can see of "the dead. They lay alone or in clumps in the high grass of the field and along the road, their pockets out, and over them were flies and around each body or group of bodies were the scattered papers" (*CSS* 306).

Hemingway would use the image of meaningless paper, all importance erased, throughout his writing about war. It seems as if the human need to record suddenly crashes through the violence of war. A tellingly ironic scene, for example, occurs when the American soldier tries to reassure the Italian, Paravicini, that *capable* Americans are coming, "Americans twice as large as myself, healthy, with clean hearts, sleep at night, never been wounded, never been blown up, never had their heads caved in, never been scared" (*CSS* 311).

The following dialogue reinforces the reader's understanding that Nick is caught in a discomfiting post-traumatic mode: when he and the Italian, for example, discuss the new helmets, Nick notes, "You know they're absolutely no damned good. I remember when they were a comfort when we first had them, but I've seen them full of brains too many times." Shocking as this comment is, the Italian's warning that Nick needs to rest brings the situation home. "Lie down a little while, Nicolo."

Hemingway's description of what occurs when Nick's eyes close is the most revealing of his attempts to image the impact of war:

He shut his eyes, and in place of the man with the beard who looked at him over the sights of the rifle, quite calmly before squeezing off, the white flash and clublike impact, on his knees, hot-sweet choking, coughing it onto the rock while they went past him, he saw a long, yellow house with a low stable and the river much wider than it was and stiller. "Christ," he said, "I might as well go." (*CSS* 314)

The fusion of his own wounding with the image of the yellow house as the site of war's slaughter and his extant mission—to appear in uniform so as to mislead viewers—illustrates the likely effects of not only post-traumatic stress disorder (PTSD) but traumatic brain injury.[7] Even as he reassures his friend that "I'm all right now for quite a while. I had one then but it was easy. They're getting much better. I can tell when I'm going to have one because I talk so much," the reader is sobered by the recognition of ungovernable fantasy as it clouds Nick's damaged mind.

In "A Way You'll Never Be," the third of his acknowledged World War I stories, Hemingway charted visible responses to trauma. According to Judith Herman, the PTSD survivor experiences "altered states of consciousness. . . . It is as if time stops at the moment of trauma [and] the traumatic moment becomes encoded in an abnormal form of memory." She adds, "The traumatized person startles easily, reacts irritably to small provocations, and sleeps poorly."[8] Cathy Caruth explains that what she calls *the trauma story* is an "attempt to tell us of a reality or truth that is not otherwise available." The narration, however, occurs in "the complex ways that knowing and not knowing are entangled in the language of trauma and in the stories associated with it."[9]

More specific than Hemingway's other "war stories," "A Way You'll Never Be" is squarely focused on the war scene, the men dead near that yellow house that lives within Nick's memory. All Hemingway's war stories have titles that reflect their languages of both sorrow and destruction (as do his more oblique conflict stories "The Undefeated" and "A Clean, Well-Lighted Place") and that return the reader to the author's earlier stories of war and its effects, "Soldier's Home" and "Big Two-Hearted River." The sonority of these titles strikes the reader hard, as if the subject of war called from Hemingway the writer a steady, poignant sound, sometimes indistinguishable from a guttural moan, as he recognizes, again and again, the permanence of loss and absence.

As if signaling that the story that closes *Winner Take Nothing* would also be a powerful story about loss and absence, Hemingway chose "Fathers and Sons" to occupy that place. He might have seen the story as both a culmination and an encapsulation. His careful positioning of "Indian Camp" and "The Doctor and the Doctor's Wife" to open *In Our Time* had introduced the role of the well-intentioned though misguided father to the boy, whether or not the child was identified as Nick Adams. As the young male character matured through Hemingway's three collections of stories, he turned at times to older men—some of them unrelated—as well as to such contemporaries as his drinking buddies or his skiing partners. But the basic structure of many of these first Hemingway stories was the *bildungsroman*, the young male character searching for answers to life's questions among the other men who surround him.[10]

Here in "Fathers and Sons," Hemingway's aim in drawing the son who has now become the father was to suggest the process of relinquishing that boyhood. He wrote about the inherent loneliness of growing away from *home*, describing "the heavy trees of the small town that are a part of your heart if it is your town and you have walked under them, but that are only too heavy, that shut out the sun and that dampen the houses for a stranger" (*CSS* 369). In this pastiche of instructions about shooting quail, about making love with Trudy, about hating his father's smell on the hand-me-down clothing he was required to wear, and above all, about reconstructing his memory of his father after his suicide, Hemingway chronicled the son-now-father's emotional life in only several thousand words. As author, he apologized for his selectivity, noting, "When you have shot one bird flying you have shot all birds flying. They are all different and they fly in different ways but the sensation is the same and the last one is as good as the first. He could thank his father for that" (*CSS* 376). Hemingway appended a "conclusion," although his point here is that such making of memories cannot ever conclude. The life in human beings continues long past their deaths.

Hemingway showed his sly side as well in writing about war. As Alex Vernon points out, a story such as "An Alpine Idyl" from *Men Without Women* also testifies to the effects of war. Vernon reads the story of the veteran using his dead wife's jaw as a mount for his lantern (until the snow melts and he can carry her body to town for burial) as an account of life in the trenches—many such stories circulated after World War I. Vernon notes,

> If the unnamed narrator is Nick Adams, then the story offers us a sympathetic position toward a fellow veteran, Olz, a man alone and utterly misunderstood by his own community. Several times the innkeeper refers to Olz as a beast, while the narrator and John hardly blanch at Olz's tale because veterans of the Great War's Western Front wouldn't. . . . It was not rare for corpses, unable to be removed for any number of reasons (bad weather being one) to linger in the trenches for some time. And not only linger but be used. . . . Where trench walls threatened to collapse, corpses were used to buttress them until better materials could be brought forward. For the millions of troops who over the course of four years lived such a life with corpses, it would not be difficult to imagine a corpse as the best place for hanging a lantern for lighting a nighttime task—and most work in the trenches took place at night. Soldiers living so much around corpses soon enough became inured to their presence.[11]

Vernon also reads "Cross-Country Snow" and the friendship between men who have endured as a kind of war story; and to that pair of stories one might add the unsympathetic husbands from "Cat in the Rain" and "Out of Season." In Vernon's assessment, "Hemingway's warring and wounding are an essential element of the man he afterward became."[12]

It was Ray B. West Jr. whose insight led the reader to attend to the unity within what he considered Hemingway's war writing in the 1920s. "Ernest Hemingway's first three important works were *In Our Time*, a collection of curiously related short stories; *The Sun Also Rises*, his first serious and successful novel; and *A Farewell to Arms*. All three deal with the same subject: the condition of man in a society upset by the violence of war." West continued about the latter, "*A Farewell to Arms* is set in the war itself, and the romance of Frederic Henry and Catherine Barkley, their attempt to escape the war and its resulting chaos, is a parable of twentieth-century man's disgust and disillusionment at the failure of civilization to achieve the ideas it had been promising throughout the nineteenth century."[13] This historical reading, apt for West's essay, which was first published in 1945, might lead today's readers to an impasse: the continuum of war, coupled with whatever puny attempts to avoid its destruction are made, and the general malaise of wounds and death made Hemingway's 1929 book a classic novel of pain and renunciation, but in this first quarter of the twenty-first century, the novel provides fewer legitimate answers.

Hovering in the background of Hemingway's writing about war is always a sense of religious belief. It is as if Hemingway, having declared himself a professional writer for the previous ten years, thought he was going to be, in fact, a *moral* writer. He had made that claim with *The Sun Also Rises*, only to be disappointed that his readers found little morality in the 1926 novel. His use of the "lost generation" epigraph was ironic, because for him the novel testified to the values of steadfastness in friendship and love, as well as the vestiges of religious belief a reader could find in Jake Barnes's willingness to learn about—and pay homage to—the Spanish Catholic world.[14]

It was Hemingway's most diligent late-twentieth-century biographer, Michael Reynolds, who unearthed Hemingway's promise to himself, written when he was in high school and signed as if it were a pledge, that he would lead a moral life, one dedicated to the study of science:

. . . I believe that the Science, English and to a certain extent the Latin that I am now studying in high school will help me in this object [to do pioneering or exploring work in the three last great frontiers: Africa, central South America, or the country around and north of Hudson Bay]. I believe that any training that I get by hiking in the spring or from work in the summer or any work in the woods which tends to develop resourcefulness and self-reliance is of inestimable value to the work I intend to pursue. . . . I do intend to do something toward the scientific interests of the world.[15]

Reading through Hemingway's writing accomplished between those naïve high school years and his professional publications of poems, journalism, story collections, and novels, one could sense that the impressionistic young man of this promissory pledge still existed. Hemingway's war wounding, like his various emotional rejections, had not changed that earnest temperament: Hemingway was bent on doing *good*.

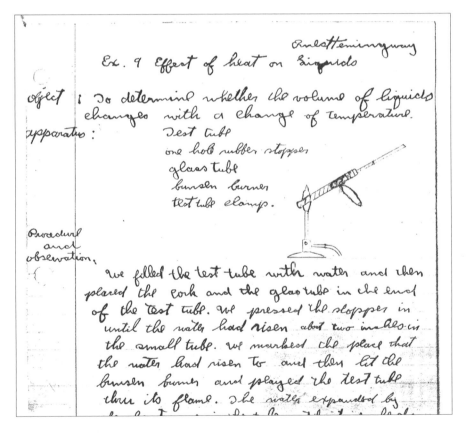

Figure 5. A high school science experiment, in Hemingway's handwriting (detail).

When Hemingway wrote to Max Perkins on March 17, 1928, when his Scribner's editor was waiting impatiently for the novel he thought was in progress, Hemingway could only apologize. The novel was not finished. In fact he had put that manuscript (*Jimmy Breen*) away and started a new book, a reasonably short novel about the war. This segment of his letter to Perkins shows that same almost devout attention to his work, which for Hemingway was the single consistent drive of his life.

Midway through the letter, Hemingway resorted to a list:

I would like to have finished the novel—but (1) I have been laid up and out a good deal.[16]
(2) It took me 5 years to write all the stories in In Our Time.
(3) It took 5 years to write the ones in Men Without Women.
(4) I wrote Sun Also Rises in 6 weeks but then did not look at it for 3 months—and then rewrote it for another three months. How much time I wasted in drinking around before I wrote it and how badly I busted up my life in one way or another I can't fit exactly in time.

Hemingway then reminded Perkins, "I work *all* the time" (*SL* 273). He had also given Perkins that seemingly casual aside: he had "busted up" his life, leaving Hadley and their son, Jack ("Bumby"), for Pauline Pfeiffer, then divorcing Hadley, then marrying Pauline, creating dissension among their friends and in the process alienating many of the people he loved.

By April 21, 1928, only a month later, he wrote Perkins that he was writing well on the war story (*SL* 276), without details. For readers who know *A Farewell to Arms*, the assumption might be that he began with the description of the land (quoted above) and then introduced Frederic Henry (named Emmet Hancock in manuscript); Rinaldi, Frederic Henry's Italian friend and his competitor for Catherine Barkley's affection; and the steady, young Italian priest. In the tripartite male friendship within the Italian camp, it seems that Hemingway had returned to his familiar theme: men's bonding in friendship, sometimes in the spirit of religion, again in the spirit of camaraderie. But the 2012 edition of *A Farewell to Arms*, published in what is called the Hemingway Library Edition by Scribner's, shows, through the inclusion of previously unpublished materials, that Hemingway began the novel at a different place. The book in first draft begins with Frederic Henry's arrival at the Milan hospital (the scene that, in the published version, is the start of book 2). Such a choice in the early draft allowed Hemingway to concentrate on the incredible physical pain the wounded American experienced.

The manuscript draft opens with direct description: "The train came into the station at Milan early in the morning." As Frederic Henry is carried by stretcher from the ambulance to the door of the hospital, all attention falls on the wounded man's pain: "At the moment of lifting him off the stretcher there was the pain and he waited, knowing it never went past a certain point. That was his theory but the pain kept on and passed that point and he was suddenly sick cold inside and in back of his ears, far inside between the bones." Through Henry's subsequent journey from area to area within the vacant hospital, he battles the pain and the nurse's formidable regulations. She was not expecting anybody; the hospital is new; there are no bed linens—and no doctors. Finally the wounded man is lying in a bed, and he controls his anger, which the extreme pain has triggered, to tell the nurse, "I think I can go to sleep. I have not been to sleep for five days." He smiles. "No that's my bowels. I haven't moved my bowels for five days. No seven days. I haven't been to sleep for five months" (*FTA* 2012 285–87). Unsuitable as this angry quip is, Hemingway followed it with a paragraph drawn partly from other of his recent fictions, including the Jake Barnes mirror scene from *The Sun Also Rises*. In that paragraph, Hemingway returned the prose to its sonority, removed anything unseemly, and lulled the reader into believing that Frederic Henry, despite his anguish, was in control.

> He was alone in the room. It was cool and did not smell like a hospital. There was a big armoire with a mirror. He could not see himself in the mirror. He knew he had a beard and he would have liked to see it. It was the first beard he had ever grown. He rubbed his cheek very softly against the pillow, barely moving it. Moving his head started the pain again and he lay still feeling it lessen. (*FTA* 2012 288)

Mixed with the pacific description that eventually marked much of *A Farewell to Arms*, these early lines suggest the way Hemingway moved from past writing into current work.

The manuscript inclusions from the first draft show that he tried to write about overwhelming pain. One paragraph describes having anesthesia for surgery, after which Frederic Henry reflects, "I had not been away. You do not go away. They only choke you. . . . I saw sandbags at the end of the bed. They were on pipes that came out of the cast. And my legs hurt so that I tried to get back into the choked place I had come from but I could not get back in there and threw up again and again and nothing came." In this description of the unbearable pain, Hemingway located it "in the bone and everywhere there was and then inside my chest it started to jerk and jerk and then I cried and cried without any noise, only the diaphragm jerking and jerking, and then it was better and I knew I could bear it" (*FTA* 2012 299).

There are sections in the manuscript draft that describe the fears the character comes to know during postwar recovery. As Hemingway wrote about the progression, the young soldier "had a feeling that other people died but I did not die." But then he is wounded. Yet "the spells of fear were always physical, always caused by an imminent danger, and always transitory. I was in the second healthy stage, that of not being afraid when I was not in danger. I suppose the third stage, of being afraid at night, started about this point" (*FTA* 2012 300).[17] In a 1929 letter to Owen Wister, Hemingway admitted that "in 1919 I had . . . after effects of concussion of brain couldn't sleep, etc."[18]

The deleted passages, some quite effective, are nearly all about Henry's physical state. One long section, for example, describes his having made four "messes" in the bed (noting that after the second one, the nurses put on a rubber sheet), with Henry feeling acute embarrassment. There are also lengthy versions of dialogue passages that appear in the published book, there much shortened. Again, Hemingway seemed to know when his reader would lose patience with a conversation that might be too aimless.

There are scattered yet always detailed passages about other instances of war brutality: "I have seen men shot, slumping quickly and hanged twirling slowly, and kneeling, arms behind the back, chest on a table, that tripped quickly forward the knife falling into a slot and thunking on wood while boy soldiers presented arms and looked sideways at the basket that had been empty and now had a head in it" (*FTA* 2012 300).

None of these sections quoted here appear in the finished novel; in fact, Hemingway seemed to shift entirely from these descriptions of pain as his character experienced it to his focus on the war-torn country of Italy and its people. Much of what Hemingway cut showed that he had both the eyes and the ears of a trained copy editor. One of the lines he deleted from the passage above about pain, for instance, showed his ability to condense: "It was dim and cool in the room. The pain was *very light* [crossed out] thin *as a spider web* [crossed out] now." In finished form before he deleted it completely, the sentence read, "The pain was thin now."

A Farewell to Arms as published in 1929 is divided into five sections, the first—which takes place *before* Frederic Henry's arrival in Milan—focuses on the condition of war, as well as on male friendships in the Italian camp, on meeting Catherine Barkley, and on his being wounded. Book 2 begins with his arrival in Milan and his convalescence—and his deepening love for Catherine. Book 3 (shorter than either of the first two books) opens with a long discussion between the young Italian priest and Frederic Henry, after he has returned to his home camp. Here Hemingway wrote a kind of reprise to the conversations that had appeared in book 1, with the priest now fearful for the outcome of war:

> "We are all gentler now because we are beaten. How would Our Lord have been if Peter had rescued him in the Garden?"
> "He would have been just the same."
> "I don't think so," I said.
> "You discourage me," he said. "I believe and I pray that something will happen. I have felt it very close." (*FTA* 156)

Studded within the seemingly aimless dialogue sections are the friends' musings about their religious beliefs. Most of these passages occur in book 1, both before and after Henry's wounding, which comes at the midpoint of that first section. The famous passages about the priest's love of Abruzzi ("where the roads were frozen and hard as iron, where it was clear cold and dry and the snow was dry and powdery and hare-tracks in the snow and peasants took off their hats and called you Lord and there was good hunting") occur early. It is there that the priest tries to explain to Henry that he does not understand *selfless* love.

The structure of the novel, however, makes the reader aware of the conflicts inherent in caring for others amid the devastation of war. As Robert Martin points out, the four men who serve with Frederic Henry as ambulance drivers before his wounding and the three men who serve once he returns to the front are not patriots: they are young Italians who have no choice about serving their country. Of the first four, Passini is killed when the shell explodes, losing his legs and dying immediately. Of the three who serve during the evacuation, Aymo (meaning "love") dies in a misdirected shooting. Bonello deserts after he executes the sergeant who has earlier been shot for desertion—an act that remains questionable—by Henry. Martin's point is that the seven men "reflect and foreshadow the course of the Frederic-Catherine love affair from beginning to end," providing emotional information about the lovers that is often only implied.[19] For example, after Aymo's death in the mud, Henry says only, "I had liked him as well as anyone I ever knew" (*FTA* 214). Some of this somber mourning occurs as well when Henry is being driven by ambulance

and the blood dripping down on him from the stretcher above him eventually
slows. He muses about the blood, "Where it had run down under my shirt it
was warm and sticky. I was cold and my leg hurt so that it made me sick." But
after the stream of blood stops, and that stretcher is taken out and replaced
with another, Henry sees only the image of "an icicle melting after the sun has
gone" (*FTA* 52–53).

After the two long books that provide factual information about war, as
well as the premises of both military action and the Frederic-Catherine love
affair, book 3 charts the retreat from Caporetto, the magnificent scene of the
army in disarray (drawn mostly from historical accounts, as Michael Reynolds proves).[20] Book 3 also presents Henry's desertion and his later escape
with Catherine. Rhythmically, as if the narrative itself offers no escape—either
from their condition as deserters or from Catherine's of pregnancy—the story
rolls into ever-shortening sections. Book 4 is only four chapters long, taking
up only forty-four pages. Book 5 is five chapters, but some of those chapters
are even shorter. Nearly all the chapters, as well as each book, open with a
description of time: "That fall the snow came very late" opens chapter 38, the
first in book 5. Chapter 39 opens, "By the middle of January I had a beard and
the winter had settled into bright cold days and hard cold nights." Chapter
40, recounted seemingly without irony, begins, "We had a fine life. We lived
through the months of January and February and the winter was very fine and
we were very happy."

Resonant with the possible disaster that could come with either Henry's
capture or Catherine's giving birth, Hemingway's prose becomes less descriptive. By the closing sentences, the reader can think of nothing "fine" or "happy."
The last section, chapter 41, begins with the physical labor of childbirth. There
is no amelioration. No one else enters the story: Rinaldi's false good cheer is
months and countries behind them, as is the reconciliation the humble priest
could have provided. The reader accepts the relentless horror of things going wrong as the baby boy is born dead, Catherine hemorrhages, and no one
stops the inevitable—a gripping denouement that comes as no surprise to the
reader. For Frederic Henry, however, Catherine's death is impossible either to
understand or to accept.

The latter half of the novel is—deftly and intentionally—grounded in bereavement. Because Henry tells the story in his own voice, the reader knows
that his earlier damage from the war will be intensified through the death of
his beloved Catherine. There was no need for Hemingway to say more than
he did:

After I had got them [the nurses] out and shut the door and turned off the light it wasn't any good. It was like saying good-by to a statue. After a while I went out and left the hospital and walked back to the hotel in the rain. (*FTA* 284)

Intensifying the protagonist's grief and the tone of lament that the novel conveys is the fact that Hemingway's father, Dr. Clarence Hemingway, had committed suicide at home on December 6, 1928. Hemingway had then traveled by train from the eastern United States to Oak Park to attend the funeral and to help with his mother's finances. *A Farewell to Arms* was finished and retyped by the end of January 1929, and by early June, Hemingway was correcting the galley proofs. The novel was published on September 27.

Summarizing the plot of *A Farewell to Arms* does little justice to the countless ways in which Hemingway saturated the text, subtly, so that *war* is never far from the reader's mind. The style of the narration itself—extensive use of metaphor and a hesitant stream of consciousness—makes the reader probe beyond Henry's literal words. Hemingway began his antiwar critique by placing all outright criticism of the conflict into the Italian ambulance drivers' mouths—and in some cases, Henry tries to argue with their pragmatic opinions. When Henry goes to the headquarters building in search of food for his men, he is shocked to hear the thump of something "set down beside the entrance," only to then hear the major say, "Bring *him* in" (*FTA* 52; my italics). The wounded soldier's body had become only a thing in the day-to-day business of fighting a war. Similarly, when Henry notices "the new graves in the [hospital] garden," he must recognize the plethora of recent deaths—perhaps of men he knew—so that war casualties become familiar. Placed close to this scene is the description of Henry's going to sleep in Milan, watching "the beams of the search-lights moving in the sky," and his subsequent waking—"sweating and scared and then [going] back to sleep trying to stay outside my dream" (*FTA* 75, 88).

In *A Farewell to Arms*, Italy is clearly a country at war, vigilant in keeping watch for any impending bombing. And Frederic Henry is clearly a man traumatized by his near-death wounding, a horrifically surprising attack that came, without warning, in the dark. Another important scene is the ambulance major's description of the war (when Henry returns to action), which he consistently calls "very bad. . . . You couldn't believe how bad it's been." In the midst of the description, the major says simply that they "lost three cars" (*FTA* 167). Because the corps owned fewer than a dozen ambulances in total, the loss of three cars and their crews meant a very high proportion of dead men. There were no "safe" roles in this, or any, war.

Just as Hemingway protested the falsely rhetorical language of war propaganda, he also worked to show readers that their assumptions about men
who go to war are erroneous. Passini and Aymo are killed; Henry is seriously
wounded—so much for the *safety* of driving ambulances. Correspondingly,
assumptions about the *safety* of modern childbirth were tragically false. Henry
thinks about these assumptions in almost the same language. The Catherine-
dying-in-childbirth scene is another of his stream-of-consciousness passages. (See *FTA* 320 for his use of insistent verbs, the quick repetition of short
phrases, and the blunted effect of the somber repetition.) That passage ends
with Henry's thinking to himself, "What if she should die? She can't die. Why
would she die? What reason is there for her to die?" By this time, the reader
understands that *reasonlessness* is precisely the point.

The enthusiasm of Robert Penn Warren shapes one of the most influential critical essays about *A Farewell to Arms*—which argues that it remained
Hemingway's best work because the simplicity of its style matched the polished structure, but more importantly, because the meaningfulness of its man-
against-world theme endeared it to readers. Or, as Frederic Svoboda writes,
A Farewell to Arms became one of Hemingway's great works because in it
"that essential sense of the seriousness of life—and sometimes of its joy—is
underscored by its occurring against a backdrop of love and war, certainly two
of the world's most serious undertakings. . . . The Hemingway protagonist
often seems to exist like Hemingway in a moment after: after the nineteenth
century, after wilderness, after innocence, after loss."[21]

Twenty years after its original publication, Hemingway was asked to write
an introduction for the 1948 edition of *A Farewell to Arms*. (The introduction
also appears in the 2012 edition.) He began with a litany of geographical
places—commemorating his marrying Pauline, the difficult birth of their first
son, Patrick, and the death of his father. His introduction opens,

> This book was written in Paris, France, Key West, Florida, Piggott, Arkansas,
> Kansas City, Missouri, Sheridan, Wyoming, and the first draft of it was finished
> near Big Horn in Wyoming. It was begun in the last winter months of 1928 and
> the first draft was finished in September of that year. It was rewritten in the fall
> and winter of 1928 in Key West and the final rewriting was finished in Paris in
> the spring of 1929.

Even as Hemingway described Patrick's birth and his father's death, he emphasized his personally joyous process of writing the book, regardless of his
father's death.

I remember living in the book and making up what happened in it every day. Making the country and the people and the things that happened I was happier than I had ever been. Each day I read the book through from the beginning to the point where I went on writing and each day I stopped when I was still going good and when I knew what would happen next.

The fact that the book was a tragic one did not make me unhappy since I believed that life was a tragedy and knew it could have only one end. But finding you were able to make something up; to create truly enough so that it made you happy to read it; and to do this every day you worked was something that gave a greater pleasure than any I had ever known. Beside it nothing else mattered. (*FTA* 2012 vii–viii)

His 1948 introduction became more noteworthy when he changed the topic to comment about the horrors of all wars. (He had written during World War II, in both his *Men at War* introduction and his various prefaces to friends' memoirs about that war, that *no* war is good or reasonable.) Here Hemingway wrote,

The title of the book is *A Farewell to Arms* and except for three years there has been a war of some kind almost ever since it has been written. Some people used to say, why is the man so preoccupied and obsessed with war, and now, since 1933 perhaps it is clear why a writer should be interested in the constant bullying, murderous, slovenly crime of war. Having been to too many of them, I am sure that I am prejudiced. . . . It is the considered belief of the writer of this book that wars . . . are made, provoked, and initiated by straight economic rivalries and by swine that stand to profit from them. (*FTA* 2012 vii, ix)

In one respect, war was an essential piece of Hemingway's journalistic treasure in his writing about politics throughout the world. In another, however, it provided a remarkable canvas that allowed room for myriad stories about bravery and sacrifice, love, male camaraderie, and the relentless parade of war's horrors.

The novel also fulfilled a political script that Hemingway had begun with his stories about Benito Mussolini in June 1922 stories for the *Toronto Star* (June 24, 1922) and the *Star Weekly* (same date). The *Star* story opens,

Benito Mussolini, head of the Fascisti movement, sits at his desk at the fuse of the great powder magazine that he has laid through all Northern and Central Italy and occasionally fondles the ears of a wolf-hound pup, looking like a short-eared jackrabbit, that plays with the papers on the floor beside the big desk. Mussolini is a big, brown-faced man with a high forehead, a slow-smiling mouth, and large, expressive hands.

Bragging about the 500,000 soldiers in his "political party organized as a military force," Mussolini told Hemingway that what he was doing was "not against the law" (*DLT* 172). It was a few months later, on January 27, 1923, that Hemingway published his most negative *Star* piece about the Italian dictator. "Mussolini, Europe's Prize Bluffer" shredded any sense that the Fascisti would work for the good—of anyone or anything in either Italy or Europe. As Hemingway wrote about the attendees at the Lausanne, Switzerland, peace conference, he commented about their physical appearances (most of these comments were very negative). With Mussolini, Hemingway described "the weakness in his mouth which forces him to scowl the famous Mussolini scowl that is imitated by every 19-year-old Fascisto in Italy." More damaging were the anecdotes Hemingway ascribed to Mussolini: When he invited the press for an interview, Mussolini was reading a book. When Hemingway managed to see what the book was, it turned out to be a French-English dictionary— "held upside down." At a later event, when six wives of members of the working class awaited him with a bouquet of roses, Mussolini, Hemingway wrote with sly attention to unmanly behavior, "scowled, sneered, let his big-whited African eyes roll over the . . . women and went back into the room. The unattractive peasant women in their Sunday clothes were left holding their roses" (*DLT* 255–56). Hemingway closed his article by predicting that a "new opposition will rise, it is forming already."

Throughout his journalism during the early and middle 1930s, Hemingway similarly kept his attention on Mussolini's inhuman behavior. Mark Cirino argues that Hemingway did so because Mussolini had tried to erase knowledge of the Caporetto retreat from history; in the novel, Hemingway had chosen to feature it,[22] which Cirino saw as an intentional insult to Mussolini:

> Mussolini had forbidden any published mention of the retreat from Caporetto, hoping Italy's humiliation could be effaced from the national consciousness. Because the Caporetto debacle plays a central role in *A Farewell to Arms*, the novel was censored by the Italian government and would not be translated into Italian until 1945.[23]

As with a great deal of Hemingway's writing, critics have often been blind to the suffusion of political beliefs and attitudes that mark the author's choices.

Just as Hemingway wrote his vivid description of the retreat from Caporetto in *A Farewell to Arms*—perhaps to anger Mussolini rather than simply writing about a great war event in the literary terms of his choice—he had the audacity to also include a chapter about the retreat in his 1942 *Men at War*. Hemingway seldom forgot an affront. What he saw as Mussolini's insult to the welcoming peasant women might have played out in unexpected ways.

Twenty-first-century critics bring new attention to the depictions of masculinity in the novel. They find that Frederic Henry's laconic narrative is an outward sign of his assumed toughness. Diane Price Herndl notes that Hemingway's male characters obey social norms, and, in doing so, believe they should not be focused on describing their pain. She says specifically that Henry must play a masculine role: he cannot "tell about his horrific experiences of war—watching his comrades Passini and Aymo die, his own suffering and wounding, the shooting of the sergeant, his forced desertion, and Catherine's death."[24] She places at the center of her reading the passage about the language of war, as well as the passage where he explains, "If people bring so much courage to this world the world has to kill them to break them, so of course it kills them" (*FTA* 249). Herndl sees Hemingway's presentation of war as only, frustratingly, *waiting*.

One of her strongest points is that *A Farewell to Arms* does not so much end with Catherine's death as it ends with "Frederic's surrender of narration, which is itself a kind of death—certainly he becomes as silent as she. . . . He can no more save Catherine than he could save his comrades."[25]

For Trevor Dodman, Frederic Henry's reticence reveals part masculinity and part trauma survivor. Yet at times, he points out, Henry talks too much, and that speech pattern, along with his personal disorganization, could be an index of his trauma: "Frederic's narrative suffers at times from troubling and uncontrolled *outflow*."[26]

Dodman's reading of the novel emphasizes details that are not often quoted: for example, he sees Henry's interest in the scarring any Caesarean delivery would leave as a reference to war's bodily damage. In this as in much of Henry's dialogue, trauma, or the fear of it, guides his speech: "Frederic's traumatic memories bleed into and disrupt his present. . . . [His] telling of his past instead goes 'all to pieces' in the enduring presence of pain and trauma." In Dodman's reading of *A Farewell to Arms* as a trauma narrative, Henry's voice "is always already the voice of a traumatized survivor of grievous wounds and losses." One might also note that Henry's aim to tell his story *perfectly* in itself represents a fixation on his life at war: "Looking back on events, reconstructing his memories, Frederic reveals a desire for a whole and perfect retelling of the past; his narrative functions as a prosthesis meant to stave off a sense of the self as a disarticulated scar."[27] Whereas Jeffrey Hart says little about Frederic Henry's speech, he privileges the character of Catherine Barkley (a woman protagonist very different from Brett Ashley) because she tells the truth in her direct manner. Hart echoes Hemingway's personal belief that *A Farewell to Arms* was his best novel.[28]

William Dow emphasizes that some of the power in the novel originates with Hemingway's borrowing from what he considered the best World War I novel, *Under Fire*, by Henri Barbusse (translated by W. Fitzwater Wray). This account of brutal warfare by a good journalist, the story of the battles won and lost by Barbusse's squad at Crouy and Hill 119 (during January, May, and September 1915), benefited from stylistic innovation: alternation of pacific natural scenes with those of rampant destruction, all segments written with what Barbusse referred to as "constater" ("a boiling down from which a condensed, authoritative, and truthful story emerges").[29] Barbusse played the changes on abstract language, agreeing with Frederic Henry that "abstract words such as glory, honor, courage, or hallow" should never be used to create real meaning. Instead, the numbers and names of men in war should provide the essential delineation.

As these twenty-first-century critics suggest, for today's readers, the continuing power of Hemingway's *A Farewell to Arms* accrues in its presenting damage, loss, and grief so evocatively that Frederic Henry's imperiled condition becomes the reader's condition as well.

When Hemingway later described one of his most important aims as a writer, he conveyed the implicit sense that *A Farewell to Arms* had achieved that aim. As he wrote in his introduction to *Men at War*,

> A writer's job is to tell the truth. His standard of fidelity to the truth should be so high that his invention, out of his experience, should produce a truer account than anything factual can be. For facts can be observed badly; but when a good writer is creating something he has time and scope to make it of an absolute truth. (*MAW* 7–8)

Jackson Benson uses a slightly different phrasing to echo Hemingway's insistence on truth telling. Benson writes, particularly about *A Farewell to Arms*,

> What carried Hemingway along his path was a total dedication to art: an unrelenting will to make his writing *true*. Perhaps his range of vision can be seen in

some respects as limited, but his aim was penetration, not comprehensiveness. Hemingway, unlike many of his contemporaries, was *there* during the wars, the evacuations, the social convulsions. . . . This effort to sense the actual event and to reproduce its emotional effect artistically as precisely as possible is precisely what we need in an age when even war itself has become a spectator sport and our sensitivity to the suffering of others has diminished.[30]

CHAPTER FIVE

Politics and Celebrity

An EVALUATION OF Hemingway by one who knew him well is that of Charles Scribner Jr., his publisher, who marveled at the ways in which Hemingway *used* everything he experienced. In his publisher's preface to *The Complete Short Stories of Ernest Hemingway*, Scribner remarked, "Hemingway must have been one of the most perceptive travelers in the history of literature, and his stories taken as a whole present a world of experience." Scribner illustrated the way journalism and fiction sprang together out of Hemingway's travels by discussing his essay about an Italian trip that was first published in *New Republic* as "Italy, 1927" and later appeared as a short story in *Men Without Women*: "In the 1920s he revisited Italy several times; sometimes as a professional journalist and sometimes for pleasure. His short story about a motor trip with a friend through Mussolini's Italy, 'Che Ti Dice La Patria?' succeeds in conveying the harsh atmosphere of a totalitarian regime."[1]

In a later foreword, this time to William White's collection of all the *Toronto Star* articles, Scribner continued his discussion of Hemingway's superlative journalism: "One of Hemingway's passions was to get the inside story, the 'true gen,' and there was a touch of punditry in his journalism whenever he could set the record straight—whether it had to do with the superiority of one boxer over another, or the 'true facts' about something like rum-running into the United States. Even though he was still in his twenties, this 'persona' is probably the first appearance of the subsequently famous 'Papa Hemingway' figure—that voice of experience and much traveled source of inside information." It is also worth noting, as Scribner did here, that "throughout his life he would continue to accept journalistic assignments whenever they led to places that interested him. He covered postwar Italy for *The New Republic*, the

Spanish Civil War for the North American Newspaper Alliance, China for *PM*, the Royal Air Force for *Collier's*, and bullfights for *Life*."[2]

As the notes and fragmentary notebooks, as well as pieces of typed sketches and dialogue, housed in the various Hemingway collections suggest, Hemingway was a person with an eye—and an ear—for materials he could use in his writing, however that writing was categorized. As Paul Smith says in his book about Hemingway's short stories, his writing process began with notes. He calls Hemingway's process his "usual sequence of composition." Notes led to a kind of manuscript, handwritten, with some sentences unfinished. Later there would be the first typescript (but it might not have much relationship to the earlier notes). Then there would be later typescripts.[3]

In Hemingway's own statements about aesthetics, he sometimes ignored the quantity of journalism that he had published. For the *Kansas City Star* as well as for the *Toronto Star* and the *Star Weekly*, his articles (most of them with his byline) totaled between 150 and 200 items. When he stopped writing for the Toronto papers in 1924, the accumulation of his journalism still grew—but more slowly.

Many of Hemingway's assignments for the *Toronto Star* had to do with European politics—particularly with a major economic conference in Genoa, Italy; the Greco-Turkish War during 1922 and 1923; the flight of refugees from the battle site in Asia Minor; and the Conference of Lausanne, organized to end that conflict. While his political articles had good information, they also showed the dynamism of a man writing to be read: he covered Germany's inflationary problems with some humor, and he was evenhanded in describing the Russian delegates, "Tchitcherin, Joffe, Korassin, and Litvinoff, as looking, talking, and acting like businessmen."[4]

In addition to this quantity of journalism, running to more than a hundred articles that covered politics, Hemingway often commented in letters to friends about the state of the world—from perspectives economic, military, and political. Because early critiques of Hemingway and his writing ordinarily came from the perspective of the literary world, his journalism was relegated to "work" he did, without much consideration that he was personally interested in the subjects for that "work." The notion that Hemingway was somehow an *apolitical* writer, which held sway during the early years of his career as novelist, now seems very dated. In the words of Peter L. Hays, "Political ideology was not Hemingway's main focus ever . . . but his work does explore the intrusion of economics and politics into daily life as part of his intense scrutiny of his characters' lives."[5]

In the same essay, Hays emphasizes the fusion between Hemingway's journalistic coverage and the prose poems and fiction he began writing in 1922 and 1923. He points out the ways Hemingway moved from his journalism about the European conflicts to his *in our time* vignettes. Hays is correct in thinking that many of Hemingway's readers did not understand the history he was reporting; he used as illustration "On the Quai at Smyrna," which Hays says "describes a British ship . . . loading Greek refugees for Smyrna, now ruled by Turkey under Kemal Ataturk. Kemal dismisses his port commander for firing blanks at the British ship; actual rounds would have caused the British ship to fire into the town, killing many, before being destroyed by Turkish short batteries, drawing Britain into the war. The ship's commander . . . laments the actions of the departing Greek army, breaking the legs of their baggage animals and pushing them into the harbor to drown."[6] The vignette, which Hemingway used to preface *In Our Time*, the book version that combined stories with vignettes, was seldom treated as informative. It was instead seen as Hemingway's attempt to portray clipped, ironic British speech.[7]

One of Stephen Cooper's conclusions in his book about Hemingway's politics parallels Hays's readings. Cooper summarizes, "Hemingway hated big government, believed in individual initiative, and was always willing to serve his country loyally in wartime. . . . His opposition to Fascism and censorship was liberal, whereas his dislike of the New Deal and increasingly centralized government authority was conservative."[8] The difficulty this critic has with labeling Hemingway (he calls him a "libertarian") points to the dichotomy of considering a person's politics without seeing his entire persona through that political lens. For Hays, who defines *politics* in twenty-first-century terms— to include ethnic prejudice, the world of the Ku Klux Klan, and the eugenics movement—Hemingway drew throughout his *in our time* prose vignettes on matters that could be considered political—the Irish cop shooting two Hungarians, thinking they are Italian "wops"; the violent execution of people throughout the world; bullfighting; organized crime; Chicago corruption; war itself.

The definitive study of Hemingway's journalism remains Robert Stephens's *Hemingway's Nonfiction: The Public Voice*. Essential in tracing all the author's work in both journalism and the essay, the study provides a set of capacious relationships between much of the fiction in relation to the nonfiction. Stephens's attention to Hemingway's writing about politics, as well as military conflicts and war, is exhaustive. Yet perhaps his designation of the journalism as "public" when compared with the opposing caveat (is all Hemingway's fiction, then, *not* public?) may obscure some of his stronger readings. It is clear that for Hemingway's readers who knew him as a story writer and a novelist, particularly the novelist of *The Sun Also Rises* and *A Farewell to Arms*, his journalism from the early 1920s seemed to be a separate entity, but Stephens sees that Hemingway's style was often germane to both his fiction and his articles. At one point Stephens says,

> For his readers . . . the real Hemingway at war was not so much interpreter or even reporter of events and moods, but renderer of the sensations of war. There is little doubt that this is what John Wheeler wanted for N. A. N. A., Ralph Ingersoll for *PM*, and Joseph Knapp for *Collier's*. They wanted him to do for their journals what he had done in his fiction: make the experience so palpable that every reader could have it as his own.[9]

The issue in placing Hemingway's writing—whether journalism or fiction—was to keep in view the writer's important parameters: his originality, no matter his models; his drive to include the detail that showed the truth; his lifelong concentration on learning to write better and better. He said in *Death in the Afternoon* that the beginning writer has to learn "what the actual things were which produced the emotion that you experienced" (*DIA* 2). Later in that treatise he added that the great artist respects innovation. He "goes beyond what has been done or known and makes something of his own" (*DIA* 100).

By 1935, the time Hemingway had written his nonfiction book about the African safari (*Green Hills of Africa*), his dialogue about aesthetics seemed to answer some of those personal dilemmas about the craft of writing. Early in *Green Hills of Africa*, the narrator admits, "Some writers are only born to help another writer to write one sentence." And, considering entire books, he added, "But it cannot derive from or resemble a previous classic" (*GHOA* 21). Hemingway here chose to emphasize the writers he considered the best in American literature: "The good writers are Henry James, Stephen Crane, and Mark Twain. That's not the order they're good in. There is no order for good writers" (*GHOA* 22).

Self-conscious about his almost exclusive production of nonfiction during the early 1930s, Hemingway wrote very few stories—and no novels. After *A Farewell to Arms* appeared in late September of 1929, his writing life was terrifically disrupted by his newfound fame. The novel had been serialized in *Scribner's Magazine* in early summer (each issue banned in Boston because of the "dirty" romance content—a situation that evoked a media blitz), and its prepublication reviews were positive. Scribner's paid Hemingway $16,000 for the book's serialization; about six weeks after the book appeared in the fall, more than 45,000 copies had sold. (The following year Paramount paid $80,000 for film rights, though Hemingway saw only $24,000 of that amount.)

Set against a hugely distracting agenda of travel—to New York, to Paris, to Switzerland, to Pamplona, to Key West, to Havana, to Montana, to Kansas and Arkansas—this immediate fame (with Hemingway finding and reading every review that appeared) was disconcerting. Finally, in late spring of 1930, Hemingway had written a new short story, "Wine of Wyoming," a mixed French dialogue and American English account of a wine-making western family, based on his friends the Moncini family (called the Pichotes in the text). The story appeared in the August 1930 issue of *Scribner's Magazine*. Hemingway also worked diligently on his bullfighting book, hauling materials with him from location to location. But he was far from calm.[10]

Biographer Bernice Kert sees the 1930s as a difficult time for Hemingway; she points out that with his marriage to Pauline and his integration into the wealthy Pfeiffer family, Hemingway was "more on the defensive" than he had been while married to Hadley. According to Kert, Pauline used her family funds for their travels—and they, either separately or together, were becoming visible worldwide. While the 1930s became more and more fraught with financial troubles for many people, Hemingway was able to spend conspicuously on travel, but he felt the need to defend himself: "As the Depression deepened and fewer and fewer people could live as they did, Ernest became more prickly and tended to exaggerate the extent of his expenses and the number of people dependent on him."[11] His visibility as world traveler and adventurer hurt his comparatively recent literary reputation.

In a gesture of clear and perhaps surprising goodwill, Hemingway set up a trust fund for his mother and his younger siblings who still lived at his Oak Park boyhood home. He had talked about doing this at the time of his father's suicide, but only if *A Farewell to Arms* brought in adequate income. Because he had transferred all the income from his 1926 novel *The Sun Also Rises* to Hadley, and because he had no way to earn money except through publishing his writing, his financial cautiousness was reasonable: writing was not only his passion, it was his "work," and he counted on it to create at least some income for him and his family. In February 1930, then, Hemingway put $30,000 into the trust, and that amount was augmented by another $20,000 from Pauline and her uncle Gus Pfeiffer. (*A Farewell to Arms* was dedicated to Uncle Gus.)

In mid-July, the Hemingways gathered at the Lawrence Nordquist ranch outside Cooke City, Montana. The family fished, swam, and rode horses, and Hemingway went hunting for mountain sheep, elk, and bear. In October 1930, John Dos Passos joined Hemingway there for hunting. Driving his Ford on narrow gravel roads into Billings, Montana, Hemingway swerved and ended up in a ditch and the car overturned. Other occupants were thrown out of the car, but Hemingway was trapped upside-down behind the steering wheel. Getting him out of the car was difficult; the pain was immense. After surgeries at St. Vincent Hospital in Billings, he was hospitalized for over seven weeks, the first month *immobilized* so that his right arm—broken in four places—might heal. Kert describes the breaks as "an oblique spiral fracture, nearly compound, three inches above the elbow."[12] In a later account, Michael Reynolds emphasizes not only the unremitting pain but the fact that Hemingway was sure the injury, even if healed, would impair his writing ability. "After the fifth day, the doctor takes him off the morphine, leaving him alone with the pain and his night thoughts. For three weeks, unable to move for fear of ruining his writing arm, he has plenty of time to think, too much time. He has been there before, badly wounded in the Milan hospital twelve years earlier, worrying then whether he might lose his leg, and sometimes now in the night he wonders which hospital he is in this time."[13]

Except for his writing the short story "The Gambler, the Nun, and the Radio," these long weeks were necessarily unproductive for Hemingway in terms of writing. He had earlier been disappointed when Lawrence Stallings's production of *A Farewell to Arms* had not played for long on the New York stage; and even as he kept working—now slowly—on his bullfighting book, he knew it was not the kind of publication that would bring him either fame or income.

The book about bullfighting did give him reason to return to Spain, however, and the year 1931 was divided into winter in Key West (where Uncle Gus Pfeiffer bought them the house at 907 Whitehead Street for $12,500) and summer and fall in Paris and Spain, Santiago de Compostela and Madrid and Pamplona—and then their return to the States because their second child was to be born in November. After another excruciating delivery, Pauline was told she must have no more children and—as the Catholic Church mandated—she was to use coitus interruptus as her method of birth control.

Living in the Key West house after their return from the West provided stability for Hemingway, though he remained bothered by all the care necessary for both little Patrick and baby Gregory. As noted by his biographers, and occasionally by Hemingway himself, he did not enjoy the presence of toddlers in his life.[14] He did, however, enjoy fishing with his buddies, and his stream of invitations to friends to come visit often garnered results.

Already in 1932–1933, Hemingway was feeling that his lack of a clear leftist political position was hurting the world's response to his writing; he said this often to Max Perkins about the reviews of *Death in the Afternoon*. Similarly, in an August 9, 1932, letter to Paul Romaine, Hemingway took on this implied criticism, telling Romaine, "I will not outline my political beliefs to you since I have no need to and since I would be jailed for their publication but if they are not much further left than yours which sound like a sentimental socialism I will move them further over. . . . I have never felt myself anything but a part of the world I live in and know how lousily that world is organized and run" (*SL* 365–66). In answer to Romaine's criticism that Hemingway wrote primarily about the Lost Generation and about bullfights, he noted, "I have to live sometime and I have quite a few things to write and my mind is not occupied with lost generations and bulls" (*SL* 366).

Somewhat later, Hemingway wrote at length to Russian critic Ivan Kashkeen. Here he spoke defensively about not being able to become communist: "I believe in only one thing: liberty. . . . The state I care nothing for. All the state has ever meant to me is unjust taxation." He praised Kashkeen for reviewing his work accurately, saying, "Here [in the United States] criticism is a joke. The bourgeois critics do not know their ass from a hole in the ground and the newly-converted communists are like all new converts. They are so anxious to be orthodox" (*SL* 418–19). As he told Perkins, "I stink so to the New York critics that if I bring out a book of stories no matter how good . . . they will all try to kill it" (*SL* 448).

Hemingway was not overly sensitive. It was the condition of the United States and its Great Depression that occupied the minds of many literary people—from the textile-strike novels of Mary Heaton Vorse, Clara Weatherwax, and Grace Lumpkin, to the "lost boys" novels of Nelson Algren, Tom Kromer, James T. Farrell, and Albert Maltz, to the many novels about unemployed workers who no longer believed in their American dream (written by Meridel LeSueur, Thomas Bell, Robert Cantwell, Jack Conroy, Harriette Arnow, Michael Gold, Josephine Johnson, Arna Bontemps, William Rollins, John Steinbeck, and others). In the midst of the chorus of approval given writers who recognized, and tried to re-create, this *lost* dream culture stood John Dos Passos, whose *42nd Parallel* had been published at the start of the 1930s and was followed even more successfully in 1932 with what would become the second volume of his trilogy (later named *U.S.A.*), a book titled *1919*.

Hemingway responded enthusiastically upon reading *1919*. On March 26, 1932, he wrote Dos Passos,

> The book is bloody splendid—it's four times the book the 42nd [*Parallel*] was—and that was damned good. It comes off all the time and you can write so damned well it spooks me that something might happen to you—wash and peel all the fruit you get. . . . You can write the best of any of the bastards writing now and you've been around the most—you write better all the time. For Christ sake don't try to *do good*. Keep on showing it as it is. If you can show it as it really is you *will* do good. (*SL* 354)

Knowing that Dos Passos had become the "poster child" of the left-leaning literati, and trying himself to survive pressure from that echelon, Hemingway added a paragraph about politics, or perhaps about *disguised* politics:

> Now watch one thing. In the 3rd volume don't let yourself slip and get any perfect characters in—no Stephen Daedeluses—remember it was Bloom and Mrs. Bloom saved Joyce—that is the only thing could ruin the bastard [Dos Passos's trilogy] from being a great piece of literature. If you get a noble communist remember the bastard probably masturbates and is jallous [jealous?] as a cat. Keep them people, people, people, and don't let them get to be symbols. Remember the race is older than the economic system—and that the Y. M. C. A. was once a noble movement—as was the Methodist church—the Lutheran church—the French Revolution—the Commune—the Xstian Religion—all badly managed and run by human beings. . . . Don't let them suck you in on any economic Y. M. C. A. (*SL* 354)

Taking Dos Passos back to the literature they knew, and at times had read together, Hemingway here pointed out that what made Joyce's *Ulysses* great was not its linguistic difficulty so much as it was "Bloom and Mrs. Bloom" (especially the latter) that "saved" Joyce. The remarkable stream of consciousness that Joyce had created for Molly Bloom was not only a literary tour de force but a window into the common—"people, people, people, and don't let them get to be symbols."

In some ways, the writing that Hemingway attempted after the publication of *A Farewell to Arms* was a probe into those all-too-common lives. The Montana family that made wine, the talk between the hospitalized gambler and the nun, the drafts of Cuban fishing-boat operators like Harry Morgan—these were not Hemingway's usual topics for his short fiction. As he wrote to his newspaper friend Guy Hickok on October 14, 1932, from his Key West home,

> Country is all busted. . . . 1/2 schools closed, 200,000 guys on the road, like the wild kids in Russia—Scribners only printed 10,000 copies of [*Death in the Afternoon*]—thought that would last till Xmas probably and sold them all out first day of publication. . . . Don't ever come home thinking U.S.A. [is] interesting— It is just the same as ever only now they are all broke where before they were lousy with cash. The scene hasn't changed. Just the condition of the actors. (*SL* 372–73)

In that long letter to Hickok,[15] Hemingway gave detailed descriptions of his fishing and hunting ("We've killed 3 big bull elk—2 bulls—2 bear—an eagle and a coyote. Grouse all the time"). More significantly, he explained to Hickok what a *learning* experience he was having: "In April went to Cuba for ten days and stayed 65—caught 32 *Swordfish*—learned a lot about Cuba" (*SL* 372).[16]

That Hemingway was learning an immense amount not only about Key West and its waters but about Cuba became clear as he wrote enthusiastically to friends—usually inviting them to come fish the amazingly fecund waters. But he was also gathering stories for the next collection of short fiction, which Perkins planned to bring out in 1933, hoping to create a kind of corrective to the less-than-enthusiastic reception that had greeted *Death in the Afternoon*.

To the stories already mentioned, Hemingway had added (in a comparatively short time) "The Light of the World," dealing with remarkably complex prostitutes; "Fathers and Sons"; "A Clean, Well-Lighted Place"; "A Way You'll Never Be"; and some less well-defined works, including (from *Death in the Afternoon*) "A Natural History of the Dead." Hemingway's organization of the stories in *Winner Take Nothing* once again shows his acute editorial eye: grouped at the beginning of *Winner Take Nothing*, itself a clearly political title, comes "After the Storm" and "A Clean, Well-Lighted Place," followed by Hemingway's favorite story, "The Light of the World." Two stories later, he placed his remarkable war-trauma narrative "A Way You'll Never Be." A similarly strong grouping closes the collection. The last three stories are "Wine of Wyoming," "The Gambler, the Nun, and the Radio," and "Fathers and Sons." Both he and Perkins knew this was going to be a successful book. Hemingway received an advance of $6,000 for it.

As Hemingway wrote these stories, he began the novel that would become *To Have and Have Not*, although some sections of that book had already been published as stories. This account of the brusque seaman, Harry Morgan, who had few choices about earning money was Hemingway's most extended exploration into socially coerced poverty: *To Have and Have Not* was intended to become a part of the leftist outcry heard throughout the United States. It was, however, not published until 1937.

In late 1932, Paramount released its film of *A Farewell to Arms*, starring Gary Cooper and Helen Hayes. Unfortunately, the scriptwriters had created a happy ending for the film, a change that so angered Hemingway that he did not go to the world premiere, which had been specifically planned for Piggott, Arkansas, Pauline's hometown, so that the Pfeiffers and their friends could all attend. Added to what he saw as this professional insult, Hemingway realized that his younger sister Carol was not going to listen to him in his paterfamilias role: he had forbidden her marrying John Gardner, her college boyfriend, but the two were married while Carol was studying in Vienna. Biographer Bernice Kert summarizes, drawing on a number of family letters, "He never forgave Carol for marrying against his wishes."[17]

Two positive turns for Hemingway and his writing occurred in 1932 and 1933. After he had met the beautiful Jane Mason in the spring of 1932 and begun his sometimes fanciful quest for her in Cuba, where she lived with her husband, Pan American executive Grant Mason, he spent more and more time in Havana. For instance, he moved to the Hotel Ambos Mundos for two months while he fished and corrected the proofs for *Death in the Afternoon*.[18] A more literarily useful meeting occurred in early 1933, when Arnold Gingrich approached Hemingway about writing for the men's magazine he was going to launch, *Esquire*, which would be sold in high-end men's clothing stores and would become American men's source of cultural information. Gingrich asked Hemingway to write a "letter" or essay for him, to appear in each issue. While the payment he offered was small, Gingrich was correct in telling Hemingway that he would be widely read by a group of elite men interested in the same sports that the writer was. So wide-reaching was the influence of *Esquire* during the 1930s that cultural historian John Raeburn claims that Hemingway's monthly letters made him into the kind of celebrity he had longed to become (and not just a toy of the literary critics who dogged his *personal* life as if it took precedence over his *writing* life).[19]

Raeburn describes Hemingway by the mid-1930s as "a public figure," saying that "much of Hemingway's appeal as a celebrity stemmed from his reconciliation of the gospels of work and leisure."[20] Glamorous as his fishing and bullfighting lives appeared to be—those activities augmented in the public awareness with big-game hunting in 1935, with the publication of his nonfiction book about hunting on his African safari, *Green Hills of Africa*— Hemingway wrote consistently about the hard work, the study, the sometimes profound knowledge that served as the foundation for the glamour.

Hemingway also capitalized on the commonness of both himself as writer and his subjects as characters. In Raeburn's consideration, "One of the sources of Hemingway's public fame was his ability to step outside his artist role and assume other guises. His worlds appeared boundless, his aptitude for confronting experience unlimited. His mastery in so many arenas of activity suggested that he was a modern Renaissance man."[21] Cultural critic Marilyn Elkins assesses Hemingway's usually informal dress as part of his emphasis on this commonness, as well as his sportsman's need for costuming. Despite his wife Pauline's disapproval, Hemingway was often "informal in formal situations and often unkempt when neatness was the norm." According to Elkins, his dress choices "communicated the power of the artist and his ability to withstand the pressure to conform. . . . Hemingway's public attire reflects the private nature he hoped to project: strong, self-reliant, realistic, and capable of handling the challenges of nature or man."[22]

The journalism Hemingway wrote for Gingrich's *Esquire* was among the best he had ever produced. His personal letters show that he worked hard on these pieces, wanting to give Gingrich—who had become a good friend and a fishing buddy—the right kinds of material, all of it based on "the true gen" about countries, sport, or life itself. In all, *Esquire* published twenty-five of his letters and six short stories (usually appearing when he did not have time to write new essays for Gingrich). Appearing in the first issue of *Esquire* (in autumn 1933) was Hemingway's "Cuban Letter," titled by Gingrich "Marlin off the Morro."

Written with steady excitement and verve, this essay involves the reader and typifies what Hemingway achieved in nearly every one of these letters:

> Getting up to close the shutter you look across the harbor to the flag on the fortress and see it is straightened out toward you. You look out the north window past the Morro and see that the smooth morning sheen is rippling over and you know the trade wind is coming up early. . . . There are two opposing schools about breakfast. If you knew you were not going to be into fish for two or three hours, a good big breakfast would be the thing. Maybe it is a good thing anyway but I do not want to trust it, so I drink a glass of vichy, a glass of cold milk and eat a piece of Cuban bread. (*BL* 137)

The essay continues, reaffirming the second-person address ("you") and keeping the reader involved in the proceedings. More specifically written to introduce readers to the routines and the processes of marlin fishing, Hemingway described the boat he rented—the *Anita*, thirty-four feet long—which belonged to Captain Joe Russell of Key West, a swordfish expert. The other person in the trio fishing that day is Carlos Gutierrez of Havana, "the best marlin and swordfisherman around Cuba. . . . He has studied the habits of the marlin since he first went fishing for them as a boy of twelve with his father."

Hemingway described the small-boat fishermen, as well as the marlin and their habits. He gave the reader figures about the quantity of the fish—11,000 small marlin and 150 large marlin were caught between March and July of 1933, the large weighing between 83 and 468 pounds. Added to this factual descriptive base, Hemingway discussed lunch, pointing out that the boat carries in its cooler "Filipino mangoes, iced pineapple, and alligator pears [avocados]." The latter are so large that a few will feed five people, for a cost of only fifteen cents.

In the January 1934 issue of *Esquire*, Hemingway wrote "The Friend of Spain: A Spanish Letter," which mixed tones. First he commented on the visible prosperity of the country, though he awaited a tragedy. To support his contention that people had more money than they had had in recent years, he wrote, "People are traveling who never traveled before; people go to bull fights who could not afford it before; and many people are swimming who never took a bath before" (*BL* 146). He then described and discussed a number of the current matadors, ending that listing with the lament that changes were occurring: "The old café Fornos is gone, torn down to put up an office building" (*BL* 147).

Hemingway's third essay, "A Paris Letter," in the February 1934 *Esquire*, begins with his memory of shooting a moose and braving storms in Cooke City, Montana. Currently, however, a year later, he was visiting Paris and finding much sorrow. France had not escaped the effects of the United States depression: "This old friend shot himself. That old friend took an overdose of something. That old friend went back to New York and jumped out, or rather fell from, a high window" (*BL* 155). He noted that there was a lot of discouragement, especially among painters, who could sell nothing. The list that occupies the center of the letter is of the French boxers who were among the greatest of Europe. Hemingway segued into that discussion with a nod to his epicure readers: "Food is as good as ever and very expensive" (*BL* 156).

He gave deft attention to the closing, where he worried that war was imminent:

What makes you feel bad is the perfectly calm way everyone speaks about the next war. It is accepted and taken for granted. All right. Europe has always had

Figure 6. Hemingway and his sons, Patrick, John, and Gregory, with a good catch of marlin, mid-1930s.

war. But we can keep out of this next one. And the only way to keep out of it is not to go in it; not for any reason. There will be plenty of good reasons. But we must keep out of it. (*BL* 158)

For the April 1934 issue, Hemingway wrote in a pseudo-comic style about his serious attack of amoebic dysentery. Titling the essay "A. D. in Africa: A Tanganyika Letter," he confessed that he no longer was on safari in Africa, but rather that he had been flown 400 miles to Nairobi in order to be cured of his dysentery through emetine doses. The essay begins by clarifying the designation of the "A. D." in the title; Hemingway then complained that he had no typewriter and therefore could not write his essay. From his bed, instead, he recollected the way the African highland country looked:

When there has been rain the plains roll green against the blue hills the way the western end of Nebraska lifts as you approach Wyoming when it has gone too long without rain. It is a brown land like Wyoming and Montana but with greater roll and distance. Much of the upland bush country that you hunt through looks exactly like an abandoned New England orchard until you top a hill and see the orchard runs on for fifty miles. Nothing that I have ever read has given any idea of the beauty of the country or the still remaining quantity of game. (*BL* 160)

Although Hemingway's usual letters for *Esquire* were focused on activity—or at least on detailed information that made the reader believe he was a part of whatever action existed—here he justified some accurate *description* about the land. Because his next letters dealt with the safari and its hunting, this quiet prefatory piece evoked a contrasting nonviolent moment.

Hemingway's June 1934 essay is titled "Shootism versus Sport: The Second Tanganyika Letter," and it opens compellingly: "There are two ways to murder a lion. One is to shoot him from a motor car, the other, to shoot him at night with a flashlight from a platform or the shelter of a thorn boma, or blind, as he comes to feed on a bait placed by the shootist or his guide." Filled with dialogue about the expedition to kill the lion, this essay was complemented by his July 1934 *Esquire* letter titled "Notes on Dangerous Game: The Third Tanganyika Letter." Focused on dialogue between Hemingway and his reader (or perhaps between Hemingway and his friend Philip Percival, the white hunter who led the Hemingways' safari), this postmodern essay did everything from give novice hunters advice to correct the author's own grammar. It also injected a tone of comic argument into the placid surface of reportorial journalism, as when Hemingway noted about one of Percival's shots, "Mr. P. took the top of the head off one [a leopard] once with a load of number sevens and the leopard came right on by and on for fifteen yards. Didn't know he was dead it seems. Tripped on a blade of grass or something finally" (*BL* 169).

Most of Hemingway's effective *Esquire* letters described his fishing in the Cuban waters. In these his great love for both the waters and the marlin absorbed both the writer and the reader.[23] Nearly half the letters written to fulfill his monthly contract with *Esquire* were about fishing, though some moved into writings about the sport, and others—more and more frequently—moved into Hemingway's meditations on the coming war. For instance, his December 1934 letter plays on his earlier career as journalist ("Old Newsman Writes: A Letter from Cuba"), but rather than tell nostalgic stories, Hemingway focused on "Mustapha Kemal" as he prepared to destroy Smyrna. Immediately turning political, this essay was nostalgic only in the writer's conviction that reporters in the early 1920s had known little about what was happening in Europe. Hemingway contended that at least some journalists in 1934 were better prepared: "If the men who write editorials for the New Republic and The Monthly Review, say, had to take an examination on what they actually know about the mechanics, theory, past performance and practice of actual revolution, as it is made, not as it is hoped for, I doubt if any one of them would have one hundredth part of the knowledge of his subject that the average sensible follower of the horses has of the animals" (*BL* 181).

Hemingway then dissected the decade following World War I, moving country by country, and then returned to his deepest passion, his assessment of the *writing* people did about wars: he referenced John O'Hara's *Appointment in Samarra* but more particularly Tolstoy's *War and Peace*. He warned readers to beware of fiction written by people who did not know what they were writing about, saying,

> You must be prepared to work always without applause. When you are excited about something is when the first draft is done. But no one can see it until you have gone over it again and again until you have communicated the emotion, the sights and the sounds to the reader, and by the time you have completed this the words, sometimes, will not make sense to you as you read them, so many times have you re-read them. . . . But if the book is good, is about something that you know, and is truly written and reading it over you see that this is so you can let the boys [the critics] yip and the noise will have that pleasant sound coyotes make on a very cold night when they are out in the snow and you are in your own cabin that you have built or paid for with your work. (*BL* 185)

Without helping his reader to link this essay with its sequel ("Remembering Shooting-Flying: A Key West Letter," which appeared in the February 1935 issue), Hemingway aligned his writing/reading life with his love of both fishing and shooting:

> When you have loved three things all your life, from the earliest you can remember: to fish, to shoot and, later, to read; and when, all your life, the necessity to write has been your master, you learn to remember and, when you think back you remember more fishing and shooting and reading than anything else and that is a pleasure. (*BL* 187)

Besides Hemingway's comments on writing, he drew heavily on his hatred of fear—as displayed by boxer Max Baer in his defeat by Joe Louis ("the most disgusting public spectacle, outside of a hanging, that your correspondent has ever witnessed. What made it disgusting was fear").[24]

He also gave space to describing the political chicanery he found operative as the bullies of Europe began to coerce other countries into doing their evil will. Published in the September 1935 *Esquire* was his incisive "Notes on the Next War: A Serious Topical Letter" (followed two issues later by "The Malady of Power: A Second Serious Letter" and capped by his January 1936 "Wings over Africa: An Ornithological Letter"). These three essays make up a hard-hitting text about the usurpation of human rights. Evincing brutality of a psychological as well as a physical kind, the marauding countries—according to Hemingway—were poisoning themselves and their compatriots by adding ingredients to "the hell broth that is brewing in Europe" (*BL* 212).

Hemingway began the first essay of this group calmly:

> Not this August, nor this September; you have this year to do in what you like. Not next August, nor next September; that is still too soon; they are still too prosperous from the way things pick up when armament factories start at near capacity; they never fight as long as money can still be made without. So you can fish that summer and shoot that fall or do whatever you do, go home at nights, sleep with your wife, go to the ball game, make a bet, take a drink when you want to, or enjoy whatever liberties are left for anyone who has a dollar or a dime. But the year after that or the year after that they fight. (*BL* 205)

As the essay continued, the pacifistic Hemingway became vituperative: "The only way to combat the murder that is war is to show the dirty combinations that make it and the criminals and swine that hope for it and the idiotic way they run it when they get it so that the honest man will distrust it as he should a racket and refuse to be enslaved into it" (*BL* 210). No shred of patriotic valor lightened Hemingway's view. He predicted that the coming conflict would be even worse than what occurred during World War I because of the current death-dealing technology: "No one wins a modern war because it is fought to such a point that everyone must lose. The troops that are fighting at the end are incapable of winning. It is only a question of which government rots the first or which side can get in a new ally with fresh troops." He lamented those seven million dead during the First World War. He warned about the coming conflict, to be orchestrated by "an ex-corporal in the German army [Hitler] and an ex-aviator and former morphine addict [Mussolini]" (*BL* 211).

Hemingway warned American readers, looking through their "blood-stained merk of misty patriotism," not to be lured into European conflicts because of humanistic/patriotic motives. It was a malevolent activity: "War is no longer made by simply analysed economic forces if it ever was. War is made or planned now by individual men, demagogues and dictators who play on the patriotism of their people to mislead them into a belief in the great fallacy of war. . . . France is a country and Great Britain is several countries but Italy is a man, Mussolini, and Germany is a man, Hitler. A man has ambitions, a man rules until he gets into economic trouble; he tries to get out of this trouble by war" (*BL* 209).

Denunciatory, delivered without amelioration, Hemingway's *Esquire* letters about the coming war left no room for misunderstanding. Part of the relentless bile that readers absorbed may have stemmed from the unnerving experience the author had just undergone when he volunteered himself and his boat, the *Pilar*, to help find bodies of the dead after the early September, 1935, Florida hurricane. Predicted to hit Key West, this hurricane instead traveled north to the Upper Keys, killing hundreds of the inhabitants of Matecumbe Key. The usual population was swelled temporarily by nearly a thousand veterans who had been brought to the area to build a bridge linking Lower Matecumbe Key with Jewfish Key, which was itself part of a Florida initiative to span the thirty-five-mile gap in the Overseas Highway. (That project was funded by the federal government to create employment for the vets and avoid a reprise of the 1932 Bonus March on Washington, DC.) The vets, living in temporary housing, did not realize what dangers the hurricane might bring.

The storm winds were estimated at 185 miles per hour, with a storm surge of nearly twenty feet.[25] When Hemingway arrived two days after the storm, he wrote to Perkins, "Nothing could give an idea of the destruction. Between 700 and 1000 dead. Many, today, still unburied. The foliage absolutely stripped as though by fire for forty miles and the land looking like the abandoned bed of a river. Not a building of any sort standing" (*SL* 421). He closed his account with this comment: "Saw more dead than I'd seen in one place since the lower Piave in June of 1918."

When *New Masses* invited Hemingway to write about the hurricane for them, he did so with alacrity. In "Who Murdered the Vets?" he did not go easy on Franklin D. Roosevelt's administration—insisting that it had abandoned the vets to their deaths. In a series of questions, he made this indictment clear:

> Whom did [the veterans] annoy and to whom was their possible presence a political danger?
>
> Who sent them down to the Florida Keys and left them there in hurricane months?
>
> Who is responsible for their deaths?
>
> The writer of this article lives a long way from Washington and would not know the answers to these questions. But he does know that wealthy people, yachtsmen, fishermen such as President Hoover and President Roosevelt, do not come to the Florida Keys in hurricane months.[26]

The essay was filled with rancor as well as blame. At one point Hemingway referred to the veterans as "bonus-marching veterans" and pointed out that they were "unsuccessful" human beings, "doing coolie labor for a top wage of $45 a month. . . . All they have to lose is their lives." Hemingway enumerated those to be "442 veterans lost, and 70 civilians."[27] Because so many dead were swept out to sea, that total would increase.

It was a pivotal period for Hemingway—celebrity enough to be invited by journals to write (as he was by both *Esquire* and *New Masses*) but still close to counting himself among the commoners who had survived World War I and now the Depression, a man trying with effort to avoid becoming a malcontent, a person dissatisfied with the world's ravaging and pillaging.

Some of these conflicts worked themselves through his 1937 novel *To Have and Have Not*, the first two sections of which had already seen print: "One Trip Across," the opening section of the Harry Morgan story, appeared in *Cosmopolitan* in April 1934, and "The Tradesman's Return," the second section of the novel, appeared in *Esquire* in February 1936.

Had these first long stories not already been published, Hemingway might have had a clearer notion of what the import of the full Harry Morgan—his 1930s version of an American pirate—story would be. But the late fall of 1935 and the winter of 1936 was one of Hemingway's most prolific periods of writing. During those months he wrote "The Short, Happy Life of Francis Macomber," "The Capital of the World," "The Snows of Kilimanjaro," these *Esquire* essays, and the novel-in-progress. He also, perhaps more intensely, watched the conflicts in Spain develop, knowing that war in Spain would be only a preamble to the next world conflict. He could not sort through all aspects of his writing from any long-term perspective. As he wrote to Perkins on September 26, 1936, he wanted only to finish *To Have and Have Not* so he could begin traveling to Spain (the conflict had erupted on July 3, 1936): "When finish this book hope to go to Spain. . . . Will leave the completed Mss. in a vault so you will be covered on it. I will go over it again when I come back. In case anything should happen to me you would always be covered financially even without this novel by the book of stories. . . . I hate to have missed this Spanish thing worse than anything in the world but have to have this book finished first" (*SL* 454–55).

CHAPTER SIX

Hemingway's Epics

"The Snows of Kilimanjaro" and
For Whom the Bell Tolls

MICHAEL REYNOLDS IS the most persuasive biographer to link Hemingway's 1936 masterpiece of a story, "The Snows of Kilimanjaro," with his 1940 novel about the Spanish Civil War, *For Whom the Bell Tolls*. He sees that each of these works used up enough material—characters, events, plots and subplots, language experiments, structural innovations, and wide-ranging metaphor that circumscribed the world of literature as well as the ecological provinces surrounding that world—to be classified as an *epic* in both structure and intent. In Reynolds's words, in both these fictions Hemingway "gave the reader a story within which was embedded an entire collection of short stories. . . . [He was] always experimenting, always reaching beyond his last effort."[1]

Implicit in the use of the term *epic* is the figure of the hero. Critics are divided over the role Robert Jordan played in *For Whom the Bell Tolls*, but they are less divided about the role Harry Walden admitted to in "The Snows of Kilimanjaro." While Jordan had gone to Spain to fight for the Spanish people, Harry seemed content to die with most of his work—that of writing—incomplete. Perhaps John Teunissen's categorization of Hemingway's novel as not a historical fiction but rather a *mythic* one adds a helpful perspective. For a novel that drew from ages of mythic beliefs, the role of hero was less central: what dominated was a generational progression of right thinking (and right acting) that kept the human fires of trust and morality lit.

Discussing *For Whom the Bell Tolls*, Teunissen states that the novel's theme was not the military conflict so much as it was the line from the Gypsy song, "I had an inheritance from my father" (*FWBT* 59).[2] In the mythic melding of chronologically defined times, Jordan saw *his* life repeating the bravery his grandfather had evinced during the Civil War. Mythically, chronological time is subsumed into "dream time," an accurate description of Harry Walden's experience as he is transported to the top of Kilimanjaro. Rather than emphasizing the quantity of events as key for an epic, the role of the fictional hero—whether the term *epic* or *mythic* is used for a work—may be a more significant factor.[3]

Hemingway's enthusiasm for his accomplishments in "The Snows of Kilimanjaro" was clear: he allowed Scribner's to use it as the title story for a 1936 collection (*"The Snows of Kilimanjaro" and Other Stories*). Paul Smith describes the late 1930s as another of the author's periods of great fertility. Smith uses the term *miraculous* and first applies it to the fiction Hemingway wrote between February of 1924 and February of 1925, a period in which he finished a dozen of his most famous stories. Another such period occurred, Smith notes, when "he wrote the first draft of *The Sun Also Rises* in six weeks of the summer of 1925."[4] Drawing on the various biographies and the ever-revelatory caches of Hemingway's letters, one could guess that the winter and spring of 1934–1935 was another such miracle period. For Hemingway, such a stretch constituted what he called "a belle époque," as he wrote on November 16, 1934, to his friend Arnold Gingrich: "Finished the long book [*Green Hills of Africa*] this morning, 492 pages of my handwriting. Going to start a story tomorrow. Might as well take advantage of a belle époque while I'm in one" (*SL* 410).

Much of Hemingway's life from early in 1933 till early in 1934 had been devoted to planning and then undertaking his African safari (*Green Hills of Africa* would narrate key episodes from his and Pauline's three months in Africa). As he was leaving Havana on August 7, 1933, aboard the *Reine de la Pacifice* (with Pauline to follow later), he watched the evidence of the leftist revolution against Cuban dictator Geraldo Machado. He mourned the general strikes that were shutting down Cuban cities. On that August day, "crowds prematurely cheered news of Machado's resignation only to be gunned down in the streets by squads of the dictator's brutal *porristas*."[5] Several days later Machado disappeared, to be replaced by Dr. Carlos Manuel de Céspedes. In Spain, similarly, where Hemingway spent the next two months as he waited for Pauline, the people's needs were being ignored; try as he did to stay away from political issues, Hemingway saw that unrest was growing.

Hemingway's letters to Gingrich established his lack of interest in moving back into the heart of American civilization; he saw Key West as a fringe location, suitable for himself as writer. He told Ivan Kashkeen that a writer "is an outlier like a Gypsy. He can be class conscious only if his talent is limited. If he has enough talent all classes are his province" (*SL* 419). When Gingrich suggested that he write for *Esquire* about topics germane to American interests, Hemingway replied, "[America] doesn't move me and hasn't moved me for a long time and still I can be moved. It's like trying to imagine Sarah Bernhardt good, because she was good once. I say the hell with it. I've been better places and better people (Spain)" (*SL* 410). He had earlier written even more sharply,

> As far as I know I have only one life to live and I have worked hard and written good stories, pieces, etc. and by Jesus I want to live it where it interests me, and I have no romantic feeling about the American scene. Also pretty soon I will be a long time dead and outside of writing I have two well-developed talents; for sea fishing when there is a current . . . and shooting with a rifle on targets at unknown ranges where the vital spots are not marked but have to be understood to be hit and for Christ sake why not go where I can use them . . . . If I don't give a goddamn about America, I can't help it. (*SL* 409)[6]

Part of his distaste for the United States had come from Franklin Roosevelt's increases in income taxes. Although he wanted to help the poor improve their lives, Hemingway was angry at what were extremely high rates (especially for a writer, whose income came in much higher amounts in some years than others, thus pushing up his tax rates). He was accustomed to the low rates that had been in effect since the tax's inception in 1913—the 1 percent originally charged was not a problem. But by the late 1930s and increasingly during the 1940s, rates for some brackets were climbing above 60 percent (with the high of 91 percent coming).[7] Because Hemingway was a writer, and did not work for corporations abroad, he could not qualify for the "earned income" deductions that could have lowered his taxes, even during years when he lived largely outside the United States. He also could not qualify for much of a deduction under the cost of doing business—the IRS would not have been sympathetic, for instance, to his claiming the cost of a second African safari. Though he had excellent tax representation from Maurice Speiser and, later, Alfred Rice, the law itself was the problem—there was no way around his required large tax payments. Because the IRS demanded estimated payments throughout the year before the taxes fell due in March, Hemingway continuously faced tax issues—often borrowing money to make the estimated payments.[8]

After Hemingway was audited by the IRS in the early 1940s, he became more and more agitated about paying these taxes, although in a letter to Rice in 1948 he expressed an attitude that Carlos Baker says was customary for him: "I need money, badly, but not badly enough to do one dishonorable, shady, borderline, or 'fast' thing to get it" (*SL* 655). He complained at every opportunity, however; as he told Hadley, "I happen to have worked hard all my life and made a fortune at a time when whatever you make is confiscated by the govt. That's bad luck" (*SL* 537).[9]

Rather than being woven around memories or accounts of wartime, although it includes the Machado revolts, *To Have and Have Not* gives readers a subtext of money problems. The novel was written in four different segments—in the first is the Harry Morgan story, in which he strangles the Chinese expediter; the second is the trip across, when he loses his arm to gunfire wounding; in the third section the rich are set against the common and criminal culture now represented by Harry and Marie Morgan and their children; and the fourth is the bifurcated conclusion. The first part of the last section focuses on the naïve novelist Richard Gordon, beset with marital problems and trying to learn enough about the bank robbery and the robbers' escape—in Harry Morgan's boat—to write the story; the brief second part is given over to Marie Morgan's stream-of-consciousness lament for Harry, who has been killed in his confiscated boat as he was trying to kill the bank robbers—particularly after they had executed his friend Albert.

Ivan Kashkeen says briefly about *To Have and Have Not* that Hemingway had not known enough to write this novel, particularly in terms of the characters' language; Delbert Wylder points out that the reader cannot sympathize with Marie's grieving monologue because she has played such a small part in the book.[10] Frederic Svoboda stresses that it was the dismal state of the area's economy (after both the Machado revolts in Cuba and the hurricane devastation in the Keys) that forced Harry Morgan to become a criminal. A former Miami policeman and the owner of his fishing boat, Harry begins his life of crime when Johnson, the wealthy American, bilks him out of the $825 charter bill—and Harry has no recourse. Down to his last forty cents, he takes on the dozen "Chinks" to cross into the States—but kills unnecessarily in order to get that cargo. The rest of Harry's earning a living is built on one illegality after another. As Svoboda states, "His double dealing in the smuggling of booze and illegal immigrants between Cuba and Key West leads to his fatal wounding and to his less than completely revolutionary realization that 'a man alone ain't got no bloody fucking chance.'"[11]

Toni Morrison, in *Playing in the Dark*, her 1992 Harvard lectures, comments on Hemingway's language in the first books of the novel—"Chinks," "niggers," "black Cubans," "rummies"—seeing these terms as examples of the literary problem of "an almost completely buried subject" and of Hemingway's dealing blatantly with untoward racial and social matters. In "One Trip Across," Harry knows he cannot trust Eddy, the rummy, to steer the boat, so the black man—whose job is only to fix bait—is given that responsibility. He is, however, *not* given language. In the second segment, the black man—now named Wesley—has been shot, as has Harry. In this section, Wesley asks the white boss why he had to fight over the rum they were carrying.

Whatever sensible thought occurs in Harry's boat, it comes from those characters unable to even speak because of their powerlessness. As Morrison says,

> Something very curious happens to this namelessness when, in part two, the author shifts voices. Part one is told in the first person, and whenever Harry thinks about this black man he thinks "nigger." In part two, where Hemingway uses the third-person point of view in narrating and representing Harry's speech, two formulations of the black man occur: he both remains nameless and stereotyped and becomes named and personalized.
>
> Harry *says* "Wesley" when speaking to the black man in direct dialogue; Hemingway *writes* "nigger" when as narrator he refers to him. . . .
>
> . . . [Finally, it is Wesley who manages to tell Harry,] "You don't care what happens to a man. . . . You ain't hardly human. . . . You ain't got human feelings."[12]

As Morrison analyzes Hemingway's choices in portraying nearly all the violent characters in the novel, she insists that his distinction between "Cubans" and "niggers"—to refer to Cubans who are darker in color—especially in the robbery scenes and in the concluding escape scenes are markers of Hemingway's racism. She brings in sexual topics as well, such as when the "nigger" speaks to Marie on the street and Harry reacts violently to him, smacking him and crushing his hat, and when Harry answers Marie's curiosity about his sleeping with black women, saying a black woman is like a "nurse shark." Much of what Morrison explicates, particularly about Hemingway's posthumously published novel *The Garden of Eden*, is dramatically significant—in terms of both race and gender. But few of her comments are as incisive as these remarks about Hemingway's language choices in *To Have and Have Not*, choices that unfold to reveal attitudes about race and class.

Much of the last hundred pages of *To Have and Have Not* tries to comment on the wealthy tourist class—Richard Gordon, the novelist, embroiled in romantic situations, is the key player here. With a heavy-handed swipe at privilege, Hemingway voided any finer sensibility that might have driven this class of characters. Just as Harry Morgan seems unrealistic, falling as he does into the use of crude names for his companions, so too are the machinations of the swingers who find Cuba and Key West more exotic than naturally beautiful. Had the novel been able to show the discrepancies between classes, *To Have and Have Not* might have landed Hemingway in the more often approved liberal camp of class-conscious novelists.[13]

That Harry Morgan dies at the end of this book indicates a significant change in Hemingway's philosophy of writing. None of his protagonists had died before—though the deaths of Catherine Barkley and her baby might suggest a kind of surrogate death.[14] In a cluster of these fictions—what one might label his "death" stories—Hemingway might have been working through his deepest, unalleviated fears.

Paco dies, unintentionally, in "The Capital of the World." Macomber dies, unexpectedly, in "The Short Happy Life of Francis Macomber." Harry Walden dies after a novel's worth of unrealized memories—all stories he was saving to write—in "The Snows of Kilimanjaro." For Harry Morgan, living outside the law as he tries to provide for Marie and their daughters, death echoes his brutal murder of the Chinese profiteer. As Harry's ruinous attempts to earn money cost him first his right arm and then his life, there is little sympathy created by Hemingway for the seaman's choices. The most memorable death, which is implied rather than described, of Hemingway's middle- and late-1930s protagonists is that in *For Whom the Bell Tolls* of Robert Jordan, whose self-sacrifice is legitimated by his giving Maria, Pilar, and Pablo time to escape. But even Jordan's death is not so obviously heroic as that of Sordo, lying in cunning wait behind his dead horse on the bare hilltop.[15] His death is the fault of a war that, by the time of the action in the novel, has been recognized as futile. The presence of Jordan, the American college teacher, volunteering in Spain has itself sometimes been considered puzzling in the novel.

In this cluster of "death" stories, Hemingway usually used narratives that do *not* describe characters' deaths. Harry Morgan's speech fades into his ending, Harry Walden disappears into the blinding whiteness, Francis Macomber seems to die instantaneously—and he is given *no* opportunity to recognize that death is coming. But Hemingway chose to describe the act of dying in Paco's story, "The Capital of the World." Paco, the least experienced, already on his way to death, chronicles his dying in disbelief:

Paco was alone, first sitting up, then huddled over, then slumped on the floor, until it was over, feeling his life go out of him as dirty water empties from a bathtub. . . . He was frightened and he felt faint and he tried to say an act of contrition and he remembered how it started but before he had said, as fast as he could, "Oh, my God, I am heartily sorry for having offended Thee who art worthy of all my love and I firmly resolve . . . ," he felt too faint and he was lying face down on the floor and it was over very quickly. (*CSS* 37)

The postscript sentence repeats what the narrator has earlier said: "A severed femoral artery empties itself faster than you can believe."

Paco's inability to find the words that might save his soul parallels the gritty scene of both blood and fear: dying even in these fictions about death is not memorable. As Hemingway was fond of saying, "All stories, if continued far enough, end in death, and he is no true-story teller who would keep that from you" (*DIA* 122).

In 1965, Frederick Hoffman wrote with his usual perspicacity about what he called Hemingway's own "unreasonable" wounding/possible death during World War I. He tied the suddenness of the shell's exploding to the mechanization of modern warfare, making these representations of possible death in Hemingway's fiction come to stand for many of the twentieth century's deaths. In Hoffman's considered words,

> Among other distinctions, Hemingway can claim that of having honestly attempted an explanation of a form of death to which the twentieth century is particularly heir—death that comes as a violent disruption of life. It is unreasonable (that is, it is not properly "motivated," cannot be understood in terms of any ordinary system of motivation); it puts traditional securities to shame, since they cannot satisfactorily keep pace with its indiscriminate destructiveness. It demands a new form of resourcefulness and courage, and—in Hemingway's case—a new type of moral improvisation. The sudden violent injury inflicted impersonally by efficient guns or planes too remote from the victim to "hold him any special grudge" is the symbol of this type of death and of the death-in-life which is its consequence.[16]

What Hoffman described could have been a kind of delayed memory, or it could have been that Hemingway's own acute understanding of the coming war prompted him to recall the casualties of the war he had been in, including his own wounding. Perhaps his turn to the nonfiction of both *Death in the Afternoon* and *Green Hills of Africa* had made him more self-conscious than he customarily was. Or perhaps his honesty in a letter to Marjorie Kinnan Rawlings, another Scribner's novelist, was an accurate representation of his omnipresent psychic life.

In his August 16, 1936, letter to Rawlings, Hemingway answered her question about the *real* Hemingway identity—was he sportsman or writer? Hemingway equivocated:

> As for being Sportsman being Artist, I always fished and shot since I could carry a canepole or a single barreled shotgun; not to show off but for great inner pleasure and almost complete satisfaction. Have not been writing as long but get the same pleasure, and you do it alone, only it is a goddamned sight harder to do and if I did nothing else (no fish, no shoot, no drink) would probably go nuts doing it with the difficulty, the times in between when you can't do it, the always being short of what you want to do, the rest of it with all of which you have probably lived some time and various places. (*SL* 449)

His honest ending to this section—about the sheer difficulty of the writing trade—then took him to this uncharacteristic admission:

> *Lately I have felt I was going to die in a short time* (hope that is nuts and that live to be a wise old man with white beard and chew tobacco) and so I have been having more fun maybe than I deserve because in a way I have done my work as well as I could as went along. (*SL* 449–50; my italics)

Pressured by Max Perkins to write enough new stories so that Scribner's could bring out a new story collection, Hemingway told him about "The Capital of the World" ("one of the best I've ever written") as well as "The Short Happy Life of Francis Macomber," which he titled in this letter "A Budding Friendship," and the story that became "The Snows of Kilimanjaro"—here referred to as "another story of Africa" titled "The Happy Ending" (*SL* 442). His letter to Perkins suggests that he wrote these three stories so quickly that he had not yet absorbed their complexity. Known for his careful attention to choosing titles, Hemingway here remarked about the Macomber story as if it placed the war veteran, the white hunter Wilson, into some kind of rapport with the fearful Francis Macomber. Such a rapport seemed unlikely.

Placing "Short Happy Life" in the context of Hemingway's condemnation of people who fear—anything—makes it a more moving story, with Macomber's final changed demeanor truly remarkable. Early in the story, the author spent a long paragraph describing why the nighttime sound of a lion's roar so disorients the American hunter. Hemingway gave the reader few details about this man, simply that he is wealthy and has a wife who is unsympathetic. Into that shadowy characterization comes this statement: "He had heard the lion roaring somewhere up along the river." Prefacing the planned hunt for lions the next day, this sound is ominous.

> When Francis Macomber woke in the night to hear it he was afraid. . . . There was no one to tell he was afraid, nor to be afraid with him, and, lying alone, he did not know the Somali proverb that says a brave man is always frightened three times by a lion; when he first sees his track, when he first hears him roar and when he first confronts him. (*CSS* 11)

Hemingway made an unexpected narrative move when he described the way the *lion* feels as he is being shot. In the midst of pages of dialogue among Macomber, Margot, and Wilson, nothing that is said seems out of the ordinary. But to put his readers into the mind of the proud, defiant lion was to change the dynamics of the story. (Hemingway remembered this technique when he came to write Santiago's story about capturing the magnificent marlin and its death.)

Just as both stories are set in Africa, so both have as women protagonists the rich and generally thoughtless (and once-beautiful) American wife. For Hemingway to develop both Margot Macomber and Helen Walden in the same pattern he had used for Helene Bradley in *To Have and Have Not* suggests that he might have been distancing himself from his own wealthy American wife, Pauline Pfeiffer.[17] When Rose Marie Burwell analyzed these stories in the company of Hemingway's posthumously published African works, she found the same pattern of unspecified hostility toward the author's past wives, particularly Pauline; Burwell phrases her observation this way: Hemingway attempted in his fiction to express "a knowledge he cannot think."[18]

Similarly, to first title "The Snows of Kilimanjaro" "The Happy Ending" was to underscore the story's closing fantasy—taking Harry Walden to the apex of the mountain and transmuting his death into a mystical arrival.[19] Again, the story moves intentionally toward the protagonist's realization that he has not been simply a spy in the house of the wealthy, waiting to write about their foibles, but that he is, in fact, as corrupt as they.

Whereas "The Short Happy Life of Francis Macomber" is an efficient story, not leaving much to a reader's imagination in drawing the triangle of brave versus weak characters, "The Snows of Kilimanjaro" is a compendium of Harry's lifetime of possible written fictions. To show the collectivity of Harry's failing imagination as he nears death and faces the truth about himself,

Hemingway used the italic type font. In each occurrence of italics, the memory Harry retrieves is somehow related to the various wars or other military action he has known. The first four lengthy italicized passages are apparently "unwritten." They move between the 1930s and World War I and the Greco-Turkish War (1919–1922), usually without signals as to time. Peter Hays sees these flashbacks as conveying even wider meanings: for instance, the use of the word *snows*. Hays points out that the Greek refugees tramped through the snow on the Bulgarian mountains, as ordered by Fridtjof Nansen, the League of Nations High Commissioner for Refugees who in 1922 won the Nobel Peace Prize. Nansen pretended it was too early for the snow that he knew would kill the refugees, but he was himself an expert skier; he knew what the snow would do.[20]

Even though Harry reflects that "he had seen the world change . . . and it was his duty to write of it," reader sympathy does not track with this character's musings. The only flashback that appears to be relevant is the late one, and in it, Harry's memory gives the reader Williamson, "the bombing officer" who was hit by a German stick bomb "as he was coming in through the wire that night and, screaming, had begged every one to kill him." The graphic details ("his bowels spilled out into the wire") led to Harry's giving the irreparably injured man "all his morphine tablets . . . and then they did not work right away" (*CSS* 53). Worn down to a state well past language, well past the comforts that religious belief might provide ("our Lord never sending you anything you could not bear . . . meant that at a certain time the pain passed you out automatically"), the image of the near-dead Williamson foreshadows the death that Harry also comes to face.

Rather than finding layers of additional meaning in what the leopard was hunting as he traveled near the apex of Kilimanjaro, or questioning why Hemingway chose the hyena to describe Harry's fear of his coming death, the reader may instead focus on Hemingway's choice to paint the voyage of death in the snowy brilliance of nature's peaks. Toni Morrison notes that the use of snow suggests "unfathomable whiteness. Harry's destiny and death dream in Hemingway's Africa is focused on the mountain top, 'great, high, and unbelievably white in the sun.'"[21] If the sinister blackness of unknown existences—here, the threatening and inscrutable African continent, feared since long before the days of Joseph Conrad—can be lightened or even transmuted by the blinding whiteness to come, surely the protagonist's innate fear of *any* unknown can be ameliorated. (Unknown experiences occur in places both psychological and geographical; Hemingway's fascination with exploration accrued throughout his active years as writer.)

In both "The Short Happy Life of Francis Macomber" and "The Snows of Kilimanjaro," Hemingway continued his experimental story of Harry Morgan (suggested by his choice of Harry as the name of several of these male protagonists). Frustrated by the critical reception of *Green Hills of Africa*, Hemingway wrote these stories about Africa (as was, obviously, his nonfiction *Green Hills of Africa*), predicated on the geographic and psychic differences the white protagonist feels in the African surroundings. For both the fearful Francis Macomber and the fearless Harry Walden, *Africa* becomes *destiny*. Harry Walden, for all the flashbacks to the conflicts and wars, all the white lives with which he has surrounded himself, lives his last few days *in* Africa. And it is in *Africa* that he dies.

Hemingway himself was not tempted to avoid conflicts of any kind. He planned carefully for his travels to Spain, writing Mary Pfeiffer, his mother-in-law, that the Spanish conflict was only "a dress rehearsal for the inevitable European war." He also apologized for taking the communist side, telling her that "the Reds may be as bad as they say but they are the people of the country versus the absentee landlords, the Moors, the Italians, and the Germans" (*SL* 457–58). Perkins warned Hemingway *not* to go, but as the writer worked with Perkins to plan a new story collection, Hemingway wrote a preface in which he defined himself as far different from Harry Walden. Hemingway saw himself as an accomplished and active writer:

> In going where you have to go, and doing what you have to do, and seeing what you have to see, you dull and blunt the instrument you write with. But I would rather have it bent and dull and know that I had to put it on the grindstone again and hammer it into shape . . . and know that I had something to write about, than to have it bright and shining and nothing to say, or smooth and well-oiled in the closet, but unused.[22]

* * * * *

Alex Vernon's carefully detailed book about Hemingway's writing activities during the Spanish Civil War, *Hemingway's Second War: Bearing Witness to the Spanish Civil War*, provides both factual and critical materials, including much about the film script that he, in collaboration, wrote for fund-raising purposes. Vernon thoroughly explicates the conception and execution of *The Spanish Earth*, the 1937 Joris Ivens film created by John Dos Passos, Lillian Hellman, Archibald MacLeish, Ivens, and Hemingway, with the latter doing the voice-overs. Vernon acknowledges the role of Hemingway's powerful North American Newspaper Alliance (NANA) dispatches and of his presence in Spain—particularly in Madrid—during the first year of the war. He then develops a wide-reaching analysis of Hemingway's short fiction, his play *The Fifth Column*,[23] and his novel *For Whom the Bell Tolls*. Filled with new information, Vernon's work provides essential insights into the prolegomenon that shaped Hemingway's writing, and his political beliefs, from the mid-1930s to the very visible end of the Spanish conflict in 1939.

Vernon, a military historian, is strong in discussions of Hemingway's reluctance to admit that he had, to some extent, been taken in by the antifascist propaganda—although Hemingway had been writing throughout the 1930s about the prospects of a coming European war. But as Jose Luis Castillo-Puche points out accurately, Hemingway went to Madrid because "he had to come, because when he was in Spain, he was more like one of us and more like himself, more his own master and more the lover of his art. Boredom and despair could not touch him here. Here he would discover the truth, *his* truth."[24]

Vernon acknowledges that Hemingway wanted to do his part to save the lives and hopes of the Spanish people but categorizes the writer's enthusiasm as at times "blind acceptance of the Republican and sometimes the Comintern line." Even if Hemingway had bought into the government's and the communists' positions, by the time of writing *The Fifth Column* in late 1937, he understood that the executions he mentioned there were frightening. In the play, Vernon notes, Philip Rawlings "has wearied of the killing and the lies, and by play's end asks to be shipped out as soon as possible." There, it is Robert Preston, the journalist, who more nearly reflects Hemingway's attitude. Vernon concludes, "At the very least one should acknowledge the play's . . . wartime acknowledgment of the political executions."[25]

Had Hemingway not gone to Spain, there would have been no play, no Spanish War stories, and no major war novel. He had rushed to finish *To Have and Have Not* in order to go; he had signed a lucrative contract with NANA—with payment set at $1,000 per dispatch—to legitimate his presence in Madrid. And, in December of 1936, he had met fellow journalist Martha Gellhorn when she had introduced herself, her mother, and her brother to him in Sloppy Joe's Bar in Key West: part of Spain's attraction early on might have been Hemingway's flirtation with the young blonde (who had, not incidentally, been featured on the September cover of *The Saturday Review of Literature*).

Amanda Vaill points out in her work *Hotel Florida: Truth, Love, and Death in the Spanish Civil War* that the irregularities of the Spanish conflict were striking; seldom were war correspondents elsewhere allowed to be in so much personal danger. Journalists were at "particular risk and they were able to cover this war more closely and thoroughly than they had any previous conflict." Vaill describes the letters Gellhorn wrote to Eleanor Roosevelt (with whom she was friends) about Hemingway's involvement and his generosity. According to Gellhorn, Hemingway had "paid passage for two volunteers who were going to Spain to join the International Brigade." He had also borrowed $1,500 to buy ambulances for the Medical Bureau of the American Friends for Spanish Democracy (and he was chairman of the ambulance fund-raising drive for the bureau).[26]

Hemingway's first stay in Madrid was from March 14 to May 9, 1937—his NANA dispatches from this trip are among the best journalism he ever wrote. From the various approaches illustrated in my introduction, through his modestly evocative "The Old Man at the Bridge," to the searing descriptions of the Tortosa battles—with much attention to the effectiveness of the German bombings—Hemingway wrote his dispatches with color and accuracy. Back in Key West, Pauline Hemingway thought her husband's being in Spain was not only unreasonable but unpatriotic. While he was away, she added an in-ground saltwater pool, a rarity in that area.

To Pauline's mother, Mary Pfeiffer, Hemingway wrote that his time in Spain was "mystical," and that being there in the fighting had given him new personal courage: he had lost his fear of dying (*SL* 460–61). Absorbed totally in the daily carnage of the Spanish war, Hemingway was living outside his normal expressive range. As he wrote in his publisher's note to *The Fifth Column*, "Each day we were shelled by the guns beyond Leganes or behind the folds of Garabites hill, and while I was writing the play the Hotel Florida, where we lived and worked, was struck by more than thirty high explosive shells" (*FC* v).

In an April 14, 1937, NANA dispatch, Hemingway wrote,

> The roaring burst of a high explosive shell wakes you and you go to the window and look out to see a man, his head down, his coat collar up, sprinting desperately across the paved square. There is the acrid smell of high explosive you hoped you'd never smell again . . . [and there is] a middle-aged woman, wounded in the abdomen, who is being helped into the hotel entrance by two men in blue workmen's smocks. She has her two hands crossed below her big, old-style Spanish bosom and from between her fingers the blood is spurting in a thin stream. On the corner, twenty yards away, in a heap of rubble, smashed cement and thrown up dirt, a single dead man. (*BL* 262)

Hemingway's April 11 dispatch left the bombings and instead gave his readers this: "After fifteen minutes of the heaviest artillery fire, which with direct hit after direct hit, hid the five houses in one rolling cloud of white and orange smoky dust, I watched the infantry attack. . . . The machine gun and rifle fire made one solid crackling whisper in the air and then we saw another tank coming up with a moving shadow behind it that the glasses showed to be a solid square of men" (*BL* 260–61).

Vaill, who focuses often on Gellhorn's experiences, recounts that early one morning Gellhorn "heard the sickening whine of a shell approaching, then a noise 'like granite thunder' as it hit just outside the hotel. . . . She [Gellhorn] discovered that the shell had decapitated a man standing on the corner."[27]

His words indelibly inscribed in his readers' minds, Hemingway through his NANA articles was becoming the voice of the Spanish Civil War; he was adding to his burgeoning celebrity. In early June, 1937, he flew to New York to speak at the American Writers Congress, giving a talk titled "Fascism Is a Lie." One thousand people were turned away, but the crowd still numbered 3,500. Hemingway spoke only seven minutes, emphasizing the discrepancies between

Figure 7. Hemingway with fighters during the Spanish Civil War, 1937. © Robert Capa/ Magnum Photos.

fascism's mandates and the work of writers who wanted to tell the truth; he illustrated his beliefs with such information as this: "In Madrid, where it costs every British newspaper 57 pounds or $280 a month to insure a correspondent's life and where American correspondents work at an average wage of $65 a week *uninsured*, we of the working press watched murder done last month for nineteen days. It was done by German artillery, and it was highly efficient murder." He emphasized that "when a man goes to seek the truth in war he may find death instead." True to his larger beliefs, Hemingway digressed to note that "there are worse things than war. Cowardice is worse, treachery is worse, and simple selfishness is worse."[28] With Donald Ogden Stewart, Archibald MacLeish, and Martha Gellhorn in the audience, Hemingway realized a new kind of identity as spokesperson for the comparatively voiceless.

A few weeks later he traveled from Bimini, the fertile Bahamian fishing spot forty-five miles east of Miami, back to New York for the premiere of *The Spanish Earth*; there was another showing later at the White House. But by September 6, 1937, he was back in Spain, this time accompanying Gellhorn throughout not only Madrid and Barcelona but Teruel's offensives—and then its defeats. *Time* magazine featured Hemingway on its October 18 cover—*To Have and Have Not* had been published, to reasonably good reviews.

Again between March 31 and May 3, 1938, Hemingway returned to Spain. This would be his last visit to the front except for a few weeks in November of 1938. The saddening destruction of both the country and its people can be traced through his articles for NANA and *Ken* (the short-lived liberal journal edited by Gingrich)—some dispatches were heavily personal, with Hemingway as journalist participating in the military action; others maintained journalistic objectivity. As the months passed, Hemingway's reportage steadily lost its hopeful tone. In an April 21, 1938, article for *Ken*, he began with descriptions of the dead from photographs:

> The man at the bottom of the left-hand page was hit by a high explosive. There are no feet to his legs.
>
> The man at the bottom of the other page was hit by a tank shell which exploded in the little pile of rocks where he was working an automatic rifle. The other man . . . looks all right . . . but he is quite dead.
>
> The man at the top of the right-hand page was hit by a light bomb dropped from a pursuit plane which was ground-strafing, impressive to those who are not accustomed to a battle-field. But in your time you've seen good friends look as bad or worse. (*HOW* 292–93)

This dispatch was primarily about the wearying effects of prolonged war. But as Hemingway learned about the Loyalist methods of survival, his horror at the conflict turned to admiration for the people involved, and that admiration deepened until it seemed exaggerated. Later came his disillusionment with the mechanics of the cause, its politics and leaders,[29] and its damning lack of concern for the Spanish people.

The intensity of Hemingway's personal experience colored not only his journalism but also both his play and the short stories he published during the late thirties: "The Denunciation," "The Butterfly and the Tank," "Night before Battle," "Under the Ridge," and "Nobody Ever Dies." It also warped any hope of having his second marriage—that to Pauline Pfeiffer—survive. As the couple's personal conflicts became more and more visible, and as Hemingway and Martha Gellhorn were more and more frequently together, American observers accepted that the practice of changing wives—especially for celebrities—had become a cultural given.

For Hemingway, set within Pauline's trips to France to be with him and Martha's trips to both Spain and France for the same reason, the malaise of traveling to escape the pressures of loves and family responsibilities took a heavy toll. In frustration, he turned repeatedly to the useful occupation of writing. As Gregory, his youngest son, wrote years later about the slammed doors, the verbal clashes, the pain during the separations (which were never quite separations), and eventually the impending divorce, he told the story of Hemingway's skill at "destroying people with words." He used as illustration his father's writing a letter to Pauline titled "How Green Was My Valet" in which "Pauline was the *millionairess* and he [Hemingway] was the *valet*."[30]

The dissolution of the Hemingway-Pfeiffer marriage went on for two years, as Pauline, Martha, and Hemingway traveled in and out of Key West, New York, Cuba, France, and Spain. It was December of 1939 before Pauline closed the Key West home and moved with her two boys to New York.

Hemingway began the novel that would become *For Whom the Bell Tolls* in April of 1939, living some of the time with Martha in Cuba at the Finca Vigia, a house she had rented ten miles east of Havana. By July of the following year, the novel was finished. When it was published on October 21, 1940, it received the best reviews of any Hemingway work since *A Farewell to Arms*. Paramount offered $100,000 for the film rights, and that holiday season, in 1940, Hemingway bought the Finca Vigia for $12,500. Six months after *For Whom the Bell Tolls* was published, Hemingway wrote to Perkins, complaining about what he saw as inadequate efforts by Scribner's to market the book (though it was approaching sales of half a million copies), telling Perkins that writing the book had been—for him—a huge and protracted effort, that he had done it even though much of the time "it was *impossible*" (*SL* 523).

In Hemingway's correspondence with both Perkins and Charlie Scribner during the months of setting copy and correcting proofs, his weariness had shown. Arguments over language choices had been the least of Scribner's worries.[31] In an August 15, 1940, letter to Scribner, Hemingway reminded his publisher, "This book is *one whole thing*; not just a lot of parts." The novel's *wholeness* supported Hemingway's rationale for including Pilar's account of the execution of the fascist villagers, telling Scribner, "There is a goddamned horribleness about part of Madrid like no other place in the world." The early "smell of death" scene—the inclusion of which Scribner questioned—"seems to me to be an integral and valid part. . . . You remember there is a whole dark business about that from the very start. The man Kashkeen who has killed himself, the same necessity which faces Jordan, the question about forebodeings which I know is not phony, from having seen people walking around with it sitting on their shoulders. . . . There is the balancing of Jordan's good sense and sound skepticism against this gypsy crap which isn't all crap" (*SL* 508). As if in dialogue with himself, Hemingway had added a paragraph to his preface to Gustav Regler's novel, *The Great Crusade* (1940), about his belief that

> the greatest novels are all made-up. Everything in them is created by the writer. He must create from knowledge, of course, unless his book is to be a tour de force. There have been great tours de force too: *The Red Badge of Courage* and *Wuthering Heights*. But the authors of those books are usually poets who happen to be writing prose. But there are *events which are so great* that if a writer has participated in them his obligation is to try to write them truly rather than assume the presumption of altering them with invention. It is events of this importance that have produced Regler's book.[32]

And Hemingway could well have added "and *For Whom the Bell Tolls*." Drawing from information he could authenticate, creating characters no more imaginary than the people who fought in the Spanish Civil War, Hemingway did not admit to Scribner that Pilar's account of her village was fabricated. Scribner might not have understood where *truth* really lies in any successful novel.

Reviewers did not seem worried about the authenticity, or lack thereof, of Hemingway's characterization of the Spanish people. Most of them compared

For Whom the Bell Tolls with *A Farewell to Arms*, as though both these great works were generic *war* novels. In Hemingway's mind, however, the books were only distantly related. His 1929 novel had grown out of his (and others') experiences on the Italian front during World War I, but the military narrative was eventually usurped by the love story. *For Whom the Bell Tolls*, in contrast, was a monumental assemblage of various war stories—parts of it told by men doomed to die, like Sordo and Anselmo; other strands of it observed by the protagonist, Robert Jordan; still other narratives that illustrated the brutality of all war told by the strong women of the novel, such as Pilar and Maria. The shifting points of view allowed Hemingway freedom to be inclusive, a technique he had been experimenting with during his writing of such short stories as "The Snows of Kilimanjaro."

Whereas *A Farewell to Arms* includes several military-based actions, *For Whom the Bell Tolls* is little *except* military action. When Hemingway chose to include Sordo's story as "The Fight on the Hilltop" in his *Men at War* anthology, he was paying tribute to the thousands of great soldiers lost in war. In this instance, as in several others, the protagonist—facing sure death—speaks for the privilege of dying nobly.

> Dying was nothing and he had no picture of it nor fear of it in his mind. But living was a field of grain blowing in the wind on the side of a hill. Living was a hawk in the sky. Living was an earthen jar of water. (*FWBT* 312–13)

None of the men in *For Whom the Bell Tolls* look forward to death, even though they know that death is likely. Sordo, at age fifty-two, and Anselmo, at age sixty-eight, look with sympathy on their younger compatriots, and Anselmo tries to educate them. When Agustin brags about the people he will kill, should the revolutionaries win, Anselmo says mildly, "That we should win this war and shoot nobody. . . . That we should govern justly and that all should participate in the benefits according as they have striven for them. And that those who have fought against us should be educated to see their error." When Agustin seems not to be listening, but repeats, "We will have to shoot many. . . . Many, many, many,"[33] Anselmo in turn says, "That we should shoot none. Not even the leaders" (*FWBT* 285–86).[34]

Meditating about his own long life, Anselmo considers, "One thing I have that no man nor any God can take from me and that is that I have worked well for the Republic. I have worked hard for the good that we will all share later; . . . and I have done nothing that I am ashamed of" (*FWBT* 197).

Stories of deaths—both good and shameful—appear throughout *For Whom the Bell Tolls*. As Pilar tells about Pablo's execution of the fascist town leaders, she gives moral weight to each experience. One of the better deaths is illustrated in her narrative of "Don Ricardo," "a short man with gray hair and a thick neck and he had a shirt on with no collar. He was bow-legged from much horseback riding. 'Good-by,' he said to all those who were kneeling. 'Don't be sad. To die is nothing. The only bad thing is to die at the hands of this *canalla*'" (*FWBT* 111).

Included in the tapestry of grief that the war story presents is the traumatic fallout of experiencing the war's losses. In Jordan's memory, for instance, lives the youngster from Belgium, a vivid cameo, a character who enlisted with five other boys from his village. All his five friends were killed. Back at home, working in a menial job, the bereaved young man could only cry. "Everyone was very gentle with him but it did no good." The damage to his psyche was permanent (*FWBT* 136).

On the final morning, going to make preparations to blow the bridge, it is Jordan who recognizes these sorts of wisdom. On the previous day, he had not allowed any of his group to attempt to help Sordo's band, though the beheadings of the five men killed on the hilltop saddened them all. But Jordan knew he needed each of his people for the work of blowing the bridge. He thought to himself, "This was the greatest gift that he had, the talent that fitted him for war; that ability not to ignore but to despise whatever bad ending there could be. . . . He knew he himself was nothing, and he knew death was nothing" (*FWBT* 393).[35] As he had earlier claimed to Pilar, he had no fear of dying but "only of not doing my duty as I should" (*FWBT* 91).

Repetition might not create conviction, but it can reinforce beliefs. When Hemingway turned to the long section after the bridge has been successfully destroyed, keeping the reader within Jordan's mind was one of his most effective strategies. At that moment of quietude, while Jordan observes *his* band, the action of the novel slows:

> *He saw them all ahead in the edge of the timber, watching him*, and he said *"Arre caballo!* Go on, horse!" and felt his big horse's chest surging with the steepening of the slope and saw the gray neck stretching and the gray ears ahead and he reached and patted the wet gray neck, and he looked back at the bridge and saw the bright flash from the heavy, squat, mud-colored tank there on the road and then he did not hear any whish but only a banging acrid smelling clang like a boiler being ripped apart and he was under the gray horse and the gray horse was

kicking and he was trying to pull out from under the weight. (*FWBT* 460–61; my italics)[36]

Hemingway's alternation of tempo here is masterful. As Jordan sees *his* band as his *family*, and recognizes his own role within their lives, he is about to relinquish whatever claim he has earned to *their* affection. He is already living his death in life.

Hemingway had described this familial bonding occurring a few hours earlier, but because that scene followed Jordan and Maria's making love, readers might have identified the bonds as sexual. Here Jordan meditates, "Anselmo is my oldest friend. I know him better than I know Charles, than I know Chub, than I know Guy, than I know Mike, and I know them well. Agustin . . . is my brother, and I never had a brother. Maria is my true love and my wife. I never had a true love. I never had a wife. She is also my sister, and I never had a sister, and my daughter, and I never will have a daughter" (*FWBT* 381). Both Allen Josephs and John Teunissen link this scene with mythic readings of the novel. Teunissen defends Hemingway's language here, saying that it is not sentimental. Rather, "it emerges from and strikes back down into the most basic and primitive yearnings of mankind, yearnings which primitive man seeks to realize through myth and ritual."[37] For Josephs, Jordan's feelings stem more directly from Maria, whom he describes as "the shining incarnation of Robert Jordan's other half." Jordan himself was, accordingly, Hemingway's first real hero, "someone who sacrifices himself . . . for something larger (the cause) or for someone else (Maria and the band)."[38]

Another of Hemingway's effective strategies was to alternate story lines. Nearly the entire second half of the novel deals with blowing the bridge. The truly energizing part of that action is the sub-story of Andres making his way to find Golz, with the near-comic scene of the Russian general Andre Marty's madness. Long aggrieved at the mishandling of war by obtuse military leaders, Hemingway here attempted to show this travesty of "leadership" so vividly that readers would not question his attitude. The effectiveness of his delaying tactics (by making readers fear for Andres's life) comes as a surprise—in terms of both its length and its inevitability. The infusion of near-comedy takes the reader, momentarily, away from the possible deaths of both Jordan and the Loyalist cause in Spain.

Both Teunissen and Josephs use the term *hierogamy*, a kind of sacred union that unites Maria with Jordan, and accordingly fuses Spain and America; they explain that the novel becomes a spiritual quest even as the accompanying political quest fails. For H. R. Stoneback, *For Whom the Bell Tolls* is shot through with the anxiety that Hemingway's personal life contributed to its writing—he was effectively demolishing his Catholic marriage with Pauline in order to live with Martha and support the Spanish antifascist movement, which was also an anticlerical movement (reflected in Pablo's murder of the Catholic priest, a figure he took into his own hands to define as fascist). In Stoneback's analysis, this book was intended to be a novel "in which he [Hemingway] would try to tell the truth of the Spanish tragedy, not as a Catholic writer, not as a Party writer, but as an artist profoundly engaged by the tragic complexity of Spain and by his own deep participation in that tragedy." Stoneback chooses to call the novel itself "a political novitiate," representing a "naïve . . . state of grace."[39]

Nearly every critic who writes about *For Whom the Bell Tolls* discusses the way the ending echoes the beginning, with Jordan pressed against the Spanish earth itself—and, one might note, remaining alive to kill the young lieutenant (he who had ordered the beheadings of Sordo's men the day before). In this circularity lies even more of the book's meaning. Critics also repeat the fact that seventy hours was all the time that had elapsed in this hegira, echoing Jordan's own recognition of the deep-rooted meaningfulness of his role: "I suppose it is possible to live as full a life in seventy hours as in seventy years" (*FWBT* 166). But, allowing for the complexity of both his role and his understanding of it, Jordan contradicts his complacency, "What nonsense, he thought." From the initial characterization of Robert Jordan as a self-indulgent and privileged man, feigning indifference to his father's suicide so that he can trace his origins back to his grandfather's military role during the Civil War, Hemingway created the Jordan who acknowledged how little he knew as he began his career as bridge-blower in Spain.

Lawrence Broer argues that it is crucial to connect Jordan with the country of Spain. Beginning with the shout "Let the bull out!" when Pablo's forces begin to execute the fascist townsmen, the history of Spain floods the novel.

> Jordan recognizes too that the absurdity of war requires the killing of people labeled "enemy" whom one might otherwise befriend. . . . Anselmo observes about the Fascists at the bridge, "I have watched them all day and they are the same men that we are." . . . The novel's title might have been "A Meditation on Inhumanity." Nothing confounds Jordan's efforts to simplify the Spanish people more than the character of Pablo, who is sometimes cowardly and cynical but at other times brave and sincere. Pablo, Jordan concludes, is "all of them."[40]

Broer employs various kinds of fusions in his reading, but they do not move the novel's meanings as far into new perspectives as does the work of Donald Bouchard, who adds to Michael Reynolds's categorization of "epic" Hemingway's *Green Hills of Africa*.[41] Part of his argument stems from the parallel descriptions of land that he draws from Hemingway's writing in both *Green Hills of Africa* and *For Whom the Bell Tolls*. Bouchard takes segments of the *Green Hills* text to emphasize the author's fascination with "time, the recaptured past and the overcoming of the negative effects of time." One exemplary section of text is the simply cast "Now, looking out the tunnel of trees over the ravine at the sky with the white clouds moving across in the wind, I loved the country" (*GHOA* 72). More dramatically epic is Hemingway's scene with the wounded Jordan watching intently, holding himself into a useful consciousness, scrutinizing the landscape for the forces that will end his life:

> Below he saw the road and the bridge and the long lines of vehicles below it. He was completely integrated now and he took a good long look at everything. Then he looked up at the sky. There were big white clouds in it. He touched the palm of his hand against the pine needles where he lay and he touched the bark of the pine trunk that he lay behind. (*FWBT* 471)[42]

As he had throughout *Green Hills of Africa*, Hemingway here described the visual, physical surroundings that gave his narrative place, locus, a compelling point of view, always rooted in the genuine, the countryside. That he had titled *For Whom the Bell Tolls* "The Undiscovered Country" during the novel's writing suggests that a mythic reading of his important novel is in no way fanciful.

Dead as Fernando and Eladio and Anselmo are, as well as the new men riding with Pablo, Jordan is slated to succeed in his planned delaying action. For all the good their survival will accomplish, Pilar and Maria and Pablo will last through at least another battle. And Hemingway would continue to judge *For Whom the Bell Tolls* a great success, because in it he had brought one single character into a selfless maturity that allowed him to act for the benefit of other human beings.

CHAPTER SEVEN

To the War Once Again

Despite hemingway's disappointment over the Pulitzer judges' denying *For Whom the Bell Tolls* the 1940 Pulitzer Prize for Fiction,[1] he continued on with his personal plans: Martha Gellhorn and he were married November 21, 1940, in Cheyenne, Wyoming, by a justice of the peace, and friends then gave the couple a celebratory dinner of roast moose.[2]

The Gellhorn-Hemingway love affair had endured through four years of war in Spain as well as domestic war in Key West, Cuba, and France. Earlier in 1940, Hemingway wrote to Charlie Scribner, perhaps tongue-in-cheek,

> Charlie, there is no future in anything. I hope you agree. That's why I like it at a war. Every day and every night there is a strong possibility that you will get killed and not have to write. I have to write to be happy, whether I get paid for it or not. But it is a hell of a disease to be born with. (*SL* 503)

After finishing all phases of *For Whom the Bell Tolls*—the writing, the negotiations over language with his editor as well as his publisher, the several stages of proofing, and the publication—Hemingway wrote nothing but journalism for months.

In December, Hemingway bought the Finca Vigia for his primary home; not only did his three sons enjoy Cuba, but he had learned that fishing in the Cuban waters was almost as good an elixir as successful writing. Gellhorn finished her collection of short stories, *The Heart of Another*, and accepted work with *Collier's* to report on the war in China. Her friend Robert Capa shot a photo essay of the newly married couple to appear in the January 6, 1941, issue of *Life*. After some days in New York, the Hemingways flew to Los Angeles

and spent time with Gary Cooper and his wife; in San Francisco they met
Ingrid Bergman, who would play Maria in the *For Whom the Bell Tolls* film.

Gellhorn and Hemingway sailed for Hawaii on the *Matsonia*; then they
flew to Hong Kong, where they waited for clearance to enter China. Martha,
now working for *Collier's*, went alone to visit the Burma Road. When she returned, she could see that Hemingway was upset because of her absence—and
because she was publishing her new book as Martha *Gellhorn*, not as Martha
Hemingway. As James Meredith emphasizes, the trip—from one coast of the
States to the other, then to Hawaii, and then to Hong Kong—was "arduous."
For Gellhorn, whose life was built around travel for her journalism, the trip
was less wearing than it was for Hemingway, who seldom traveled on this
scale. Meredith makes the point that Hemingway had already been involved
in difficult travel to war fronts since 1935—and he would remain involved
until the end of the World War II.[3]

There was a great deal to be learned in China. Few journalists had been
allowed access to the nationalist China war effort (Chiang Kai-shek fighting
the invading Japanese). Hemingway, however, had difficulty accepting the trip
because Martha had initiated it. In her account of going to China (*Travels
with Myself and Another*, in which she referred to Hemingway as "U.C." for
"Unwilling Companion"), she made no bones about his "face of black hate,"
his recalcitrant pettiness. She got him to sign the *PM* contract and the travel
documents, but she admitted that their crossing from Honolulu was rough
and interminable.[4]

In Gellhorn's absence, Hemingway managed to meet both Japanese and
Chinese officials in Hong Kong, as well as British, South American, and
American contacts. He used mealtimes to initiate conversation: he met such
key business and political figures as Carl Blum, a US Rubber Co. executive;
Major Charles Boxer, head of British intelligence in Hong Kong; Morris Cohen, an expert on China and warlords; W. Longhorn Bond, an aviation expert;
Ramon Lavalle, an Argentine diplomat; Rewi Alley, a New Zealand industri-
alist; Emily Hahn, a journalist; and others. He grew friendly with H. H. Kung,
Chiang Kai-shek's brother-in-law, who served as China's minister of finance;
he also met the ministers of education, of communications, and of war. He was
developing the series of essays contracted by *PM* publisher Ralph Ingersoll—
none of which were to be published until his return from the Pacific Rim (the
series began on June 10, 1941, after Ingersoll printed his own interview with
Hemingway in the June 9 *PM*).

As historian Peter Moreira suggests, however, Hemingway was on the trip
to help the United States spy on Chinese government activities. His convivial

Figure 8. Martha Gellhorn and Hemingway with Chinese soldiers on their 1941 tour of the Burma Road and the mainland.

talking was an excellent means of finding information useful to American readers (although when he and Gellhorn toured Pearl Harbor on their stopover in Hawaii, they did not suspect what an advantageous site it would prove to be for the Japanese attack less than a year later). Moreira believes that the experiences Hemingway had in China intrigued him so much that after returning to Cuba, he "spent most of the next four years as a government operative."[5]

Staying first in Hong Kong, Hemingway laid the foundation for later interviews throughout China. He and Gellhorn flew to Nam Yung by Chinese airline, and then went by car to Shaikwan, the headquarters of the 7th War Zone (of eight such divisions), and then he went alone to visit Chengtu, where the Chinese Military Academy was located: Hemingway's interest throughout the trip was both economic and military. Although he later wrote that the Japanese would have an "enormous problem" defeating the Chinese, he knew the Chinese military was weak—at least partly because it had neither planes nor pilots to fly them. It also had little artillery. Always aware of politics, Hemingway knew better than to affront the Chinese, particularly Chiang Kai-shek and his wife, with whom Hemingway and Gellhorn had several personal interviews.

Hemingway and Gellhorn then spent a month at the front, traveling down-river by sampan, on horseback, and on foot. According to Ingersoll, "There were twelve days during a wet spell when he and Mrs. Hemingway never had dry clothes to put on" (*BL* 307). He also spent several weeks on the Burma Road (from Lashio, traveling by car to Mandalay and then by train down to Rangoon, where he spent a week seeing the immense amount of corruption in all the Chinese business dealings).[6]

Returning to Hong Kong in late April, Hemingway flew out alone on May 6 and island hopped. Gellhorn had left earlier by ship, traveling to Jakarta, Java, Singapore, and then the United States.[7] *PM* published the Ingersoll interview and then Hemingway's sequential articles from June 10 through June 18, 1941. These essays included "Russo-Japanese Pact," "Rubber Supplies in Dutch East Indies," "Japan Must Conquer China," and other, more military-oriented articles, such as "China's Air Needs" and "Chinese Build Air Field." Terse and businesslike, Hemingway's pieces read like dispatches, built at times around well-chosen, even metaphoric, images. In "U.S. Aid to China," for example, Hemingway wrote,

> The Generalissimo is a military leader who goes through the motions of being a statesman. This is important. Hitler is a statesman who employs military force. Mussolini is a statesman who is unable to employ military force. The Generalissimo's objectives are always military. (*BL* 327)

Hemingway's articles provided useful foundational information, as in "Russo-Japanese Pact" when he pointed out that Russia had given China "planes, pilots, trucks, some artillery, gasoline, military instructors and staff officers," along with the equivalent of more than 200,000 US dollars, which China repaid by barter in tea and tungsten ore. Hemingway warned that once Russia began removing its technical personnel, the partnership would be finished.

One of the more interesting pieces of writing about the Chinese political and economic situation in early 1941 is a letter Moreira includes as the first appendix to *Hemingway on the China Front*. Hemingway wrote on July 30, 1941, to Secretary of the Treasury Henry Morgenthau, fearing that he had not explained enough about his observations in China and offering to write a more complete report should Morgenthau be interested. This previously unpublished letter, set against the *PM* essays, shows the depth of Hemingway's reservations about China's future. He rehearsed the fact that Chiang Kai-shek had fought hard against the Communists for more than a decade, but then they had kidnapped him and gradually turned him against the Japanese. Hemingway said bluntly that the country suffered from a "lack of true democracy." And, contrary to his reports while he traveled throughout China, in this letter he said, "Life in Chungking is unbelievably difficult and unpleasant."[8]

Patrick Hemingway later said that his father's *PM* articles were among his "most prescient military journalism."[9] Yet for Doug Underwood, who conflates this run of articles with the journalism Hemingway wrote during 1944, Hemingway's war writing remained inferior to Gellhorn's. Underwood objects to Hemingway's tendency to shape his journalism around his own presence, producing a kind of memoir that was far from standard journalistic practice. Underwood also criticizes Hemingway's "self-referential glibness."[10] When Meredith assesses Hemingway's role as war journalist, he places his professional competitiveness within a more personal context. "Hemingway's lifetime of competing urges to participate and to cover the story may have gotten the best of him, inflaming his already pronounced tendency to paranoia and further damaging him psychologically. In brief, Hemingway's intense involvement in the war effort, which spanned almost a decade, harmed him severely, both professionally and personally."[11]

Separate from his journalism, Hemingway's personal behavior, even as early as the mid-1930s, was occasionally offensive, although most of his biographers downplay his sullenness. Several friends, however—Arnold Gingrich, Archibald MacLeish, and Hemingway's young hunting friend Thomas Shevlin—told Denis Brian about his episodes of unexpected anger. Gingrich equated Hemingway at times with "the high school bully . . . very, very bad about losing," whereas Shevlin recalled his throwing an early manuscript version of *To Have and Have Not* out a cabin window (after Shevlin—at Hemingway's request—had made suggestions for improving it) and leaving it in the snow for three days before he retrieved it. MacLeish, who knew Hemingway better than did either Shevlin or Gingrich, assessed his temperament in this way: "These moods of real rage at people would come on him from the earliest time I'd known him."[12]

Given that Prohibition had ended, Hemingway's reliance on alcohol seemed less dramatic, especially since he was often a cordial, pleasant drunk. But the decades of drinking had already taken their toll; he was damaging his body at a quick pace. As he matured, he developed some personality traits that could be identified as alcoholic behavior. He was erratic and increasingly unpredictable; he liked to blame others for whatever happened to him. He also embellished his stories to fantastic degrees. Many people thought this embellishment was

Hemingway's humor, but as Gellhorn finally realized, her husband had no idea how far from reality he lived.

After much investigative work, Susan F. Beegel suggests that Hemingway may already have been seeing symptoms of the hemochromatosis (iron-storage disease) that one of his doctors at the Mayo Clinic suggested as a diagnosis years later. Although this disease is comparatively rare—it is no doubt underdiagnosed because its symptoms can be misread as effects of either cirrhosis of the liver or diabetes mellitus—it could have been genetically predicted for the Hemingway family. Its signs sometimes appear first during a person's thirties or forties. Hemingway's sensitivity to his personal health, particularly his mood swings and his erectile dysfunction, would have made him conscious of any changes.[13]

Biographer Paul Hendrickson points out Hemingway's increasing use of voluble prose, with disconnected thoughts, run-on constructions, and perhaps inappropriate content, as early as a July 10, 1935, letter to friends Sara and Gerald Murphy.[14] At several places in his novels, too, a character comments on a kind of verbosity connected with war trauma, as when Robert Jordan in *For Whom the Bell Tolls* realizes he has talked too much to Agustin: "He felt the need to talk that, with him, was a sign that there had just been much danger. He could always tell how bad it had been by the strength of the desire to talk that came after" (*FWBT* 87). Similarly, in *Across the River and into the Trees*, Cantwell knows he is "talking too much" (*ARIT* 197). In psychological studies, this loquacity is sometimes paired with sleeplessness, which marks many of Hemingway's early fictions about war survivors. His own inability to sleep alone—intensified particularly in the period during which he was separated from Hadley—gave him insight into this condition, as did his awareness that such sleeplessness marred the lives of a number of the wounded men he had known after World War I.

In one of his more candid moments, Hemingway wrote to Scott Fitzgerald about his own sleeplessness. After he had commiserated with all the health problems Fitzgerald described, Hemingway wrote,

> Non-sleeping is a hell of a damned thing too. Have been having a big dose of it now. . . . No matter what time I go to sleep wake and hear the clock strike either one or two then lie wide awake and hear three, four, and five. But since I have stopped giving a good goddamn about anything in the past it doesn't bother much and I just lie there and keep perfectly still and rest through it. . . . If I get exercise and go out in the boat sleep like a log. (*SL* 428)

For Alex Vernon, discussing Cantwell in *Across the River and into the Trees*, night is the time "when Hemingway's other wounded veterans, like Nick Adams and Jake Barnes, are most vulnerable to the memories and fears. For such Hemingway veterans, the vulnerability induced by wartime trauma becomes associated with emasculation (psychological or literal) by a power outside their control."[15]

Hemingway's return from China seemed to confirm his decision to stay in Cuba, to enjoy the Finca Vigia for a time. Gellhorn's biographer points out that she too refused journalistic assignments for more than a year: with visits from Hemingway's sons, and friends, and fishing, and working (Hemingway edited the anthology of war writing, *Men at War*, while Gellhorn worked on her next novel, *Liana*), the Hemingways knew the only period of stability in their lives as a married couple.[16] It was not peaceful, however, despite Gellhorn's efforts, once the United States entered the war in December 1941. Hemingway knew his wife would return to active journalism, and his anger at her planning another absence from their life distorted what remained of their time in Cuba. In July of 1942, Gellhorn went back to traveling for *Collier's*, visiting Haiti, Puerto Rico, and other Caribbean locations to survey people's worries about the possible presence of German submarines. Hemingway, meanwhile, early in 1942 had contacted Naval Intelligence through the American embassy in Havana, offering to help with intelligence work related to "the arrest of German agents as they tried to disembark in Cuba from Spanish vessels the Falangist political clubs in Spain had helped them travel through Spain to board, vessels which as neutrals could make port in Havana and other destinations in Latin America." That activity led to Hemingway's being given what his son Patrick called "paramilitary status as captain of his sport-fishing boat, *Pilar*, to play a small part in a large operation to contain and turn back Operation *Paukenschlag*, the all-out U-boat assault on American coastal shipping lanes."[17]

As Terry Mort points out in his book *The Hemingway Patrols*, the author's sleuthing for German U-boats from the *Pilar* "was a legitimate contribution." The U-boats had been destroying merchant ships just a few miles from Havana. In 1942, on July 13, U84 torpedoed and sank the *Andrew Jackson*; on July 16, U166 blasted and sank the *Gertrude*; and on July 30, the *Robert E. Lee* was torpedoed and sunk. (On May 2, 1942, U507 sank the *Federal*, though reports were somewhat delayed.) Mort notes that even though Hemingway did not find a U-boat, he could have: "It does not matter. The search is what matters, the quest, the adventure, the serious purpose, the voluntary service, the fun, the

satisfaction of command and comradeship, the joy of being at sea." Mort adds
a sober reminder, the fact that if the *Pilar* had found a U-boat, it would most
likely have meant Hemingway's death.[18]

Short-lived as Hemingway's expeditions into the Cuban waters were—with
the German U-boats soon rumored to be working, instead, along the Atlantic
coast—they did irreparable damage to his marriage. Gellhorn saw the activity
as undermining their relationship.[19] As Hemingway briefly headquartered his
operation on Cayo Confites, a tiny offshore island, he became more and more
remote from the Finca Vigia. Watching Hemingway pour his energies into
the patrols made Gellhorn realize how different her plans for her married life
were from those of her husband. Years later she told Carlos Baker that at this
time she thought Hemingway was "literally insane."[20]

According to Baker, all the activity with his male friends led to Hemingway's increased drinking. When he was writing, he rationed his alcohol intake,
but since his return from China he had done little regular literary work: now
he seemed to see excessive drinking as a badge of defiance that would predictably offend Gellhorn, and her reaction would then feed into her usual
aversion to having sex with him. Caroline Moorehead describes this sexual
incompatibility in some detail.[21] Moorehead and Baker also tell the story of
Hemingway's being too drunk to drive his Lincoln Continental one night. Yet
when Gellhorn took the wheel, he slapped her. She then deliberately drove
the car into a tree, got out and walked home, leaving Hemingway to handle
the wreck. On another night, Hemingway drove the car home without taking
Gellhorn with him.[22]

Given that Gellhorn and Hemingway were professional writers, the
fact that she tried to live at the Finca—without traveling for journalism—
surprisingly seemed to leave Hemingway unmoved. Faced with the imbroglio
of his anger and his alcoholism, Gellhorn finally accepted an offer from *Collier's* to become their European correspondent. She sailed from New York for
Lisbon on October 25, 1943, hurt by Hemingway's announced plan to take
a three-month fishing trip on the *Pilar*. While working abroad, Gellhorn
heard rumors about the Nazi persecution of the Jews and she was stunned by
the realization of what such persecution would mean. Gellhorn's situation in
Europe made her relating to Hemingway's existence in Cuba more and more
difficult.[23]

Although their biographers describe the correspondence between them in
late 1943 and early 1944 as "loving," it was March 1944 before Gellhorn returned to Cuba for a time. There she offered to share her *Collier's* assignment

with Hemingway. He did not accept her offer; instead *he* wired *Collier's* and offered to be their war correspondent, an offer that the magazine accepted, cutting Gellhorn completely out of her previous credentials.

When the couple traveled to New York, awaiting passage to England, Gellhorn's rage knew few bounds. As a *Collier's* correspondent, Hemingway was given air passage to London, though he had to wait for an available seat; in contrast, Gellhorn had no transportation. As a result, on May 13, 1944, she sailed on a freighter loaded with dynamite. That passage took over two weeks. Finally the ship landed safely in Liverpool. During that time, Hemingway had been flown to London, housed in a comfortable hotel, and then, on one of his drinking nights, had been seriously injured in a car crash—though he had not been driving. He was treated for head injuries—a laceration that required fifty-seven stitches to close and a concussion—at St. George's Hospital. Gellhorn hurried to London, only to find Hemingway surrounded by friends and champagne bottles. By the end of her visit, she had told Hemingway that she never wanted to see him again.[24]

Hemingway's concussion did nothing to improve the headaches he had complained about since early 1944. Living as he was at the Dorchester Hotel, Hemingway drank and talked, talked and drank, exaggerating all his wartime experiences. He was clearly making his play for the younger Mary Welsh Monks, a staffer for *Time*. In fact, he had already—somewhat jokingly—proposed marriage to her.

Hemingway was seldom alone: Baker phrased his popularity as generally festive, bordering on the hysterical. "Everyone wanted to give him a party." William Walton, a British journalist who had trained with the 82nd Airborne, immediately became a new friend. Hemingway's younger brother Leicester was serving in a documentary film unit, as was Irwin Shaw; they became part of the party crowd at the Dorchester, along with Roald Dahl, Jimmy Charters, and many other younger soldiers and pilots. But as Baker notes, Hemingway's "odd combination of benignity, gaiety, and boorishness did not make him universally popular."[25]

Hemingway's popularity rested on more than his ability to provide drinks for his friends. In a late conversation Denis Brian had with William Walton, Leicester Hemingway, and journalist John Carlisle, the three men agreed that Hemingway "was marvelous company." Walton continued, "He wasn't always telling us about *his* life. We were telling him about our lives, too. He had a marvelous gift for extracting all kinds of tales from me, of my childhood, of my parents, of my loves and adventures, and he remembered them all. If you told it

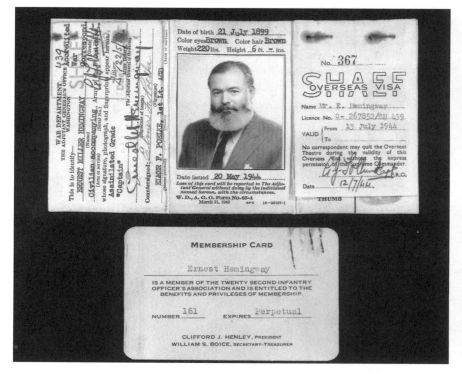

Figure 9. Hemingway's 1944 overseas visa and Officer's Club card.

again and abbreviated, he'd say, 'Ah hah, no, no, no. *That* wasn't her name. *This* was her name.'"[26] Carlisle agreed, saying that Hemingway

> seldom talked about himself. Mostly he talked about how well our guys were doing in the war. He was a great admirer of GI Joe. . . . He seemed to have a great concern for the wounded. He liked the fact that they moved the field hospitals up close. . . . He was the greatest expert I've ever seen in getting people to talk when he wanted them to. In trying to find out how you felt about things, he seemed to show genuine interest in you, the guy who was in front of him. . . . The Hemingway I saw for a month was not quarrelsome.[27]

Leicester's tribute to his older brother was not limited to those days in London. He said, "The good thing about Ernesto was . . . the guy had an absolute emotional honesty. If a thing bothered him he'd say, 'Look, this is what's really itching me.' And he'd say it right out. If everything was going well and smoothly, he'd say 'Goddamn, none of the things that used to bother me'—our bloody mother and the way she'd pick at us, or he'd cite various things that used to annoy him—'are showing up, and I feel wonderful.' And he'd just plain out with it."[28]

Part of Hemingway's attraction for the younger military men was his willingness to teach them. As John Groth wrote about Hemingway in his 1945 *Studio: Europe* book of sketches, "He showed me war. We jeeped past men and machinery moving up. Not comfortably, for jeep seats are not wide, and Hemingway is."[29]

Baker provides a detailed account of Hemingway's six weeks in London, waiting for the Allied troops to be readied for D-Day while he was also recovering from his head injuries. His status as a celebrity brought him more opportunities than were offered to most journalists. Well before D-Day, he received his blue uniform with "Correspondent" on its flash and supplies in case of being shot down; later he visited the headquarters of the 98th Squadron (under the command of G. J. C. Paul, trying to investigate buzz-bomb warfare). Hemingway asked permission to ride along on one of the air strikes. Eventually he flew—sitting beside a pilot—in a twelve-plane formation of Mitchell aircraft. Because everything happened so fast, he asked Wing Commander Alan Lynn afterward if they could return to the target area so he could view more of the site. Lynn refused: the flak was heavy, the risk great. One of the planes had already been lost in the strike.[30]

The next week Hemingway accepted an invitation from Group Captain Wykeham Barnes to visit Mosquito Attack Wing 140, located at Royal Air Force Station Thorney Island, from which site planes made nearly continuous day and night attacks on German lines of communication behind the Normandy bridgehead. Barnes told of a midnight flight with Hemingway seated next to him in the tiny plane, although he admitted that he had been told *not* to take Hemingway over enemy territory. Barnes, chasing a V1 buzz bomb, said he ended up traveling at "better than 400 miles an hour. . . . I was acting against my better judgment." As he acknowledged, "If you did blow one [a V1] up, particularly at night, it was touch and go for yourself, also."[31] Hemingway probably intended to use these exploits in his writing, but he also was fascinated by learning about the war technologies available in 1944—and he was not planning to miss any chance to experience that warfare. As John Carlisle remembered, Hemingway was truly an authority on war: "He knew more about the goddamned army than I did. He was a walking encyclopedia

on how the war was being fought. . . . Hemingway said this modern war was
made for the Germans and the Americans: they understood it better because
they both knew how to handle tanks, and how to coordinate planes with tanks.
He understood tactics."[32]

Hemingway wrote a very long article for *Collier's* about the D-Day landing.
Along with hundreds of other correspondents, Hemingway was taken to the
south coast, where the invasion flotilla was assembled. He was placed on the
attack transport *Dorothea M. Dix*, under the command of W. I. Leahy. Their
orders were to go ashore, and they were told that during the first half hour
minefields would be swept clear so that their way would be unimpeded. When
Hemingway wrote his article (several weeks after the June 6 "landing"), he
emphasized with an ironic title the ineptitude of the plan.

"Voyage to Victory" begins with nearly eight pages about the difficulty of
even *finding* "Fox Green beach." Maps were lost, as were voices between one
thirty-six-foot coffin-shaped steel boat and another, and nobody could figure
out where anyone was supposed to be landing. At least two machine-gun nests
kept hostile fire going. By the time the LCV(P) on which Hemingway rode
was near enough for him to see dead men's bodies massed along the shore and
tanks (with men inside) burning, the assault seemed doomed. This is Hemingway's key description:

> On the beach on the left where there was no sheltering overhang of shingled
> bank, the first, second, third, fourth and fifth waves lay where they had fallen,
> looking like so many heavily laden bundles on the flat pebbly stretch between
> the sea and the first cover. . . . To the right of this, two tanks were burning on
> the crest of the beach, the smoke now gray after the first violent black and yel-
> low billows. Coming in I had spotted two machine gun nests. One was firing
> intermittently from the ruins of the smashed house on the right of the small
> valley. (*BL* 349)

After more confusion about where their small boat was to head, Hemingway included a few scenes of the necessary killing: "I saw a piece of a German
about three feet long with an arm on it sail high up into the air in the foun-
taining of one shellburst." But the author also reported on saving a wounded
man from a duck boat farther out to sea, and then on the fact that their boat
"put our troops and their TNT and their bazookas and their lieutenant ashore,
and that was that" (*BL* 354). Published as his article was on July 22, every
reader would have known that the Allies had taken those beaches: what Hemingway achieved was the immortalization of a few soldiers, identified by name

and rank; a clear description of the sheer difficulty of the attack, often because of human error; and a permanent place for his own role in D-Day.

His August 19, 1944, *Collier's* article, "London Fights the Robots," followed a similar pattern—much attention to characters he thought would be both specific and illustrative, grouped into a few scenes of action, and the whole panorama given with a personal twist. Here Hemingway made use of his flying with Wing Commander Lynn, identifying the plane as a Tempest—though Baker corrects him, saying the planes were Typhoons—which were particularly good at maneuvering to destroy Germany's V1 bombs. ("Robots" in Hemingway's title indicated any "pilotless" missile.) In this article, there was little action, in contrast to much more characterization of the Hemingway figure. In one passage, the author wrote with an attempt at clarification that largely just obscured:

> The day before your pilotless aircraft editor started studying the interception angle, he or I (I guess it is I, although sometimes it doesn't seem the right man in the right place and I have thought some of leaving the whole thing and going back to writing books in stiff covers), went out in one of forty-eight Mitchell bombers—that is, eight boxes of six bombers each—to bomb one of the sites from which the pilotless aircraft are launched. (*BL* 360)

Beyond explaining to readers the separable parts of this fighting equation, Hemingway's article did little except make him the central consciousness for bombing activity over London. No reader, however, believed that a single American journalist filled that role.

Beginning on July 24, 1944, Hemingway had attached himself to the 4th Infantry Division, specifically to Colonel Charles Trueman "Buck" Lanham's 22nd Infantry Regiment, and for the following nine days he embedded himself so as to travel with that division "as it moved steadily southward through La Denisiere, Villebaudon, Hambye, Villedieules-Poeles, and St.-Pois." According to Baker, Hemingway "was clearly in his element. All his diffidence had dropped away. He called it 'a tough fine time with the infantry.'"[33] In Leicester Hemingway's memory, it was an ebullient time for his older brother: "Papa was our reigning hero then, working with Colonel Bruce of the OSS on a voluntary basis. Papa was the guy who could do no wrong. He knew both languages—French and English—perfectly, could make instant funny translations, and understood things we only vaguely guessed at."[34]

Hemingway's late-summer articles tended to repeat the mistake of self-aggrandizement, although since both recount the Allies' taking Paris—in which

Figure 10. Hemingway with Colonel Charles "Buck" Lanham, commanding officer of the 22nd Infantry Regiment, in action during World War II in Germany, 1944.

Hemingway became a part of the ground forces, particularly at Rambouillet—there may be less exaggeration in them. "Battle for Paris" appeared in the September 30, 1944, issue of *Collier's* and "How We Came to Paris" in the October 5, 1944, issue. Using first person, Hemingway as author appeared to be a person in charge: he had a driver and an aide, and he spoke French, whereas no one else in the company did. Including the names and hometowns of the men with whom he traveled, Hemingway made the point that "war correspondents are forbidden to command troops," although he seemed to be the leader of these guerrilla, or irregular, troops. Hemingway reported that the two armored reconnaissance units were withdrawn so that only those irregular troops were left to keep the area safe from German attacks. Referring to the situation as "unorthodox warfare," Hemingway made his activity the point of the first essay.

According to Robert Fuller, Hemingway's article omitted a great deal of factual information.[35] Hemingway did seem to be in charge at moments in and around Rambouillet, and complaints about his acting as more of a participant than a journalist were made to the Third Army's Inspector General. Hemingway was called to Nancy to testify on October 6, 1944.[36] In his statement, Hemingway explained that he was not armed. He allowed men to keep their guns and grenades in his hotel room; he did not use the weapons himself. In a September 15, 1944, letter to his son Patrick, Hemingway told a different story, saying that he had "commanded a French Maqis outfit [while temporarily detached from being a correspondent] that was the best time of all." Later in the letter, Hemingway told Patrick, "You will be very proud of what the Division has done and I have never been happier nor had a more useful life ever" (*SL* 571–72).[37] A man who may have been a more reliable witness than Hemingway himself, Colonel Buck Lanham, explained years later to Denis Brian, "I wrote out a statement in which I said, 'I have never seen him armed.' And I hadn't. However, I was damned sure he usually was. And I'm sure his jeep was loaded with everything in the world it could be loaded with, but he was very careful not to let me see these."[38]

In Hemingway's second essay, "How We Came to Paris," the memorable takeaway was Hemingway's great love for Paris, beginning decades earlier, during the 1920s. The article was, in fact, structured to create overwhelming nostalgia. It opened, "Never can I describe to you the emotions I felt on the arrival of the armored column of General Leclerc southeast of Paris. Having just returned from a patrol which scared the pants off of me and having been kissed by all the worst elements in a town which imagined it had been liberated through our fortuitous entry, I was informed that the general himself was just down the road and anxious to see us" (*BL* 374). In fact, the regular army and the officers in command wanted nothing to do with either war correspondents or irregular troops.

Hemingway's evocation of a grateful Paris dominated the spirit of the article. The dispatch closed as the author looked down from a height and there, "gray and always beautiful, was spread the city I love best in all the world" (*BL* 383).

Hemingway seemed to be expressing his gratitude to Lanham for supporting him, regardless of what rules he might have occasionally broken, in his November 4 *Collier's* article, "The G. I. and the General." Here, again, the authorial consciousness remained at the center but emphasized throughout was the exhaustion of all the Allied forces. Set during the summer battles, the account ascribed concern to the "general," which Lanham, a colonel, never was: "His face that was still handsome when he was rested was gray and drawn and endlessly tired. Only his eyes were alive and his kind, warm voice said, 'I was worried about you'" (*BL* 390). The reader remembers Kurt Vonnegut's coda to his praise for Hemingway as war journalist. Vonnegut there had said, "I will guess, too, that the permission for males to bond with one another, to love themselves and one another, which was given to [military expeditions] was the principal ingredient of that happiness . . . the freedom of one man to somehow express love for another one in the neighborhood of danger or bloodshed."[39]

Hemingway's friendship with Buck Lanham was an apt illustration of Terry Mort's suggestion that, as an adult, Hemingway often tried to shape "a place with innocent friendships and camaraderie of the kind" that he had known as a younger man. Just as he had on the *Pilar*, he here tried "to put together kindred spirits who would not only take orders from Hemingway the leader but also join wholeheartedly and unreservedly in Hemingway's enthusiasm of the moment, whether fishing, eating, or poking around in the mangroves."[40]

Hemingway's friendship with Lanham created a separate chapter of male bonding begun during the bloodiest battles of the closing days of war, when Lanham's troops were ordered to take the remaining German forces out of Hürtgen Forest on the Siegfried Line. James Meredith calls this, from the start, "perilous." The German forces were entrenched within "horribly fortified positions. Despite a greatly diminished military strength, the German army proved itself a deadly defensive force."[41] For nearly two weeks, the forces of both sides killed anyone who opposed them. United States casualties were numbered at 2,678 men. (Beegel points out that the regiment lost 87 percent of its strength.) One of the most costly attacks of the war, the battle that ran from November 15 to December 4, 1944, took a toll of nearly 24,000 Allied men—considering the total dead, wounded, taken prisoner, or missing in action. Biographer Jeffrey Meyers quotes statistics from three days in mid-November, that the regiment "had incurred more than 300 battle casualties, including all three battalion commanders, several key staff officers, about half the company commanders, and many key company officers and noncommissioned officers." After five days of this fighting, the forces had moved fewer than two miles in the forest.[42] Hemingway wrote to Patrick on November 19, 1944, "We are in the middle of a terrific damned battle . . . that I hope will finish off the Kraut Army and end the war" (*SL* 576).

Meredith argues that what made this battle so different for Hemingway was not the sheer carnage the fighting involved but rather the fact that for the writer, embedded within Lanham's forces, to become a part of the battle, he had had, at times, to wound and kill German soldiers. In his description of what he refers to as "astronomical" losses, Meredith says directly that

"Hemingway became so involved in the fighting in the densely packed ever-green forest that he felt compelled to take up arms and fight his way out of the danger. There is no question that Hemingway participated in the killing."[43]

The issue, as Meredith sees it, was that Hemingway was not a military man in any sense of the word. He had manned the Red Cross cart in World War I and he had been an observant journalist during the Spanish Civil War, but at no time in Hemingway's life had he ever been *trained*: he knew nothing about military discipline, or about surviving, or about injuring or killing other people. For all the aplomb he mustered as he wrote the introduction to the *Men at War* anthology, Hemingway knew less about warfare than the average Allied soldier.

As a result of Meredith's studies, he can envision the kind of devastation Hemingway was enduring as he both observed, and then participated in, the Hürtgen Forest battles. Meredith concludes that

being so close to the action, engaging in life or death circumstances, and ex-periencing the death and suffering of soldiers, proved psychologically costly for Hemingway. . . . Hemingway was traumatized not just by all the death and destruction he witnessed, but also by the fact that he became directly involved in the killing. . . . Hemingway, the forty-six-year-old world-famous novelist, who had no business being there, *was* there among this vast amount of killing and suffering. . . . In many ways, the war haunted Hemingway throughout the rest of his life.[44]

CHAPTER EIGHT

After the War

Across the River and
Into the Trees

WRITING ABOUT WAR was still Ernest Hemingway's métier, no matter how frightening or disillusioning he found his attempts at fighting in such conflicts. As his later fulsome letters to Buck Lanham show[1]—particularly those written after he had returned to Cuba to get the Finca Vigía ready for Mary's first visit—he used the written word to erase some of his worst, most vivid memories: getting rid of the vestiges of the days and nights in the Hürtgen Forest became one of his primary aims.

But before he could leave Europe, Hemingway was faced with writing about the Hürtgen Forest battle. Accordingly, he wrote "War in the Siegfried Line," which appeared in the November 18, 1944, issue of *Collier's*. This piece broke the pattern Hemingway had established for his earlier *Collier's* stories—perhaps because he was trying to maintain some personal distance from what had occurred, and was occurring, in those impenetrable forest battles. First of all, Hemingway chose to use a narrator other than himself. He focused instead on "the words of Captain Howard Blazzard of Arizona," and then once those words began coming, the author-character interposed his own views, often to clarify the action being described. The result of this postmodern alternation of voices was to downplay the slaughter: the reader became involved in sorting through several sets of remarks and therefore diverted his or her attention away from the accounts of battle. (The article was written near the start of the action and published November 18; the battle, however, raged past December 4.)

What Captain Blazzard conveyed was the shock of immense conflict, but he did so with little detail. He also used blunt language: "They were all just sort of dead," he said at one point. When he got into his narration, moving from one German bunker to the next, seeing the effects of the Wump guns and grenades on the well-fortified and well-camouflaged doors and walls, his terse expression became more effective. After the first bunker was shelled, Captain Blazzard noted, "Every one of them [the Germans in the bunker] was wounded in five or six different places, from pieces of concrete and steel . . . one fellow with both his legs cut off" (*BL* 398). After the second bunker was taken, he noted, "There were arms and legs and heads scattered all over that goddamn place" (*BL* 399).

Blazzard's emphasis was on the destruction of the German forces. A more evenhanded presentation would have taken into consideration the damage on both sides of the conflict, with particular attention to the deaths of the US infantrymen who struggled to move through the forest with few shields between their bodies and gunfire. Some of this detail accrued as the character Hemingway interposed his comments with Blazzard's, as when he added a description of the forest: "The woods were close-planted fir trees, and the shell-bursts tore and smashed them, and the splinters from the tree bursts were like javelins in the half-light of the forest." It was also the Hemingway voice that pointed out, when Blazzard seemed to be following the party line of the command, "There is a great difference in combat between the way it is supposed to be and the way it is" (*BL* 396, 394).

Hemingway wrote several pages of explanation in this article before beginning the Blazzard character's narration. There he said that the seasonal rains had come so no planes could support the ground military action. "The *infantry* cracked the Siegfried Line," he stated positively (*BL* 392; Hemingway's italics). This Hemingway narrator also made clear that because the Germans had disguised their machine-gun nests so well, at times the attack was both in front of the infantry and behind it; this situation added to the ever-increasing death toll. Similarly, the closing Hemingway gave the article suggested Blazzard's awkward delivery, as he commented that "it really would have been better for Germany not to have started this war in the first place" (*BL* 400). It was as if Hemingway's *Collier's* article assumed that readers already knew—through photographs and body count—how destructive this conflict was, for both sides. Were a reader *not* to understand the massive casualties, Hemingway's essay would have been of less value.

Robert Stephens praises Hemingway's war journalism because it both showed "the ambivalences and the ambiguities of Hemingway's thinking" and "emphasized his paradoxical notion that wars are fought by the best of people for the worst of reasons. It suggested his moral intuition, often only informally understood by himself, that good can come out of evil while acting as the agent of evil." His writing revealed the inherent conflict in Ernest Hemingway as journalist "of emotionally doing best what he was mentally reluctant to do at all." Stephens, like Michael Reynolds and other biographers, believes with Hemingway that "war is the real experience of the century—the experience that makes a man feel incomplete if he misses it, and an experience to be known directly, sensuously and emotionally rather than abstractly."[2]

Hemingway's journalism here is markedly different from his writing in the later stages of the Spanish Civil War, for example, when he wrote short fiction—and published most of it—as if to capture essential scenes, crucial explanations for the behaviors of people at war. Of the half dozen stories written about the civil war, the titles Hemingway chose show his political stance. "The Denunciation," for example, places a known fascist in his favorite bar, Chicote's, even though people there know his threatening politics (the bar has become a Loyalist center). When the fascist is arrested and taken to be executed as a traitor, the author figure asks that *he* be named the denouncer, not the waiter. The narrator tries to let the fascist keep his sense of his own earlier belonging to the community of the Madrid bar. There are similar political narratives within the other stories.

Most of Hemingway's Spanish Civil War short stories were published either during the war or soon after. They gave him a running start on the moments of political ambiguity that would mark *For Whom the Bell Tolls*, the novel about the men of the Lincoln Brigade as they joined with international forces and with the Spanish people to fight the fascists.

One of Hemingway's short stories that dates from this period but was never published is an exception to the body of his short fiction about the Spanish Civil War. In "Landscape with Figures," he created an almost unidentified set of characters, intent on viewing the scenes from a "war" playing out below them. Starkly outlined, the brutality of killing takes on a distant aura so that the girl in the cast of characters must ask for explanation from the more experienced man who accompanies her:

"Were those two men killed who went out with the stretcher?" "Yes," I said. "Positively." "They moved so *slowly*," the girl said pitifully. "Sometimes it's very hard to make the legs move," I said. "It's like walking in deep sand or in a dream." (*CSS* 595)

Hemingway placed the scene that became the mandala for the realization of death in war early in the story, but first the fiction opens with the sounds of war: "The first one hit us. It came with a noise like a bursted steam pipe combined with a ripping of canvas and with the burst and the roar and rattle of broken plaster." The scene is immediate destruction. The girl cries; then she inquires, "Are those men all dead?" The experienced observer reassures her, "No. Some are too badly wounded to move. They will bring them in in the dark." The central death scene is almost hidden within the panorama:

> We stood and watched. Through the glasses you could see two men get out of an angle of the trench and start up a slant of the hill carrying a stretcher. They seemed to move slowly and ploddingly. As you watched the man in front sank onto his knees and then sat down. The man behind had dropped to the ground. He crawled forward. Then with his arm under the first man's shoulder he started to crawl, dragging him forward toward the trench. Then he stopped moving and you saw that he was lying flat on his face. They both lay there not moving now. (*CSS* 594)

In this set piece of death, the men's bodies lying together inert, Hemingway foreshadowed what he was going to experience both at the end of the Spanish Civil War and later, in that chartless territory between Germany and Belgium—the Siegfried Line battles.

For expected writing from Hemingway about war and its slaughter, such a quiet image is both understated and provokingly distant. Much of the dialogue in the story "Landscape with Figures" emphasizes the observing character's infallible knowledge—when death occurs—and so the story seems farther reaching, as well as longer, than the events it chronicles. Hemingway wrote this story in 1938. But by the time of his participation in the Hürtgen Forest battles of November 1944, he was not sure his earlier representations of war were credible. He was not sure his writing truly described modern warfare. Years after World War II had ended, he was still writing to Charlie Scribner about those battles, reminding him that "the regimental losses were greater than any regiment at Gettysburg and the regiment took every objective" (*SL* 703).

Hemingway was clearly meditating about the battles that were bringing World War II to a close, but he had written little journalism about that warfare. In Stanley Cooperman's survey of Hemingway's postwar writing, he states that *For Whom the Bell Tolls* is, obviously, not about that war. Cooperman points out that once that novel was complete,

> Hemingway could never write about World War II. It was just too complex. How could he shape all this into art? World War II was a gigantic organization in which the politician became more important than the soldier. . . . As for the

post–World War II era of "Cold War" and continuing crisis—there was simply nothing in it for Hemingway to *use*: the swamp of ideological-political-military complexities offered no solid ground on which Hemingway could stand either as a man or as a writer.[3]

For Susan Beegel, Hemingway's new avoidance of war narratives is signaled by his turn to focusing on the majesty of the sea, the marlin and sharks, the non-manmade skirmishes that could be read metaphorically as well as literally. Beegel draws from Hemingway's letters to Mary to show "the profound impression on a man badly shaken by the military slaughter on land in Europe. In 1945 Hemingway began experimenting with writing about sharks, killing, and sin in *Islands in the Stream* that would evolve into the enduring shark passages of *The Old Man and the Sea*." This critic points out that "Huertgenwald left Hemingway with indelible memories of carnage and a legacy of anger, loss, and terror." She also traces the little-published fact that during catastrophic losses at sea, whether from German U-boat or carrier attacks, what survivors there were usually died from shark attacks.[4]

It was as if Hemingway was determined to survive the days of battle, even though his consciousness had been sure he would not live through the Hürt-gen Forest fighting. As he later told George Plimpton, when that interviewer asked him about his fondness for the paintings of Hieronymus Bosch, "I have the nightmares and know about the ones other people have."[5] Beegel points out, using evidence from Hemingway's postwar letters, that the process of forgetting—the need for which manifested itself through a chronic insomnia that sleeping pills could not touch—involved a great deal of alcohol. Beegel describes Hemingway's "night drinking" ("when you wake up in the night and things are unbearable and you take a drink to make them bearable") as well as his "wake-up drinking" in the mornings (*SL* 581, 586). Closely observed by both friends and enemies, Hemingway's thirst for alcohol had not diminished since the early 1930s.[6]

Some of the neediness that shows in Hemingway's letters and poems to Mary came at least in part from his European war experiences, and in those letters he often included memories that seem dissociated from the letters' text. He repeated that pattern in his frequent letters to Lanham, as if he were still exploring the camaraderie between them—a camaraderie they continued to share, by virtue of their both being survivors of those days of intense and bloody battle.

Part of Hemingway's difficulty with putting the 1944 battles behind him was his continuing literary reputation. He was known throughout the world for his war novels—*A Farewell to Arms* and *For Whom the Bell Tolls*—as well as for the films made from each of them. The translations into more than thirty languages meant that his reputation as a writer of war was truly worldwide. Now, having for the first time experienced the horrors of battle for himself, he realized that the words he had written about "sacrifice" were likely false. He saw that the silence that he had chosen to represent wounded and dying consciousness, as in the vignettes of *In Our Time*, was more representative than the language he had occasionally ventured to put into fictional soldiers' mouths. The truth was that Hemingway knew very little about sacrifice: he had been only an observing narrator, placed outside the parameters of death by wearing his "Correspondent" badge.

As those days in the Hürtgen Forest had taught him, there was no language for a person's ultimate sacrifice.

Hemingway realized as well that the pose he had taken in order to write his introduction to the *Men at War* anthology was also false. He was not the "scholar of war" that he had pretended to be. And just as he could not write—in his term, "truly"—about war in his fiction, because that task would lie beyond any powers of language, he could not write truly about it for his *Collier's* dispatches: he chose in those essays to create fictional characters, he dodged the facts of conflict, and he wrote about situations oblique to the real.

His realizations were less frightening while he was still in Europe. He contracted a serious case of pneumonia in December 1944, and though he was still traveling with the infantry, Lanham's physician put him to bed and dosed him with sulfa pills. He spent much of early 1945 in London, often with Mary, before leaving for the United States on March 6. Again, as his social life there showed, Hemingway the *writer* was more visibly Hemingway the *celebrity*. And what lived after the Hürtgen Forest battles, and the last of Hemingway's articles for *Collier's*, was not so much his writing as the frequently circulated "Hemingway stories." There were many such stories. Some were true. But more and more often those stories were exaggerated, or they were conflated with other stories of "war legend" and had little to do with Hemingway.

Those that did have to do with him were based, often, on what biographer Michael Reynolds describes as Hemingway's ability to compartmentalize: "His ability to shut down the normal response of fear made him invaluable to officers like Buck Lanham and a source of worry to officers more bound to the official book of war."[7] Reynolds recounts the story of the German shelling of Lanham's officers at mess, while the infantry was stalled at Buchet, waiting for supplies. As the sounds of planes penetrated the large room, all the men dove for the outside walls, but Hemingway remained in place—eating—in the then-empty room. Reynolds also tells about a time at the end of the Hürtgen Forest battles when Hemingway, Bill Walton, and Hemingway's driver, Archie Pelkey, were leaving an area and Hemingway commanded Pelkey to stop the Jeep. He had heard the faint hum of still-invisible aircraft. He told the men to jump into the ditch—as he did himself—and saved all their lives from the machine-gun stitching that was about to come.[8]

Unfortunately, Hemingway was distraught enough that he sometimes had difficulty leaving behind battlegrounds and behavior suitable to them. Carlos Baker recounts the story of Hemingway's threats of shooting up his London hotel room as he tried to fire at a photograph of Mary's husband, Noel Monks, whom she was trying to divorce. Using one of the two machine pistols Buck Lanham had given him, Hemingway agreed to move into the bathroom for his shooting spree. He then shot the man's photo to pieces, but unfortunately he also shattered the toilet bowl, so the guests spent the rest of the evening mopping up water while Hemingway tried to pacify the hotel management.[9] Baker reports that at that time Mary thought seriously of ending her relationship with Hemingway, who had immediately lapsed into bad French as if giving an official speech. She told him that Lanham had called his behavior "an adolescent trick." But Hemingway seemed less than concerned about either the episode or its fallout.[10] Whether Hemingway saw himself as an American folk hero or as an infantryman who had survived unimaginable battles, he did not try to stifle or change any of the stories that were being told about him.

It is probable that journalist Doug Underwood had, of necessity, to keep in mind these legendary stories as well as Hemingway's journalism as he assessed the work coming from Hemingway's involvement in both the Spanish Civil War and World War II. Underwood sees in these dispatches and stories a consistent urge to take risks, sometimes foolhardy ones. Many of Hemingway's articles were drawn from behavior that was far from prudent—and was no doubt unnecessary from a correspondent's point of view. "Hemingway's life on the edge of risk, in many ways, has come to define him," Underwood notes. His acknowledged and visible behavior with the irregular forces at Rambouillet is "one good example of his choice to be involved in tremendous risk." Underwood associates this quality, increasingly evident as Hemingway aged, with two other traits, one he defines as "rootlessness," the author's seeming "discomfort with life lived on ordinary terms." Perhaps even more prevalent to an observer was Hemingway's tendency toward "grandiosity," his persistent urge—both in telling his stories and in living them—to create experiences "on a mythic scale."[11]

Psychiatrist Alice Miller also frequently uses the term *grandiosity*. The larger-than-life person "must excel brilliantly in everything," she notes. The fear of not being able to sustain such performance might result in severe depression. Miller points out that "one is free from depression when self-esteem is based on the authenticity of one's own feelings and not on the possession of certain qualities." In Miller's experience, people with this type of torturing self-interest might have been children of demanding parents: "The childhood trauma is repeated: he is always the child whom his mother admires. . . . In the parents' feelings, dangerously close to pride in their child, shame is concealed—lest he should fail to fulfill their expectations." Miller also traces the ways these feelings of grandiosity can be associated with manic-depressive illness.[12]

One element of sympathy that cloaked and probably softened Hemingway during his late-war days in London was the fact that his oldest son, Jack (Bumby), was a prisoner of war in Germany, having been captured months after parachuting into France at Le Bosquet d'Orb, north of Montpellier. Hemingway did not ask for any special treatment regarding news of his son's situation. Jack had joined the Office of Strategic Services in July 1944 and was training partisans to infiltrate enemy positions. In late October, Jack was shot in the right arm and shoulder by rounds from a high-velocity carbine. Because the Austrian officer in charge had known Ernest, Hadley, and their toddler son in 1925 at Schruns, he sent the wounded Jack Hemingway to a hospital. When he recovered, he was placed in a POW camp, then liberated, and then recaptured and taken to Stalag Luft III in Nuremberg until the war ended.[13]

During Hemingway's postwar malaise in London, he realized that his place was back in Cuba—making a home for his three sons and for Mary, who would become the fourth Mrs. Hemingway, and hopefully his anchor in a world that he increasingly felt was attacking him. Rose Marie Burwell said it bluntly, "Hemingway's decision to wed Mary Welsh in 1945, although it had been reached very quickly and in a frame of mind close to *panic*, was quite calculated. The determination to marry her consciously incorporated his desire to have a wife who would remain with him, would take over the domestic and business arrangements of his life, would not be a competitor (as he now fancied Martha had been), and would produce another family for him." Perhaps having his son Jack safe led to his realization that protecting his family was an essential survival strategy for himself. For whatever reason, the life Hemingway chose to lead after the war was in part a result of his ever-increasing celebrity. Reynolds noted that "between 1941 and 1961 *Life* published sixteen feature stories on Hemingway."[14]

It is not surprising that Hemingway's return to Cuba was focused on things other than starting a new novel. He put much less emphasis on writing the great novel at this point than he had during the late thirties. Then, Hemingway seemed to feel revitalized by his physical and emotional involvement in the Spanish Civil War. In 1945, as he wrote to Lanham just after leaving Europe for the United States,

> It is a hell of a thing going away from the 22nd [Infantry Regiment] though. It probably sounds wet but I was, and am, absolutely homesick for the regiment and I miss you very badly Buck. I don't give a damn about writing. Will have to get over that. I guess I will. Have gotten over everything else.
>
> Certainly have the Black Ass today. Miss Mary so much it makes me sick. Always before we had our Double Deuce [22nd Regiment] problems and some sort of fight going on when I was away from her and I had your companionship. (*SL* 579)

It was not beyond Hemingway's expectations that replacing love with the business of war would keep him productive.[15] What may have given Lanham pause was the fact of Hemingway's sense of proprietorship about the 22nd Infantry.

As Hemingway had written to associates about the Hürtgen Forest battles, "That summer from Normandy into Germany was the happiest I ever had in spite of it being war" (*SL* 608). To Lanham, however, he admitted that when he talked with a Marine about "the Hurtgen fight . . . I could see him starting to not believe me. So I just shut up. . . . Now I just feel homesick, lonely and useless. But will pull out of it. *Because have to*" (*SL* 579; Hemingway's italics).

Hemingway closed that April 2, 1945, letter to Lanham, "I get cheered up writing to you." Less than two weeks later, he began another letter to his friend, "Certainly miss the hell out of you." In talking here about his writing about war, Hemingway lamented, "What a trade Buck. What a terrible trade" (*SL* 586, 588). In another few days, he repeated the same sentiment, adding, "So far I can't write worth a damn but I never could after any war so am not worrying." He closed with, "Honestly, Buck, I think you had a regiment before Hurtgen, that could outfight any regt. in the world" (*SL* 590). Writing to Perkins on July 23, 1945, Hemingway asked that Scribner's send copies of many of his books to Lanham, "my pal and partner and former Colonel of the 22nd Infantry Regiment." He told Perkins,

> Last year was a hard year. What we learned from it may not show for a long time. Very little of it was bought cheaply and really, Max, it probably isn't exactly what the doctor would order for a good writer 45 [46] years old, with what when it is working right, is a good, delicate instrument. But I learned more while Buck and I were together than I had learned altogether up until then so I hope we will get some decent writing from it sometime. (*SL* 594)

Years later, Lanham told Baker that he felt an equally deep rapport with the writer. He said candidly about the Hürtgen Forest battle, "After that night and the next terrible eighteen days Ernest Hemingway and I were locked into a species of brotherhood that both of us knew would last as long as we lasted. It did."[16]

The men's friendship was renewed whenever Lanham and his wife visited with Hemingway, usually in Cuba. Those visits, however, diminished in frequency with the writer's declining health.

It is hard to reconstruct the fictions Hemingway was working on after his return from World War II. Much of the manuscript material was not published until after his death, and most of the pages written between 1945 and 1949 are hard to decipher and/or categorize. Burwell remains the authority on these "posthumous" writings. In her description,

> The novel that we know as *Islands in the Stream* (1970) had its genesis in a sprawling ur-text which Hemingway began in the fall of 1945 to memorialize the experience he had shared with Buck Lanham during his ten months of covering the European war. But from its inception the narrative was also about the creative problems of a protean artist who is sometimes a writer named Roger Davis or David Bourne, and sometimes a painter named Thomas Hudson or Nick Sheldon. From this ur-text came not only the posthumous *Islands* and *The Garden of Eden* (1986), but also the two novels published during Hemingway's life, *Across the River and into the Trees* (1950) and *The Old Man and the Sea* (1952).

Burwell notes as well that Hemingway referred to the works as "The Land, Sea, and Air Book," "The Sea Book," and "the Big Book," using the titles "interchangeably."[17]

For most of the literary world, however, it looked as if Hemingway's first fiction after the war was *Across the River and into the Trees*, the novel about an aging military man living on a series of reminiscences while he courts a beautiful Italian teenager in Venice. Published in 1950, that "war" novel provoked a great deal of rancor. It was frequently criticized, for example by such reviewers as Joseph Warren Beach (who had admired *For Whom the Bell Tolls* but found this novel "ribald" instead of romantic).[18] Hemingway, furious about the bad reviews, said ironically to interviewer Harvey Breit in the *New York Times Book Review* that "*all that happens* [in the novel] is the defense of the lower Piave, the break-through in Normandy, the taking of Paris and the destruction of the 22nd Infantry Regiment in Hurtgen Forest." Hemingway continued instructively, "In the last one [*For Whom the Bell Tolls*], I had the straight narrative; Sordo on the hill for keeps; Jordan killing the cavalryman; the village; a full-scale attack presented as they go; and the unfortunate accident of the bridge." He then asked Breit, somewhat defensively, "Should I repeat myself? I don't think so."[19]

Hemingway described *Across the River and into the Trees* as a book "written for all people who had ever fought or would be capable of fighting or interested in it. It was written, as well, for people who had ever been in love or were capable of that happiness." He then referenced his *Life* magazine letter of June 24, 1940, in which he made this honest claim:

> Having fought Fascism in every way that I knew how in the places where you could really fight it, I have no remorse neither literary nor political. . . . [He mentions being at] Guadalajara, Jarema, Madrid, Teruel, first and second battles of the Ebro. . . . Young men wrote of the first war to show truly the idiocies and murderous stupidity for the way it was conducted by the Allies and Italy. Other young men wrote books that showed the same thing about the German conduct of the war. All agreed on war's violence and undesirability.[20]

As if explaining that *Across the River and into the Trees* was, necessarily, about war, and war was predictably a hated subject, Hemingway took the position of intentionally choosing controversy.

It was, too, as if Hemingway was now the *commander* of *writing about war*: in *The Sun Also Rises*, he had attempted a novel that, largely, *concealed* the war. In *A Farewell to Arms*, the war gives way to a love story. In *For Whom the Bell Tolls*, the love story becomes subordinate to the almost epic story of war.[21] But in *Across the River and into the Trees*, the war becomes the *protagonist*. It is not that Richard Cantwell becomes a heroic figure, as readers might have argued in the case of Robert Jordan; but in Cantwell's role as the repository of memories of war, he takes on some elusive characteristics of the memory of brutal and wasteful conflicts.

Another paradigm that differentiates Hemingway's war novels from one another is their narrative method. *The Sun Also Rises*, while less fragmentary in structure than his *In Our Time* vignettes and stories, is still oblique to World War I. It is, obviously, set in peacetime. Both *A Farewell to Arms* and *For Whom the Bell Tolls* are told aggressively, so that there is little confusion about characters or events. *Across the River and into the Trees*, in contrast, has a different way of narrating, the character's memory free from sequence or chronology. If Cantwell's days of duck hunting are the still point of his turning world, if his storytelling is a means of courting the young Renata, then Hemingway's highly imaged discourse forces the reader who wants to comprehend to fuse *all* memories, to make the stream of last consciousness meaningful, regardless of gaps. To read Hemingway's 1950 novel, his contemporary readers were forced into a modernist posture that meant they must learn to read accurately by experiencing Cantwell's fictional life.

The critical world would have been content had Hemingway simply repeated himself; they had liked *For Whom the Bell Tolls*, from its resounding and poetic title to its emphasis on Jordan's manly sacrifice. Within the literary world, the decade of brutal war had changed criticism and reviewing very little. People noted that Alfred Kazin complained about Hemingway's novel, even though Robert Cantwell praised it. Others remembered that John O'Hara's review on the front page of the *New York Times Book Review* called Hemingway another Shakespeare.

Criticism in retrospect has been more evenhanded, although *Across the River and into the Trees* is not considered one of Hemingway's more effective novels. In Jackson Benson's discussion of this novel as a good study of war, he supplies the context for the difficulty of writing about the varied elements of war, explaining that "the worst thing about war, even more terrible than the physical suffering, because it is more subtle and insidious, is that the individual (and along with the individual, morality and responsibility) is lost and that the loss serves little purpose except to feed irrationality. All who have been in the army of any country know that the first abiding principle of service is the loss of individual volition, a literal beating down of identity."[22]

Jeffrey Meyers points out that Cantwell was drawn in part from Hemingway's British friend Eric "Chink" Dorman-Smith, whom he knew during his early hospitalization in Milan; Dorman-Smith was godfather to Bumby. Even though Hemingway and he had lost touch, Hemingway had followed his demotion from the rank of lieutenant general—just before Bernard Montgomery assumed the Allied command—and his retirement in 1944.[23] In the novel, similarly, Cantwell loses his rank—and feels victimized by his colleagues—but he also loses his sense of being a complete human self after his first major wounding. Understated in his retrospection, Cantwell remembers, "Finally he did get hit properly and for good. No one of his other wounds had ever done to him what that first big one did. I suppose it is just the loss of the immortality, he thought. Well, in a way, that is quite a lot to lose" (*ARIT* 33).

In Michael Seefeldt's reading, the character of Cantwell is interestingly complex; he is "a rich, an individual character, even an everyman." Cantwell also speaks consistently, says Seefeldt, who observes that "dialogue among bilingual speakers not fully familiar with each other's tongues is bound to be deliberate and simple, appreciating, even cherishing, basic words."[24]

One of the responses to the book that pleased Hemingway the most was Lanham's reassurance that he was not offended by any of the portraits of military men in the novel. Lanham told Hemingway he did not take the author's criticism personally: "If anybody wants to fire me because of my friends, they can fire me. And that goes double where you are concerned for you have been my number-one friend since 1944. I find that the ability to laugh and wisecrack is as important here as it was in Hurtgen Forest."[25]

Gerry Brenner sees Hemingway attempting in the novel to create "a rendition of Dante's *Divine Comedy*. Like the poem, the novel incorporates real people and events, arcane allusions, private diatribes, encyclopedism, a double point of view, and much ado about hell and the salvation of a sinful warrior-pilgrim, Cantwell." Hemingway also used another feature of the great poem—"its merging of mimetic fiction, history, and dream fantasy."[26] By giving Hemingway's fascination with living figures this rationale, Brenner may be thinking to keep criticism away from the book and its author: the casting of a pock-faced character who resembled Sinclair Lewis, a figure often underfoot in the hotel dining room, seemed petty to many. Why would the author draw this cartoonlike character to mock one of the earliest Americans to win the Nobel Prize? (Lewis had received the prize in 1930).

The clear outsider status of the pseudo-Lewis character is set against the five-man "Order of Brusadelli," to which both Cantwell and the Gran Maestro, Giuseppe Cipriani, head waiter at the Gritti, legitimately belong—for bravery during wars. Much of Cantwell's activity outside his scenes with Renata has to do with helping his aide and driver, Jackson, understand Venetian history related to the world wars. (Jackson—named to suggest General Stonewall Jackson, who provided the title wording—seems less than interested in what Cantwell is trying to impart: Seefeldt, for example, refers to the young soldier's "patterned, uninterested conformity.")[27]

The camaraderie between Cantwell and the Gran Maestro runs throughout the book and bonds both the men to the core of Cantwell's memories. It shows the strength of the continuing male experience.

> He and the Colonel both remembered the men who decided that they did not wish to die; not thinking that he who dies on Thursday does not have to die on Friday, and how one soldier would wrap another's putteed leg in a sandbag so there would be no powder burns, and loose off at his friend from as far a distance as he figured he could hit the calf. (*ARIT* 59)

In another passage, Cantwell brings the physical bodies of his friends into his journey to the Piave during World War I, where he was himself wounded: "The iron's in the earth along with Gino's leg, both of Rudolfo's legs, and my right kneecap" (*ARIT* 19).

Significant as the men's friendships remain, the reader remembers them less than the fictionalized Renata—the reborn heart of the aging Cantwell, the muse for whom his story is evoked, his Beatrice, his Pygmalion, his well-born countess. There is little question that in drawing the young Italian woman, Hemingway was aiming to create "a goddess risen from the sea to become the presiding spirit of the ancient city of Venice," in Carlos Baker's words. "What he wanted her to represent was the spirit of youth, reborn in the mind of his fifty-year-old Colonel. She could stand for the freshness, innocence, courage, and idealism that both Ernest and Colonel Cantwell had enjoyed in the days before war had aged and embittered them."[28]

For Robert Gajdusek, the image-laden novel revolves around the focus of birds—from the early scenes of duck hunting to the late, from the Colonel's consideration of feathers that might please Renata to the author's emphasis on creating gifts for his beloved. According to Gajdusek's analysis,

> It is with an imagery of birds that this level of meaning is enunciated . . . which progresses from the first scene and its shooting of the birds to the last scenes, in which the guns are put away and the killing of birds is abjured. It is a novel studying the ritualized self-overthrow of the male who in ritual self-castration divests himself of the signs of his authority and power and transfers them to his

female consort. It is a studied examination of a shift from the patriarchal to the matriarchal mode, an understanding that the time has come culturally for that shift, and it is told to an extent in "bird language."[29]

Translated literally, Hemingway's novel based on Cantwell's memories of war must give way to the more matriarchal, preservative belief system that would find war (like hunting) as frightening as any action occurring on today's planet.

Mark Ott moves in this direction in his reading of Hemingway's Spanish Civil War stories, seeing that some of the ineffectiveness of several of the stories may stem from the author's lack of resolution—a lack that may reflect Hemingway's ambivalence about warfare. Ott asks, "How should a writer approach the horror and meaninglessness of war? Irony, the strategy employed in the 1920s by a younger Hemingway to write about World War I, is no longer adequate to the task." Instead, Ott suggests, it might be that "Hemingway has now recognized the integration of mankind in an extended brotherhood, one that foreshadows Santiago's brotherhood and unity with the marlin. . . . Amid the senseless slaughter of modern warfare, our common humanity, along with our integration with and understanding of the natural world may yet redeem us."[30]

For *Across the River and into the Trees* to end with Cantwell's death, a demise unsung or even noticed, leaves the reader questioning the rationale for the text—why devote page after page to reconstructing the Colonel's memories? Why enhance Renata's understanding of her beloved older lover if his experiences have told her little? For Adam Long, just as Renata is an idealization of Venice, intentionally exaggerated and beautified, so Cantwell's hatred for the American/Allied military powers who robbed him of his rightful rank is exaggerated. Then, rescued from his bitterness, he joins his wishes with hers—and their unified wish is to go to America, where they might find a new society where they can escape the classed formality of the older Italy. In his retelling of a life, Cantwell has received a kind of absolution. In his criticism of the military powers, he has freed himself from the existence of that power. Tellingly, he dies not in Venice but on the battlefield site in northern Italy.[31] And as Cantwell dies, he no longer thinks of Renata. He has told her goodbye with an intentional elevation to the status of Dante's Beatrice: "I'd say you were the loveliest and most beautiful girl that ever lived. Any time. Any place. Anywhere" (*ARIT* 276).[32]

The literary world came to know that Adriana Ivancich was the model for Hemingway's Renata. Even as he was able to use some of his young Italian friend's drawings for book jackets, Adriana was never seriously involved with

Papa Hemingway—though when *Across the River and into the Trees* was published, her family experienced great shame (the novel was intentionally not
translated into Italian for many years). In 2014, in Venice, Adriana Ivancich's
younger brother Giacomo Ivancich addressed the Hemingway Society, re-
hearsing the great admiration that existed between his sister and the aging
writer—and, once more, explaining that their friendship was chaste.[33]

As the archive of their letters at the John F. Kennedy Library shows, Hemingway's manner of writing to the young Adriana was formal and respectful.
He took a single liberty in his correspondence—that of telling her that they
were the same person, signing his various letters to her "A. E. Hemingstein-
Ivancich" or "A. Ivancich" with a salutation to "Adriane" or "Hemingstein." In
his courtly fashion, he told her, "I do not, and cannot, ever love anyone as I love
you," claiming that he thought of her every minute.[34]

Past the dreamlike romance (whatever was occurring in real life did not
lessen the fantastic quality of Hemingway's attachment), the key to the novel's effectiveness lies in the way Hemingway drew Cantwell. Ironically, most
reviews did not emphasize his characterization. Philip Young, one of the first
critics to publish a book about Hemingway's writing, was bothered by the
author's use of what he called the "interview technique" because by using that
structure, the character Cantwell had reason to "pontificate" rather than simply answer. Young argued that "the know-how has become show-off" and led
the reader to see other of Cantwell's "empty mannerisms."[35]

Cantwell as Hemingway drew him, however, was not intended to be a simple man. In one of his first dialogues with Jackson, the Colonel looks at his
aide "with the old deadliness" (*ARIT* 37). Irascible, dizzy, faint from taking
more mannitol hexanitrate than usual, Cantwell controls his condition by sac-
rificing pleasantries. As he recalls the three women he has loved, only to lose
them, he is rueful: "You lose them the same way you lose a battalion, by er-
rors of judgment; orders that are impossible to fulfill, and through impossible
conditions. Also through brutality" (*ARIT* 95). Critic Sarah Wood Anderson
notes that Hemingway's choice of name lent a forbidding tone: "Cantwell"
will not recover. She reads the character's demeanor as evidence of years of
not only physical injury but also the mental trauma of unending fear and loss.
Cantwell's insomnia is pervasive. He has already experienced three heart attacks and at moments in the narrative seems to be experiencing symptoms of
another. Anderson emphasizes that it is not so much this character's memories
of war that are valuable, but rather it is his willingness to retrieve the memories—a confession, a process that may have value or may not. It is Hemingway's re-creation of the *process* that makes the novel work.[36]

Many of the Colonel's remembered passages are quietly effective: memories of the blocked canals that held the dead from one of the Piave battles ("floating and bloating face up and face down regardless of nationality until they had attained colossal proportions" [*ARIT* 20]), reminiscences with the Gran Maestro about the poor soldiers who "would share the contents of a match box full of gonorrheal pus to produce the infection that would keep them from the next murderous frontal attack" (*ARIT* 59), and his more personal guilt-ridden recollections of the troops being unloaded from the trucks: "They should not have gotten out, ever. . . . That was where I grew up, he thought, and all the nights I woke screaming, dreaming I would not be able to get them out of the trucks" (*ARIT* 122). At that point, Cantwell tells Renata that he has no remorse, and no bad dreams, though he does have "strange" dreams—what he calls "combat dreams" (*ARIT* 123).

When Cantwell recounts a memory of the Hürtgen Forest, he becomes more descriptive, explaining about his regiment "how every second man in it was dead and the others nearly all were wounded. In the belly, the head, the feet or the hands, the neck, the back, the lucky buttocks, the unfortunate chest and other places. Tree burst wounds hit men where they would never be wounded in open country. And all the wounded were wounded for life" (*ARIT* 242). Hemingway frequently had used word repetition to create a mood; his repeated word in this description is *wound*.

With a kind of graphic snarl, Cantwell then segues into a meditation about death, which he calls "a lot of shit . . . in small fragments that hardly show where it has entered . . . sometimes atrociously." Unexpectedness is the key. "I have seen it come, loosening itself from the bomb rack, and falling with the strange curve. It comes in the metallic rending crash of a vehicle, or the simple lack of traction on a slippery road. It can come with the smoke-emitting arc of the grenade, or the sharp, cracking drop of the mortar" (*ARIT* 219).

Seldom had Hemingway written more tersely or effectively about the methods of warfare or the wages of battlefield killing. In its various elements, *Across the River and into the Trees* portrays a life of unbearable pain, whether or not it sanctions the unpredictability of either an aging Cantwell or the book's author.

CHAPTER NINE

The Old Man and the Sea

W<small>HEN IN A</small> 1950 Harvey Breit interview Hemingway compared his 1940 book *For Whom the Bell Tolls* to his just-published novel *Across the River and into the Trees*, he collapsed the ten years that separated the two "war novels" into a moment of time. Admitting that *For Whom the Bell Tolls* was a much more specific account of a wartime battle, Hemingway still felt disappointed with readers of *Across the River and into the Trees* who could not see how *large* a canvas of war (episodes, battles, deaths) he had achieved through the imagistic portrayals of Cantwell's memory. His focus, the author implied, was no longer on a single battle of a single war (that of Jordan's blowing the bridge during the Spanish Civil War): rather, here, his emphasis had shifted to the human qualities of the "successful" soldier, the traits of the war-damaged Colonel, whose physical survival was the immediate focus of the narrative.[1] Hemingway's canvas was intentionally large. He told Earl Wilson that he personally had much material to cover: "I lost about five years work out of my life during the war and I am trying to make up for it now."[2]

Hemingway's umbrage at what he saw as the thoughtless criticism of *Across the River and into the Trees* relates to an important 2016 commentary by James Meredith. In his assessment of Hemingway's career as writer, Meredith summarizes that—up to 1950—Hemingway's life and consciousness had been marked irretrievably by four events: 1) his 1918 wounding in Italy; 2) his 1926 divorce from Hadley Richardson Hemingway; 3) his 1937 participation in the Spanish Civil War; and 4) his 1944 experience as an embedded journalist— and participant—in the World War II infantry battles.[3]

Hemingway's catastrophic experience in the Hürtgen Forest—the need to, simply, get through hour after hour, day after day—became a significant part of the psychological basis for his creation of Santiago's will and intellect in *The Old Man and the Sea*. How can a person keep going? At what point does the "human" evaporate from "humanity"? At what point does the wellspring of *loss* distort any human patina of control? Even though Hemingway as writer had previously appeared to *insist* on an intellectual separation between the emotions and the mind's control—a balance he had worked to describe to perfection in "Big Two-Hearted River"—his life during the autumn of 1944 had taught him that such a paradigm would not always be achieved: his retrieval of the old fisherman's story became the vehicle for him to change what in retrospect appeared to be an all-too-stoic message.

The daring of Santiago's quest was no perversion of will: it was rather a way to break out of conventional ambition. Contrary to Mark Cirino's thinking that Santiago's interior conversations indicate a kind of descent into madness, Santiago *does* maintain his balance. He expresses joy at catching the marlin and then he outlines the trauma of seeing the marauding sharks destroy it, just as he castigates himself for putting the marlin in such peril. His sorrow, though it pains him, does not crush him. He docks the boat, takes down the mast and sail, walks slowly and stumblingly up the hill, with resting stops, and collapses. But he stands upright again, and walks to his shelter and his bed. He is able to sleep. He is able to recognize Manolin; he is even able to drink the coffee the boy brings him. As Hemingway wrote in the novella, "A man can be destroyed but not defeated" (*OMATS* 103).[4]

The emotional tone of *The Old Man and the Sea* is less defeat or destruction than it is exhaustion. "'You're tired, old man,' he said. 'You're tired inside'" (*OMATS* 112). Exhaustion is not despair; it is a natural physiological response to aging or to superhuman effort. The seeming simplicity of the Santiago story accrues from the intense narrative drive—Santiago must go out far enough to find the mystically large marlin, he must kill that being (the novella was earlier titled "The Sea in Being"), and then he must bring the fish back to port to sell at market: few Hemingway plots are so clearly defined, so starkly outlined. The simplicity in itself is close to parable.

Donald Bouchard observes that

Across the River and Into the Trees condenses the work of a lifetime, as does, more acutely, *The Old Man and the Sea*. Both books are lessons learned and their protagonists have completed their education. Both are now in a position to tutor the young, whether it is T5 Jackson and Renata or Santiago's disciple, Manolin. . . . The protagonists in both novels are "strange," where one speaks from bitterness and the other out of serenity. . . . Cantwell is different in that he does not play by the book. Santiago is perpetually unlucky.[5]

Most readers did not consider *The Old Man and the Sea* a "war" novel. Susan Beegel, however, points out how much war the 1952 novella contains: "The war just past is present in brief descriptions of the shark factory and of the young fishermen who have purchased motors and *palangres* with their war profits. It is present in the radios that others now have aboard their boats for communication but that Santiago cannot afford. . . . Most of all the war is present in the *galanos* who will hit a man in the water even if he has no smell of blood on him (*OMATS* 29–30, 39, 108)." Even in Santiago's language, there are signs of war—the fish's eye looks like a periscope; there are references to soldiers and to soldier business. As Beegel concludes, this novel has "an unstated interest in human violence and murder, imaged in the lost military personnel as well as in the damage from the malevolent sharks."[6] She emphasizes her point by quoting Hemingway's words in *Death in the Afternoon*: "If a writer of prose knows enough about what he is writing about he may omit the things he knows and the reader . . . will have a feeling of those things as strongly as though the writer had stated them" (*DIA* 192).

Hemingway, too, allowed the novella to be read as simply as it could have been. He often said that he had heard the story in 1936 from Carlos Gutierrez, a tale about an old Cuban fisherman. He let it be known that he had written *The Old Man and the Sea* in fewer than eight weeks and then he had put the manuscript into his safe. He was still upset at the reviews of *Across the River and into the Trees*, and he could not believe that his masterful war novel, with its hero Cantwell, was still unappreciated. The fact that the novel had appeared close in time to the Lillian Ross *New Yorker* interview with Hemingway—which was read not as a New Journalism piece, which it was, but as a parody of the author's brusque speech, complete with the slang-based title phrase ("How Do You Like It Now, Gentlemen?")—made him feel less than appreciated.

He also remained angry that Charlie Scribner had not pulled strings and gotten the book reviewed by sympathetic people; Hemingway knew that if Max Perkins had not died suddenly in 1947, Perkins would have orchestrated the reviews, and the novel's reception, differently. Missing not only Perkins but also Fitzgerald, Hemingway felt old beyond his years. Just before *Across the River and into the Trees* was published, when he was correcting galley proofs, he wrote to General Eric Dorman O'Gowan—the name his friend

Chink now used—berating him for not visiting Cuba while he was touring the States:

> Combat we have, Gentlemen, and if we do not have it we will improvise it from some other and subversive war. Hate to miss talking that stupid one [Spanish Civil War] over with you. We were beat when they took Irun but we ran it out for two and a half years into the longest holding attack in history. And, of course, the attack never came.
>
>   In this next book [*Across the River*] I speak rather irreverently of the good Monte [Bernard Montgomery] but I had hoped to speak with you so that in the after-next I could breathe down his neck in the first clinch and blind him. Why should one human (?) being rouse the dislike of another human being? I suppose only to kill him. I have it completely accurate and straight now that have killed 122 (armeds not counting possible or necessary shootings)[7] and this Monte still escapes one.

Later in this long letter, Hemingway explained the new novel *Across the River and into the Trees* to Chink, saying that the book was "about Venice and it seems very simple unless you know what it is all about. It is really about *bitterness, soldiering, honour, love and death.* I probably sound pompous in this but wanted to give you the true gen in case you ever had to read it in a hurry" (*SL* 691–92; my italics).

Being a forgiving man (much of the time), Hemingway cooled his angry missives to Scribner about the way *Across the River and into the Trees* had been reviewed. Scribner then visited Cuba and fished with his war-weary author. While he was there, he read from the ever-growing manuscript of Hemingway's "sea" novel, and one segment he read eventually became the separate novella *The Old Man and the Sea*.

Hemingway's own critique of this novella is important. In an October 5, 1951, letter to Scribner, Hemingway said,

> This is *the prose that I have been working for all my life* that should read easily and simply and seem short and yet have all the dimensions of the visible world and the world of a man's spirit. It is as good prose as I can write as of now. (*SL* 736; my italics)[8]

He went on to describe the rest of the larger manuscript that would eventually become both *Islands in the Stream* and, years later, *The Garden of Eden*, but what was significant here was his writer's pride in the consistently skillful delivery of Santiago's story. For a craftsman as well trained as Hemingway was, these 26,000 words (written without chapter or segment divisions, a continuous stream of language tied in to the character's fluidity as he narrated) were miraculous. They would have seemed miraculous to anyone who understood modern writing.[9]

Cosmopolitan had offered Hemingway $10,000 in 1951 to publish the novella; he had turned that offer down. In 1952, working through Scribner's,[10] *Life* magazine paid Hemingway $40,000 to publish the work entire in a special issue of the magazine. The publishing world had never seen such a frenzy: 5,318,650 copies of *Life* sold out in forty-eight hours. There had never been a print run of that size. *The Old Man and the Sea* was chosen a Book-of-the-Month Club selection, where it also broke sales records. Later, filming would begin on the movie, with Spencer Tracy as Santiago. The book won the Pulitzer Prize for Fiction in 1953. Although in 1950 Hemingway had been disappointed at the slim royalties (and the lack of movie sale) of *Across the River and into the Trees*, after the 1952 publication of *The Old Man and the Sea*, he would seldom mention money—or taxes—again.

The difference in reception between *Across the River and into the Trees* and *The Old Man and the Sea* made little sense to Hemingway: both were about the difficulties, and the inherent trauma, of aging. Cantwell, like Santiago, is past his prime, and both characters have been denigrated by other characters because of their faulty performances (Santiago is considered "salao" and has gone eighty-four days without catching a fish; Cantwell has been demoted and knows his military career is ending). Each man is, essentially, alone in his fast-fading life. Santiago knows that his young friend Manolin cares about him; Cantwell pretends that both Jackson, his aide, and Renata, a teenaged dreamer, care about him—but in the latter case, the painted portrait of Renata suggests the evanescent nature of any feeling between the Colonel and the living woman.

The ironies of Cantwell's life were harder for readers to comprehend than the more direct losses of Santiago's life. Cantwell dies at the end of *Across the River and into the Trees*, but Santiago appears to be still alive—though carrying the mast may symbolize his coming death. As Michael Reynolds says, "Only Mary's pleading kept Santiago alive."[11] Despite these differences between the two books, the narrative arcs are similar.

There were also, from a writer's perspective, technical choices that differed. Richard Cantwell spends little time in the blind enjoying the duck hunting that brought him to Venice. His immersion in the natural world hardly compares with the setting necessary for Santiago's fishing hegira: all *is* the natural world in *The Old Man and the Sea*. To carry the name of the fisherman disciple, a name so common in the Canary Islands, from whence Santiago came,[12] does not distinguish the character: he is an *everyman*. Better put, no one besides Manolin (and his disapproving parents) has any knowledge of Santiago.

The green world setting of the Santiago story takes the character out of the militarization that had surrounded—and perhaps destroyed—Cantwell. As Leo Marx notes, Hemingway's best work "invoke[s] the image of a green landscape—a terrain either wild or, if cultivated, rural—as a symbolic repository of meaning and value." Marx sees this comparative set of worlds as integral to the modern, terming Hemingway's "complex pastoralism" a new force in evoking history accurately. Beegel, too, sees Hemingway's choice to draw so heavily on the ocean as it represents the natural world as being in keeping with his earlier successful fiction, "the Nick Adams stories and the novels *The Sun Also Rises*, *A Farewell to Arms*, and *For Whom the Bell Tolls* . . . the ironic juxtaposition of nature, a place of refreshment and healing, with scenes of war and postwar despondency."[13]

For all the differences in the initial reception of the books, recent critics more and more often find similarities: Michael Seefeldt calls *Across the River and into the Trees* "the immediate sibling of *The Old Man and the Sea*, a partner to it as high allegory," noting that both books represent "the life journey."[14] Reynolds and others see that both these books, as well as the larger mass of "sea" writing that posthumously became *Islands in the Stream* and *The Garden of Eden*, are "war" novels, stemming from the vast experiences of characters in wartime. (Like "Big Two-Hearted River," in which the war does not appear, these fictions treat war both as memory play and as failed experience.)[15]

Another similarity is that all these fictions are built around a new concept of "family": Santiago's wife is dead, causing him much pain; he turns over her photograph. Colonel Cantwell has lost three women beloved to him, and his fantasy of replacing past love objects with the Venetian teenager is clearly that. The two men who comprise the adult cast in *Islands in the Stream* are alone, sharing the three sons of one of the men as if they were a unified family—marred by the deaths of the oldest son in wartime and the younger two in an automobile accident. The two women who pair with David Bourne in *The Garden of Eden* are fantasy figures, confused about their roles and their sexual preferences—happiest when swimming and tanning, and primarily interested in *changing*.

Debra Moddelmog describes Hemingway's late works as centered on "substitute families." She remarks that these families "stand in for the biological family, providing the community that it often fails to establish, but also that they often stand in *opposition* to this family."[16] Freed from conventional "oughts" and "shoulds," Hemingway's late characters seem able to trust their instincts about living a life that satisfies. It took him years to draw such characters—the first passes, as we have seen, were failures, as was Harry Walden, who did not fulfill his own expectations; or characters who were cut off short, as was Robert Jordan in *For Whom the Bell Tolls*. To some extent, Cantwell of *Across the River* shares that fate. He is a man barely fifty, but the wars and their related stresses have brought him to an unexpected early death.

Perhaps the concept of family ties in to Carlos Baker's early suggestion that "Renata stands in one of her aspects, for Colonel Cantwell's lost youth. Manolo fulfills a similar purpose."[17] Modern fiction provided few models for aging characters who were exemplary. After *For Whom the Bell Tolls*, Hemingway's works were based on characters that *achieved*, at whatever cost. These figures are, usually, male, and the part of a family that matters is the child, usually the son. There are no grandparents or cousins or distant aunts in these novels, and the women who bore the children seem to be somewhat disposable. As Hemingway created his ideal fictional world over and over, it was a male existence that emerged—and it was idyllic. He had written the prototype for this patterning in the early 1930s, titling it "Fathers and Sons," with echoes of Turgenev; that title would have sufficed for much of his later fiction. Here at the end the reader sees Santiago and Manolin, or Thomas Hudson and Roger Davis and Hudson's three sons, the sons and fathers shifting places, melding, merging. Male friendships—whether or not based on blood relationships—become more and more prominent in Hemingway's later fictions, whether located within the human world or the animal kingdom.

Illustrative of these themes is "An African Story," a postwar work published posthumously, both as a segment of *The Garden of Eden* and standing alone in *The Complete Short Stories of Ernest Hemingway*. Here the boy David comes to see his father, who hunts elephants for their ivory tusks, and his African partner, Juma, as intolerably vicious. (Juma had years before killed the elephant's male companion, and wounded this animal as well; he and David's father are hopeful that they can slaughter this elephant at the site of that attack.)

David's companion is his dog, Kibo, and it is he and Kibo who have first seen the ancient elephant that is the object of the story's hunt—killing the noble animal is the adults' only aim. Like Santiago's love for the marlin, Davy loves the elephant; his love for the animal turns him against his father—and he vows to lead a life of secrecy from this time forward.[18] One might read "An African Story" as Hemingway's apologia to his father for the censure he had felt after Clarence Hemingway's suicide: it might also be read as his apologia for his own incipient suicide. Men who age and know despair cannot be blamed for their acts that seem, at first, unkind: it took several decades, and many injuries, before Hemingway realized that fact. Although Ernest Hemingway, like the ancient elephant and the equally ancient Islander fisherman, had kept going, had kept recovering some quality of process for some time, he had learned what it meant to *age* years before his suicide.

Exactly when Hemingway wrote "An African Story" is unknown. But it came to him after the war, when he had seen too many deaths and maimings. As a young writer, he had looked at the human world critically. As the aging writer that he had become, he understood the pain of broken health and of lasting impairment. He especially understood the pain of losses—lost friends, lost lovers, lost memories, and, increasingly, lost abilities.

Had Stanley Cooperman ever read "An African Story," he might have paired it with *The Old Man and the Sea*. In his reading of the novella, Cooperman writes that the author's depiction of Santiago's strongly achieved free will "marks a return on Hemingway's part from some attempt at social involvement to justify action, to an examination of action itself—and a hymn of praise to the sacred nature of such action, when purified by will and uncorrupted by external cause." Cooperman summarizes that Santiago acted so that "the act becomes its own truth: that is, he achieves divinity of manhood by means of the ritual or trinity of action consisting of willed sacrifice, pride, and endurance."[19]

For Donald Bouchard, Santiago represents nearly all Hemingway's late protagonists, men whose "typical experience involves individuals at the limit, exhausted by this experience, who sketch for the moment the outline of a lost continuity and coherence. This process may imply an empty form, but, as an action found in all his works, it also achieves . . . an intensity and clarity."[20] This critic links Cantwell with Santiago on the basis of the characters' dreams. Driven as Cantwell is in his attempts to recover his lost youth, his dreams do not betray him—instead, he experiences "strange dreams . . . about places mostly. We live by accident of terrain, you know. And *terrain* is what remains in the dreaming part of your mind," he explains to Renata (*ARIT* 117). For Santiago, dreams about place are much more integral to his being.

> He dreamed of Africa when he was a boy and the long golden beaches and the white beaches, so white they hurt your eyes, and the high capes and great brown mountains. . . . He only dreamed of places now and of the lions on the beach. They played like young cats in the dusk. (*OMATS* 24–25)

Unlike Cantwell, Santiago is able to *name* the place, just as he is able to describe it: Santiago's dream of Africa is nothing strange or mysterious. It is, rather, tactile. As the mountains impinge on the low-spreading beaches, Santiago's beloved sea encroaches on his seemingly separable childhood memories. Again and again, Hemingway gave the reader the dreams both of Africa and of the majestic terrain. When Santiago first describes his comforting dream, he dwells on each part of it. The author followed that initial description with Santiago's true narrative: "He lived along that coast now every night and in his dreams he heard the surf roar and saw the native boats come riding through it" (*OMATS* 24). Santiago is completely immersed in the ocean and its beaches—hearing, seeing, and then smelling the surroundings so integral to his memories ("He smelled the tar and oakum of the deck . . . and he smelled the smell of Africa" [*OMATS* 24]). As a sentient and experienced man, Santiago lives a present-day life that is itself an anachronism: he is a creature of his African past as well as of the country that has become his immediate country, and as he rolls and unrolls his one pair of trousers before setting out to wake Manolin for their day, he remains moored in his sustaining memories.

Bouchard sees these two characters' dreams as wistful. He speaks of "youthful strength, care-free exuberance, and the resiliency found in certain places," forcing such dreams to appear nostalgic. But *Hemingway* was not using Santiago's dreams for that purpose: like a man separate from his life as it exists in the present world, Santiago draws on his entire being—"The Sea in Being" can be changed to "Santiago in Being," if the reader wishes—in order to accomplish his long-projected feats.

Santiago has become a man who no longer recognizes limits. He has become a human being at his best, unbounded by restrictive reason or practical common sense. He has become a man who *dares*. Becoming "strange," Hemingway assured his reader through the complex figure of Santiago, does not suggest madness or willed difference; it rather draws from the possible wholeness of man-in-nature, as well as man-in-life. Santiago's state in *The Old Man and the Sea* represents the tantalizing evocation of unified human power that Jake Barnes had only glimpsed, that Frederic Henry had—in his grief—relinquished, that Robert Jordan had begun to comprehend, and that Richard Cantwell had caught sight of and then plowed under his wounded bitterness. The prize of a complete, and a completed, understanding was to be only Santiago's.

Bouchard concludes his discussion by emphasizing that, in Hemingway's last-finished novel, "this sense of the marvelous found in seemingly prosaic reality infuses all aspects of *The Old Man and the Sea*. It sets the stage for

Santiago's endurance, his engagement with the marlin, and his first sight of the 'great fish,'" a kind of mystic sight and insight that baffles the simple understanding of the aging fisherman.[21]

> The line rose slowly and steadily and then the surface of the ocean bulged ahead of the boat and the fish came out. He came out unendingly and water poured from his sides. He was bright in the sun and his head and back were dark purple and in the sun the stripes on his sides showed wide and a light lavender. His sword was as long as a baseball bat and tapered like a rapier and he rose his full length from the water and then re-entered it, smoothly, like a diver and the old man saw the great scythe-blade of his tail go under and the line commenced to race out. (*OMATS* 62–63)

Characteristic of Hemingway's best writing throughout his career, this distilled moment of the marlin's imposing and regal "birth" sanctifies both the reader's and Santiago's reaction to his presence.

Written with the sonorous line of *and*'s, which Hemingway often used to create a rhythm of stately power or prayer, this excerpt immerses the reader into one of the oldest *creation* stories: arising from the sea, this primordial being first makes the sea *bulge* before he comes through the restricting waters. A vision of unendingness, with water pouring from his sides, the marlin encapsulates sunlike radiance in his royal purple and lavender colors, a totem of miraculous birth.

As he did on other quasi-mystical occasions, Hemingway here distorted the reader's grammatical expectations: the *stripes* on the marlin's sides—taking the reader to a pre-crucifixion brutality, misreading *stripes* as *strikes* or piercings—"showed wide and a light lavender." (Dimensionality and color are qualities that do *not* join with a conjunction.)

The humor inherent in comparing the marlin's *sword* to a baseball bat smacks of Santiago's references to Joe DiMaggio, but the death-dealing properties of the word *sword* are reestablished here with the word *rapier*. The marlin unfolds his being in the brilliance of his birth; Christlike, he *rises* from the all-nourishing water, just as naturally to reenter that matrix, "smoothly, like a diver," his prowess commanding.

Hemingway's grammatical break, which should isolate the last twenty words of the excerpt, only unites "the old man"—here unnamed and uncapitalized—with the power of life and death ("the great scythe-blade"), which belongs more apparently to the fish. This linguistic merging introduces, and also echoes, the poignant scene in the novella when Santiago asks, "Is he bringing me in or am I bringing him in?" (*OMATS* 99).

The deft layering that Hemingway achieved throughout Santiago's narrative makes any reduction into "meaning" difficult. Bouchard notes, "Santiago is powerless to explain what has happened; he experiences, as did Robert Jordan, the weakness of any language that tries to express the limits and the heights of his being. He is overwhelmed by what surpasses him. Silence is the only adequate response. . . . Santiago's transgression in going out too far leads to a more riddling absence."[22]

Whether today's reader adopts Frederick Carpenter's assessment of Santiago's completed being as the mystical fifth stage of human understanding, or Joseph Waldmeir's careful delineation of a religion separate from formal distinctions, or H. R. Stoneback's repeated insistence that Santiago is a saintly but flawed pilgrim, the aspects of the old fisherman's strangeness are not meant to be forbidding. Stoneback chooses to describe the Canary Islands beliefs that he found similar to Hemingway's own late belief systems. He traces the writer's attention to the concept and practice of the pilgrimage, particularly aligning it with "the Pilgrimage of Santiago de Compostala" during the mid-twenties, as Hemingway was drafting *The Sun Also Rises*.[23]

In a later essay, Stoneback repeats his conclusion that, while Jake never completed his pilgrimage, Hemingway *did*, perhaps several times. (This critic draws from the author's correspondence with both Bernard Berenson and Father Robert Brown, the latter unpublished and housed at the University of Texas.) Santiago, with his deep-rooted Canary Islands belief system, brings to the geographical accuracy of Hemingway's accounts of pilgrimage the wider significance of not only the earth and its seas but the earth and its heavens. Stoneback notes that from Santiago's Guanche culture would have come his veneration for "the sun, moon, sea, and stars," each entity appearing in the novella as participant in the fisherman's discourse. The Guanches believed in giving women "absolute respect." They "regarded suicide as honorable," and they also "believed that one of the great Spirits lived on the snowcapped peak of Mount Teide," the highest mountain on Spanish soil.[24]

The Canary Islands are also known as the Fortunate Islands and the Isles of the Blest, "the abode of the storied undead, the mortal heroes upon whom the gods confer immortality." Mystical and a part of the natural world rather than the religious world in a doctrinaire sense, Santiago has affinities with the rich heritage of "St. James the fisherman, St. Jacques/Santiago," the apostle later beheaded for his beliefs. A focus for Santiago's debility in his exhaustion, being clear in the head consequently becomes more than a physiological symptom: it prompts Hemingway's reader to recall this metaphor of death being meted out for dangerous beliefs.[25]

The second meaning in pilgrimage history for St. James/Santiago is his identity as Santiago Matamoros (which translates "Moor-slayer"). In structuring *The Old Man and the Sea* around Santiago's victory over "the negro from Cienfuegos," Hemingway was marking the pride Santiago had in being called "the champion." The reader is meant to recall this element of historiography: war is never distant from peace within either the civilized or the natural world.[26]

Stoneback concludes this essay with information about "the Virgin of Cobre," Cuba's sacred image. In the August 1956 Cuban celebration for Hemingway's receiving the Nobel Prize in Literature, Hemingway presented the medal from the Swedish Academy to the Virgin of Cobre because so much of his later writing had been both conceived and executed in the land and the waters of Cuba.[27]

As *The Old Man and the Sea* shows, writing, for Hemingway, was becoming increasingly interior. If the quality of a believable character is a factor of his or her range of mental life, the writer's obligation is to chart that intellectual existence. Hemingway thought he had drawn the wide-ranging thoughts, reactions, and memories of Richard Cantwell, hoping to create this believability. Evidently, readers of *Across the River and into the Trees* did not manage to see, or to appreciate, the activity of the Colonel's mind.

So in *The Old Man and the Sea*, with the even more aged and more experienced Santiago as protagonist, Hemingway developed different narrative techniques. Rather than drawing on memories, he created several different dialogue patterns. Often, Santiago talks, seemingly, to himself. Again, he talks to the creatures of the sea, particularly to the marlin—and later, to the vicious sharks. At times Santiago goes back in time and speaks to his beloved Joe DiMaggio, whose performance despite his painful bone spur illustrated physical bravery. Hemingway created a remote and unusual world, working from within Santiago's unexplored mind. The fragments that readers are given in the narrative movement are intentionally vague, pointing first toward the catching of the marlin and then toward its killing. For all the appearance of specificity, Santiago's story exists largely within his consciousness.

Simple in appearance and thrust, the opening of *The Old Man and the Sea* illustrates Hemingway's careful framing of the marlin story. The novella opens with one of his distinctive *and* constructions:

> He was an old man who fished alone in a skiff in the Gulf Stream *and* he had gone eighty-four days now without taking a fish.

In the first fifteen words here, only one word is not a monosyllable. Insisting on its difference, the two-syllable *alone* becomes resonant. It also falls at the midpoint of the first clause. The second clause, connected to the first with the modest *and*, includes ten words, of which seven are monosyllabic. *Eighty-four*, *without*, and *taking* are the longer, and consequently more emphatic, words.

When Hemingway added the second sentence, "In the first forty days a boy had been with him," he created the emotional nexus of the book. Of those eleven words, only one is not monosyllabic. As the paragraph continues, and coming to the concluding sentence, the first compelling metaphor takes shape—one that describes Santiago's poverty (the sail "patched with flour sacks") as well as his isolation. Adding in the metaphor itself, Hemingway closed the paragraph with "it looked like the flag of permanent defeat" (*OMATS* 9).

The metaphor sets up misleading insights, however. Whereas Hemingway had described his effective style in the novella as prose "that should read easily and simply and seem short," he was not talking about the use of monosyllabic words. He was talking about the *ease* a reader would experience. He was also talking about *access*. What about the first paragraph of *The Old Man and the Sea* would the common reader—either Hemingway's or Virginia Woolf's—*not* understand? But then in his letter to Scribner, Hemingway had remarked, about the aim of his precise writing, that he wanted his prose to have "all the dimensions of the visible world and the world of a man's spirit."

The irony Hemingway so consistently practiced came into play here: there is no "permanent defeat" either for Santiago or for his ambition. How monumental was the author's aim, to give his readers *all* the dimensions of both the visible world and a man's spirit. Only when the reader continues to track the smooth-flowing prose will he or she discover how meaty yet how amorphous Hemingway's descriptions become, how intangible, how mystic, Santiago's reactions are.

There are three repeating metaphors that guide readers through *The Old Man and the Sea*. The first, introduced in the novella's second sentence, is the great love Santiago has for Manolin, "the boy." As part of the all-important frame, the story of Manolin's having now been forbidden to fish with the old man—because of his unluckiness—shows Santiago's genuine loss of his company. The first eighteen pages of the novella establish this bereavement. So too do the last six pages, when the boy tries to care for the broken body of his friend. In the conclusion of the novella, Manolin alternates between a fierce protectiveness and a natural lament: he sheds tears three separate times for Santiago's injuries, both physical and monetary, as well as for the brutal evisceration of the eighteen-foot marlin.

Similarly, Santiago repeats his need for Manolin three times at compelling points in his narrative, the first being "If the boy was here he would wet the coils of line, he thought. Yes. If the boy were here. If the boy were here" (*OMATS* 83). This direct expression takes on weight because through the pages leading up to it, Santiago's memory-text emphasizes his aloneness ("The old man had seen many great fish. He had seen many that weighed more than a thousand pounds and he had caught two of that size in his life, but never alone. Now alone, and out of sight of land, he was fast to the biggest fish that he had ever seen and bigger than he had ever heard of" [*OMATS* 63]). In the verbal space of Santiago's recognition of his aloneness exists the presence of the boy. There are few givens in Santiago's account of this endeavor, but Manolin is one of the two dominant factors. As Santiago says in an early scene, in the second of the three statements of his need, "The boy keeps me alive" (*OMATS* 106).

The third time Santiago states his need for the boy is in his memory of—and idealization of—the place of Africa: Africa as land, Africa as place of nourishment and freedom, but particularly Africa as home of the playful young lions. As Hemingway had done, less directly, in his 1936 African story "The Snows of Kilimanjaro," in this novella too he created an exotic, semi-imaginary location so that his character's imagination could be fully expressed. Reified by the human possibility of accomplishment, the place of Africa is introduced once, early, and then recurs unexpectedly at points within *The Old Man and the Sea*. After the fish has been caught, for example, when Santiago is himself caught in a relentless round of pain from his hand injuries and his muscle strain, the dream resumes:

> After that he began to dream of the long yellow beach *and* he saw the first of the lions come down onto it in the early dark *and* then the other lions came *and* he rested his chin on the wood of the bows where the ship lay anchored with the evening off-shore breeze *and* he waited to see if there would be more lions *and* he was happy. (*OMATS* 81, italics added)

Envisioning the young lions, despite the stifling pain, Santiago relies on the commonplace *and* as if all events were equal—and equally bearable.

A stasis of imagination never affects the old fisherman. From the statement closest to outright despair ("What can a man do against them [the sharks] in the dark without a weapon?" the bewildered fisherman asks while the sharks attack) to a more sanguine acceptance ("It is silly not to hope"), Santiago wrenches meaning from the simplest of word choices (*OMATS* 117, 104). Hemingway described the fisherman's acute moment of physical fear as he loses his breath and tastes the "coppery and sweet" (*OMATS* 119) blood in his mouth as if that experience of bodily breaking was always anticipated. (Santiago's own foreknowledge had earlier been described—"but he had always known this would happen" [*OMATS* 83]).

Metaphorically, even after Santiago has docked his skiff and returned home, even after the reader feels a security in Manolin's caring for the old man, Hemingway controlled the peace that floods the ending of what might have been presented as a horrific narrative. Set opposite the language of Santiago's valid explanation for his loss of the great fish ("I went out too far") comes the closing image of Santiago's tranquility: "He was still sleeping on his face and the boy was sitting by him watching him. The old man was dreaming about the lions" (*OMATS* 127). Caught in the web of Manolin's concern, Santiago sleeps safely, assured that his prowess in living remains, imaged in the beauty of the youthful animals on the shore of the land he has long considered home.

As Bouchard says about Hemingway's technique of resting his meaning within a dream, "If dreams are indeed the mechanism for wish fulfillment, Cantwell/Santiago (nee Hemingway) seek perpetual youth and ideal conditions for the work to be done. This is a dream at the end of a career."[28]

The dedication of *The Old Man and the Sea* was changed late in the publication process, from Mary Hemingway to Charlie Scribner and Max Perkins. Both men were dead by its time of publication. But as the literary world knew, the novella was written by Scribner's most turbulent, most talented, and most searching protégé, Ernest Miller Hemingway. Its publication eventually led to that writer's being given the Nobel Prize in Literature, even though he had won very few prizes throughout his successful writing career.

CHAPTER TEN

The Late Years

H<small>EMINGWAY CONSISTENTLY DEFINED</small> *power* as his ability as a person to make unique choices. He loved the *Pilar* for the freedom it gave him to escape both domestic and professional life in order to live on the Gulf waters. He loved his income as a writer for providing his ability to make sometimes idiosyncratic choices about what he considered his responsibilities toward the people important to his life. In the labyrinth of personal choices that shaped his existence after World War II were those about how he chose to spend the remaining years of his life; his choices reified the role of writing as part of his physical well-being.

Hemingway had written cogently about these choices as early as his 1935 nonfiction book *Green Hills of Africa*. Titled with compellingly messianic optimism, this work (which few critics have seen as essential to comprehending Hemingway) created the country of *Africa* as a thoroughly positive imago for an almost mystic location. In fact, Hemingway wrote about the country while he and his party were still *within* it, in the early months of 1934: "All I wanted to do now was to get back to Africa. We had not left it, yet, but when I would wake in the night I would lie, listening, homesick for it already" (*GHOA* 72).

In this eulogistic prose, Hemingway described his truly beloved country for, first, its natural beauty ("Now, looking out the tunnel of trees over the ravine at the sky with white clouds moving across in the wind, I loved the country" [*GHOA* 72]). He also saw that country as a protected place, a site of encouragement that he keep involving himself with intense devotion to the craft of writing:

> What I had to do was work. I did not care, particularly, how it all came out. I did not take my own life seriously any more, any one else's life, yes, but not mine.

They all wanted something that I did not want. . . . To work was the only thing, it was the one thing that always made you feel good, and in the meantime it was my own damned life and I would lead it where and how I pleased. And where I had led it now pleased me very much. (*GHOA* 72)

With sentiments similar to those that he wrote to his friend Arnold Gingrich about the failure of the United States to "move" him, Hemingway here abbreviated those arguments. Later in the book, he expanded his rationale for loving *Africa*:

So if you have loved some woman and some country you are very fortunate and, if you die afterwards it makes no difference. Now, being in Africa, I was hungry for more of it, the changes of seasons, the rains . . . , the discomforts . . . , the names of the trees, of the small animals, and all the birds, to know the language and have time to be in it and to move slowly. I had loved country all my life; the country was always better than the people. I could only care about people a very few at a time. (*GHOA* 73)

Susan Beegel maintains that there is little question about Hemingway's "abiding love for Africa." She believes his attraction to the country was partly a tribute to his vivid memories of the Michigan outdoors[1] and partly owing to "his need to experience wilderness." She reasons that this explains his attraction to East Africa, "with its still intact Great Plains—the Serengeti (which in Masai means 'land that runs forever')—its vast herds of ungulates numbering in the thousands and even millions and its indigenous peoples still, to some extent, able to practice their traditional lifeways."[2]

Returning from that 1934 safari, Hemingway wrote to Ivan Kashkeen, "We go to Africa and I have the best time I have ever had" (*SL* 418). He began telling Gingrich that he *must* return: "What I want now is dough in a sufficient sum safe somewhere so I can get out to Africa. . . . I do not give a shit for anything except to get out to Africa again" (*SL* 409). As Hemingway was to write simply in *Green Hills of Africa*,

I felt at home and where a man feels at home, outside of where he's born, is where he's meant to go. (*GHOA* 284)[3]

He said that he did not intend to exploit Africa, or to emphasize its exotic qualities: "I would come back to Africa but not to make a living from it. . . .

I would come back to where it pleased me to live; to really live. Not just let my life pass" (*GHOA* 285). In many ways, Africa seemed reminiscent of his beloved Spain. "It was a new country to us but it had the marks of the oldest countries. The road was a track over shelves of solid rock, worn by the feet of the caravans and the cattle, and it rose in the boulder-strewn un-roadliness through a double line of trees and into the hills. The Country was so much like Aragon that I could not believe that we were not in Spain. . . . The high trees beside the track over those rocks was Spain" (*GHOA* 146).

Beegel equates Hemingway's joyful sense of exposure in Africa—to the natural world, to his successes in tracking and killing animals (or, more accurately, in learning to *know* those animals), and to attaching experiential knowledge to his somewhat abstract understanding of East Africa, its terrain, and its people—to the joy that his fishing in the Gulf Stream brought him. Earlier in the 1930s, before he made the trip to Africa, Hemingway wrote to journalist Janet Flanner, an old friend from Paris, about that fishing:

> We fished along that coast 65 days last year. . . . It is wonderful. The gulf stream runs almost black and comes right in to the shore. The marlin swordfish go by, swimming up the stream like cars on a highway. You go in to shore in the boat and look down to see the wrinkles in the white sand through the clear water. It looks as though you would strike bottom and when you drop anchor the rope won't reach bottom. They have beaches miles and miles long, and hard white sand and no houses for twenty miles. We go out in the morning and troll the stream, go in to swim and get back somewhere at night. Sometimes sleep on the boat. (*SL* 386)

Later in his long letter, as he invited Flanner to come for a fishing visit, Hemingway described their "fine house" (in Key West) and their flourishing children, along with "4 coons, a possum, 18 goldfish, 3 peacocks and a yard with a fig tree, lime tree." Even as he described his contentment ("I could stay here damned near all the time and have a fine time watching the things grow"), he admitted that he found himself getting "homesick for Spain and want to go [to Africa] and see the animals and hear the noises they make at night" (*SL* 387).[4]

Years after that African safari, Hemingway told Selden Rodman, who interviewed him several times, "You take Yoknapatawpha County, and I'll take the ocean. . . . It's one of the last unspoiled places . . . the place I love best and that moves me the most."[5]

Hemingway maintained his fishing and taking solace in the Gulf Stream almost to the end of his life: so long as he was physically able to handle the huge marlin that could be caught in those waters, he loved the sport. In the mid-1930s, when he thought that Max Eastman had called him a weakling, he shaped this acerbic prose poem for Perkins:

> Poor old Hem the fragile one. 99 days in the sun on the gulf stream, 54 swordfish. Seven in one day. A 468 pounder in 65 minutes, alone, no help except them holding me around the waist and pouring buckets of water on my head. Two hours and twenty minutes of straight hell with another. A 343 pounder that jumped 44 times, hooked in the bill. I killed him in an hour and forty-five minutes. Poor fragile old Hem, posing as a fisherman again. (*SL* 395)

Besides the continuity of his loving the Key West house and the Gulf Stream, the *Pilar* and his fishing conquests, Hemingway, as we have seen, kept writing, writing, writing, and as is evident from his 1930s correspondence, saw himself as the writer of great—even superlative—short stories.

When Perkins encouraged him to write new stories so that Scribner's could publish his third short story collection (*Winner Take Nothing*, which appeared late in 1933), Hemingway wrote to his then mother-in-law, Mary Pfeiffer, about his aims for short stories, which he saw as the heart of his oeuvre:

> I am trying to make, before I get through, a picture of the whole world—or as much of it as I have seen. Boiling it down always, rather than spreading it out thin. These stories are mostly about things and people that people won't care about—or will actively dislike. All right. Sooner or later as the wheel keeps turning I will have one that they *will* like. (*SL* 397)

Hemingway knew that his emphasis on the story form was both unfashionable and costly: Scribner's might pay him advances of five or six thousand dollars, but any novel would make ten times that amount in royalties. For Hemingway, however, the story form was intrinsically American. He respected Sherwood Anderson's aims when he wrote better stories than novels; he saw that the reliance on dialogue and scene that was more necessary in a short form than in longer narratives was itself American. Not for nothing had he read H. L. Mencken's book *The American Language*.

One of the clearest statements of Hemingway's belief in himself as a good practical critic can be drawn from his November 16, 1933, letter to Perkins.

Here he railed at critics who were being hostile to the stories in *Winner Take Nothing*. One had denigrated Hemingway's stories because the author was "middle-aged." Hemingway began his long letter to Perkins by asking,

> When does middle age commence? That story—Wine of Wyoming, is nothing but straight reporting of what [I] heard and saw when was finishing A Farewell to Arms out in Sheridan and Big Horn. That was in 1928 and I was just 30 [29] years old while I was out there. . . . I was 17 [18] when first went to war. . . . I write some stories absolutely as they happen i.e. Wine of Wyoming—the letter one ["One Reader Writes"], A Day's Wait, and another ["After the Storm"] word for word as it happened, The Mother of a Queen, Gambler, Nun, Radio . . . others I invent completely—Killers, Hills Like White Elephants, The Undefeated, Fifty Grand, Sea Change, A Simple Enquiry. *NOBODY* can tell which ones I make up completely.
>
> The point is I *want* them to sound as though they really happened.

In this prolegomenon, Hemingway used underlining (indicated here with italics) to make clear to Perkins that this information was crucial. He repeated several times that he would *not* bring these matters up again; he expected Perkins to *remember*.

> I invented every word and every incident of A Farewell to Arms except possibly three or four incidents. All the best part is invented. 95 percent of The Sun Also was pure imagination. I took real people in that one and I controlled what they did. I made it all up.

He reassured Perkins defiantly, "I haven't *started* to write yet."

Then his outspoken critique started. Hemingway announced,

> I can't write better stories than some that I have written because you can't write any better stories than those—and nobody else can. But every once in a long while I can write one as good—and *all the time* I can write better stories than anybody else writing. But they [the critics] want *better ones* and as good as *anyone ever* wrote. God damn it there can't be better ones. The one they pick out as "classic" Hills Like White Elephants not one damn critic thought *anything* of when it came out. I always knew how good it was but I'll be goddamned if I like to say how good my stuff is. (*SL* 401)

As we have seen, Hemingway was to write very few stories after *Winner Take Nothing* appeared in 1933. But when in 1936 he wrote "The Short Happy Life of Francis Macomber" and "The Snows of Kilimanjaro," Perkins *was* paying attention.

* * * * *

Previous chapters have outlined some of the conflicts within Hemingway's personal and literary life, those congruent with his major works. Behind the scenes of the celebrity writer's existence ran currents of worry, physical injury, depression, and other emotional disruptions. During his completion of *To Have and Have Not* and his several years working for the Loyalists in the Spanish Civil War, Hemingway left Pauline Pfeiffer to live with Martha Gellhorn. They married in November 1940 and made their home at the Finca Vigia in Cuba. *For Whom the Bell Tolls* was published in 1940; its sale for a film and the appearance of his Spanish Civil War stories and his play occurred in connection with that popular novel.

After a joint journalistic trip to China, Hemingway and Gellhorn covered World War II separately: she reported for *Collier's* while he hunted both spies and U-boats from the *Pilar*. Finally, in 1944, Hemingway went to the European theater as a journalist and a sometime participant with the 22nd Infantry. His son Jack was captured and held for several months as a German prisoner of war.

Hemingway had fallen in love with Mary Welsh while in Europe; the often-absent Gellhorn agreed to a divorce. Hemingway returned to Cuba and cared for his sons at the Finca while waiting for Mary to arrive. They married on March 14, 1946.

As chapters 7 and 8 have described, Hemingway's litany of physical injuries in car accidents and battles, along with the psychological strain of friends' deaths and wartime injuries and his increasingly visible drinking, combined to enervate his health. Just a few months after their marriage, Mary suffered a miscarriage when an ectopic pregnancy nearly cost her her life—Hemingway's hopes to have a daughter were dashed. His wife's recovery took months. Even though Hemingway wrote a great deal toward his "Land, Sea, and Air" opus during the late 1940s, he published only *Across the River and into the Trees* and *The Old Man and the Sea*, in 1950 and 1952. It was a time of dying and death. His friend and publisher Charlie Scribner, his mother, Grace Hemingway, and—even more unexpectedly—his second wife, Pauline Pfeiffer, died during 1951 and 1952. As Hemingway wrote, tersely, to Bernard Berenson in the spring of 1953, "It was a bad year for deaths and details and problems" (*SL* 780).

To Berenson also, considering the shadows of the Vietnam conflict, Hemingway wrote, "The violence is the violence of our time. . . . Any time must be a good time to me and we make each day a day. I cannot write beautifully but I can write with great accuracy (sometimes, I hope) and the accuracy makes a sort of beauty. (NOT like the camera.) I know how to make country so that you, when you wish, can walk into it and I understand tactile values. I hope sometimes I can make people because, as a writer, I have almost a perfect ear" (*SL* 808). Returning to his writing prowess, bragging about his obvious skills, Hemingway as a person seemed less confident. He was exhibiting the same kind of unpredictable (often alcoholic) behavior that had marred the mid-1930s for him and for his family.

Mary Hemingway chronicled some of these moods and events in her later memoir, *How It Was*. For the fourth Mrs. Hemingway, all the suppressed irascibility, the out-of-control drinking, the abusive behavior, and the yearning for young and beautiful women became reality rather than gossip. Mary jokingly referred to Hemingway's cadre of beautiful girls as his "vestal virgins," but the pain of his continuous flirtations ruined much of her enjoyment of being married to Hemingway.[6]

Judging from the correspondence included in Carlos Baker's *Selected Letters*, Hemingway seldom wrote to anyone about his personal life during these postwar years. He still arranged his days so that he could escape to the *Pilar*, and fishing continued to be his most consuming enjoyment. He still planned the long-awaited African safari, as if that physical and emotional voyage had ballooned into a shining image of pure ecstasy.

Arriving in Mombasa in late August of 1953, the Hemingways were met by Philip Percival, the white hunter of Hemingway's beloved memories, and *Look* photographer Earl Theisen;[7] they were encamped in nine tents on Percival's Kitanga Farm in the Mua Hills. They gathered supplies and, on one sunny morning, were able to see Mount Kilimanjaro.[8] On September 1, 1953, the Hemingways began the safari proper. Described at length in Hemingway's african journal, it was a recasting and an expansion of the 1933–1934 experience Hemingway had shared with Pauline and then recorded so satisfactorily in *Green Hills of Africa*. In the twenty years since his first safari experience, sharp differences had emerged in Hemingway's body and mind: he worried, he "trained" Mary for the skills he thought she would need, he got himself into better physical shape. The excitement of the original safari was missing for Hemingway, which sharpened his sense of nostalgia for what he had shared with Pauline, an experience darkened by her sudden death.

For the month of September, the Hemingway party was allowed to be the only hunters in the Southern Game Reserve, forty miles south of Nairobi. Rarely opened for hunting, the game preserve fulfilled all of Hemingway's dreams, although he spent as much time studying animals and birds as he did shooting them.

Hemingway became convinced he was being invited to join the Wakamba tribe. To that end he shaved his head and planned to take Debba, one of their young girls, as his bride. Mary went on a shopping trip to Nairobi; she returned to find that her spouse had dyed his clothing the Masai "rusty pink ochre" and had taken up hunting, naked, with a spear.

The holidays passed; plans were made for a tour in a Cessna 180 to see parts of Africa new to the couple. As they flew near Murchison Falls, "a flight of ibis suddenly crossed the path of the plane [and when the pilot dived to avoid the birds], the plane struck an abandoned telegraph wire." Because the propeller had been damaged, the plane had to land. It crashed on Ugandan soil. Mary was unconscious; Hemingway had, among other things, an injured shoulder. The pilot moved them away from the crash, but media reports of both the crash and the assumed deaths of the passengers were already circling the globe.

A day later, the plane that came to replace the Cessna had equally bad luck. The twelve-seater de Havilland Rapide came to pick up the Hemingways and their original pilot at the Butiaba airport. When it took off from the runway, which was only slightly better than a plowed field, it fell back onto the field and burst into flames. The pilot kicked out a window so Mary and their first pilot could escape, but Hemingway was too large for that opening. He butted the jammed door with his head, cracking his skull and doing what turned out to be irreparable harm to his body. His face, hands, and arms were badly burned, and he had internal injuries. Driven to the town of Masindi, the Hemingways did not understand how damaged their bodies were, how long even minimal recovery would take.

News headlines around the world again lamented the couple's deaths. As they tried to recuperate in Entebbe, both their injuries and the media attention only increased their discomfort. In Baker's description, Hemingway's injuries included a collapsed lower intestine, kidney damage, ruptured spleen, spine damage, and the shattered head. In Michael Reynolds's description, the most serious injuries were Hemingway's "fractured skull and concussion, two cracked spinal discs, damaged internal organs"—dire wounds that would be compounded in the coming year with his developing hepatitis, nephritis, anemia, and high blood pressure, as well as effects from the head injuries.[9] In Hemingway's descriptions, there was no part of his body that had escaped. He wrote to Berenson, "Concussion is very strange—and I have been studying it: Double vision, hearing comes and goes, your capacity for scenting something can become acute beyond belief. . . . Ruptured kidney (much blood and pieces of kidney in urine). The hell with the rest of it" (*SL* 828). He wrote to Harvey Breit, "It was more or less indecisive for a time but now have stopped bleeding from all the orifices and always had declared to win" (*SL* 830). He wrote to his son Gregory, months later, "In the aircraft nonsense I got smashed really bad. I never had a broken back before, certified anyway, and it can be uncomfortable and shitting standing up, while not a difficult feat, can get to be a bore. . . . I went 22 days when I couldn't unlock the spincter [*sic*]. Then shat a species of white hard nobby rocks about ball size."[10] He wrote to Berenson about that same time, "I had the experience of the destruction of vital organs which ordinarily would take a long time to achieve. Also the indelicacies that accompany these destructions. . . . At present I work at about 1/2 the capacity that I should have but everything is better all the time" (*SL* 837).

At the year's end, and with the candor he often showed when talking to military friends, he wrote to Chink Dorman O'Gowan,

> This has been a sort of rough year. You know we never discuss casualties but I would not have minded going for a shit at Murchison or Butiaba except I had to look after Mary and there is always the *obligation* to survive, that mis-understood obligation. But I believe I would have stayed in the kite [plane] that burned at Butiaba, once Mary was out, if I could have seen the rest of 1954 as she would be and as she'd feel. We call this 'black-ass' and one should never have it. But I get tired of pain sometimes even if that is an ignoble feeling. (*SL* 843)

The old sense of outright humor, sometimes disguised as irony, reassures the reader that Hemingway was finding some vestige of himself amid the carnage of that second plane crash. Although he here told Chink that he would have chosen to die by staying in the burning plane, he was not talking about suicide per se. He evinced the same attitude when he told Harvey Breit, "I have been beat-up worse than you can be and still be around" (*SL* 833).

Ironic as it seemed, Hemingway's second and long-awaited safari in Africa led almost directly to his own early death. In Meredith's list of the five events that shaped Hemingway's life, the African plane crashes are the final item that he considers crucial. Always conscious of the debilitating effects of the

Figure 11. Hemingway eating with Mary Hemingway and a friend (and one of his favorite cats), late in 1960. Photo by John Bryson © 2016 Bryson Photo.

damages of injury and war, both physical and mental, Meredith concludes that Hemingway was unable to recover even a semblance of his normal life.[11]

One must remember Hemingway's listing of the pervasive themes in his postwar writing: "bitterness, soldiering, honour, love and death" (*SL* 691–92). The pairing of "soldiering" with "honour" and the leap to "death" chalk a paradigm that dominates all writing about war. Hemingway's writing about war would be little different.

Buck Lanham recalled years later, "The plane crashes had ruptured his liver, and ruptured his spleen. And he had very bum kidneys that he was being treated for constantly. Of course, he was an absolutely incredible drinker. He could drink 24 hours a day. So he had a physical breakdown in all departments."[12] Hemingway's son Jack said, looking back, "He had a personality change after those crashes. I don't think there's any question of it. I always tried to deny it and found excuses for it, but looking back I think there's no doubt about it. He was easily nasty after those crashes."[13] Reynolds summarizes too that, after the second plane crash and fire, Hemingway was "incredibly changed . . . his beard whiter, his eyes frequently vacant, his moods mercurial."[14]

The almost inevitable downward spiral of Hemingway's condition after the plane crashes—and the fact that he was far from American medical attention for several months following them—was halted briefly by the October 28, 1954, phone call from Sweden telling him that he had been awarded the Nobel Prize in Literature. He explained that he was too ill to travel so far, but he accepted the honor; a month later, he made a voice recording of his acceptance speech. The speech was read at the awards ceremony by John Cabot, American ambassador to Sweden.

The remarks that accompanied the award were about Hemingway's writing's remarkable, internationally famed style and the fact that through it, Hemingway created memorable scenes: "Lieutenant Henry's flight in the rain and mud after the panic at Caporetto, the desperate blowing up of the bridge in the Spanish mountains when Jordan sacrifices his life, or the old fisherman's solitary fight with the sharks in the nocturnal glow of lights from Havana."[15] This is the Nobel Prize committee's group of pervasive images, honored so capably in their award text, so it might be said that they too found Hemingway's writing about war (and the metaphoric war of a fisherman against the natural world) his most resonant.

In answer, Hemingway gave his thanks to the Swedish Academy for the generosity of Alfred Nobel. "No writer who knows the great writers who did not receive the prize can accept it other than with humility." He then spoke about the writer's life, its loneliness: "For he does his work alone and if he is a good enough writer he must face eternity, or the lack of it, each day. For a true writer each book should be a new beginning where he tries again for something that is beyond attainment. He should always try for something that has never been done or that others have tried and failed. Then sometimes, with great luck, he will succeed."[16]

In March of 1954, Hemingway had been awarded the $1,000 Award of Merit Medal from the American Academy of Arts and Letters; in July, on his fifth-fifth birthday, he received the Order of Carlos Manuel de Céspedes, Cuba's highest honor. Both paled in comparison with the Nobel Prize.

On receiving the phone call from Sweden, Hemingway quickly phoned Buck Lanham, as if the prize itself honored Lanham, the United States military (particularly the infantry), the forces of war throughout the world: he had pledged to write fiction that would distill the greatness of the military in this country, and he could see those pages of unfinished fiction—known in his own mind as the "Land, Sea, and Air" novel—which were not yet in readable form. His frustration with his own progress as a postwar writer led him to tell Lanham immediately about the honor.

On December 13, 1954, *Time* magazine featured Hemingway on its cover, captioned "An American Storyteller."

The accolade was everything Ernest Miller Hemingway the writer had ever dreamed of achieving. And it came as a lucky reprieve. It helped to change that slow but inevitable decline in Hemingway's spirit and physical health. Years before, after suffering a concussion in London, Hemingway had written to Mary Welsh about its effects: "ringing in ears, loss of verbal memory, even a tendency to write backwards" (*SL* 584). The years and years of damages to his physical frame, particularly to his head, led to immense pain, sometimes diminished, sometimes intense, always warring at the back of Hemingway's consciousness with his desire, his need, to keep writing at the top of his ability. The motivation for Hemingway's existence was his work, and he did that work to the best of his abilities—no matter his physical state.

There have been arguments about genetic instability within the Hemingway family line, as well as speculation about possible manic-depressive symptoms. Andrew Farah's 2017 study *Hemingway's Brain* posits the existence of traumatic brain disease, recounting the many injuries to the author's skull—concussions as well as injuries that damaged the skull itself. As more and more information is known, the more plausible conjectures grow in number.

Friends, observers, and family members acknowledge visible changes between the Ernest Hemingway in his twenties and the Ernest Hemingway in his fifties. Much of what biographer Michael Reynolds delineates in his third volume remains accurate: "The boxer, the writer, the matador: age eventually diminishes their skills, judgment, and timing. Eventually the best of them are crushed if not defeated by age and death. Professionals trapped in a holding action they cannot win was ever Ernest's interest from his Paris days forward."[17] What was happening to the consciousness of Ernest Hemingway during his last years alive was much more general, and much more dire, than the simple aging process.

Seven years after receiving the Nobel Prize in Literature, Hemingway chose to commit suicide. Reported as an accidental death while he was cleaning his gun, his death was announced throughout the world—and received with the same intensity of grief that had accompanied the two reports of his and Mary's deaths in the African plane crashes in early 1954. Rather than read Hemingway's choice of location for his death as any kind of hostility toward his wife, as some observers did—the entrance and hallway to their Idaho house being a family entrance—one might place the ramifications of Hemingway's death in the context of his desperation. Physical pain and mental despair, not the least of which was prompted by his loss of memory, whether from his brain

Figure 12. Hemingway in Idaho, toward the end of his life.

disease or from the electroconvulsive shock treatments administered at the Mayo Clinic, were enemies Hemingway had grown weary of fighting.

In 1935 he had written a deeply personal letter to Sara and Gerald Murphy. In it he lamented the death of their sixteen-year-old son Baoth. As a father himself, he expressed the raging grief he felt over the boy's loss, but he reminded them that everybody will die. He also told them that their son "is spared from learning what sort of a place the world is."

> I know that anyone who dies young after a happy childhood, and no one ever made a happier childhood than you made for your children, has won a great victory. We all have to look forward to death by defeat, our bodies gone, our world destroyed.

His attempt at some kind of consolation came late in the letter, when he told Sara and Gerald, "No one you love is ever dead" (*SL* 412).

Throughout Hemingway's life, he seemed to write best about loss. Whether a physical disability or a state of mind that might be termed a "disability of death," his writer's perceptions were honed by a necessary grief. When he was asked to write an introduction for the 1948 edition of *A Farewell to Arms*, which had first been published in 1929, he opened that introduction with a litany of the dead:

> Scott Fitzgerald is dead, Tom Wolfe is dead, Jim Joyce is dead (he the fine companion, unlike the official Joyce of his biographers, who asked me one time, when drunk, if I did not think his work was too suburban), John Bishop is dead, Max Perkins is dead.[18]

The theme is consistent throughout his unfinished manuscripts and throughout his letters to friends. Seemingly at random, he wrote to Berenson, "About dying: We must do it but there is no reason we should give it importance" (*SL* 812). To that same correspondent, soon after returning from the African plane crashes, he wrote, "There is nothing like Africa as there is nothing like youth and nothing like loving who you love or waking each day not knowing what the day will bring, but knowing that it will bring something" (*SL* 838).

Always the efficient writer, Hemingway privileged his mornings, sometimes not speaking to his wife until afternoon: the break of day was *his* and his attentive consciousness. Work was all.[19] As the character Richard Cantwell thinks retrospectively, knowing that he is nearing his own death, "he had never been sad one waking morning of his life. . . . He had experienced anguish and sorrow. But he had never been sad in the mornings" (*ARIT* 289).[20]

The sobriety of Hemingway's reflections on his writing life—whether his statements occur in fiction or in drafts or in letters—is nowhere more compelling than in *Islands in the Stream*. In that unfinished novel, Roger does *not* tell his divorced wife that their son has been killed in the war. Bereft of all three boys, two having died earlier in a car crash, Roger realizes that his life must continue past this threnody of death and loss, and that his son's mother will find her own way to get past the devastation that he knows she will feel: the death of a child creates a crucible of pain. There are no answers; there are no words. Everyone that experiences this loss remains alone, isolated from the human condition, even that of grief.

Hemingway wrote his most significant letters late in his life to Berenson, a man who seems to have replaced both of his mentors at Scribner's, Max Perkins and Charlie Scribner. He clung, too, to the friendship he had found within the military, particularly that with Lanham. He also took on a number of younger writers—Harvey Breit, Aaron Hotchner, and other, more tangential figures—as well as the young women who admired him. But Hemingway remained essentially alone, whether from his own debilities or from his writerly stance toward existence. He once wrote with genuine candor to Berenson, about the joy of writing: "You are very right about how we never achieve what we set out to do. We do make it come off sometimes as we know when we re-read it after a long time. It always reads to me, then, when it's very good as though I must have stolen it from somebody else and then I think and remember that nobody else knew about it and that it never really happened and so I must have invented it and I feel very happy" (*SL* 836).

Poised to feature the writer as conqueror, Hemingway's fiction and his correspondence consistently show how tenuous that hold on life—and achievement, and honor, and bravery, and nobility—truly is. Many of his principles of living a useful life came from his encounters with literal battle; sometimes he wrote about those battles realistically and sometimes metaphorically. As he wrote to Wallace Meyer, his new Scribner's editor after Perkins's death, he was deeply satisfied with what he had achieved in *The Old Man and the Sea*. He called it a book "where a man shows what a human being is capable of and the dignity of the human soul without the word soul being capitalized" (*SL* 758).

Hemingway aimed high and he aimed large, and he knew what his chances were of living very long: one of his constant refrains in his letters to Berenson is a kind of implied lament that he would never reach the age of real wisdom, which he saw in Berenson's existence. Had it not been for his physical debilities, Hemingway would have lived past 1961. But as his son Patrick recently wrote in his introduction to the restored edition of *A Moveable Feast*,

> In later life the idea of a moveable feast for Hemingway [became] a memory or even a state of being that had become a part of you, a thing that you could have always with you . . . that you could never lose. . . . Hemingway had many moveable feasts besides Paris: D-Day on a landing craft going in to Omaha Beach, among many others. For this to work, however, you need memory. With memory gone, and knowing that it is gone, is likely to come despair, the sin against the Holy Ghost. Electric shock therapy can destroy memory like dementia or death does, but, unlike dementia or death, you are left aware that it has been destroyed. (*MF* restored xiv)

✳ ✳ ✳ ✳ ✳

Hemingway's recognition of the destruction of both his memory and his acute awareness lives on in this fragment of his writing—undated, but surely coming late in his life—preserved at the John F. Kennedy Library. This is the commentary:

> When he awoke he knew he had been out of his head in the night and after eating his breakfast he unloaded his pistol and placed the loaded magazine in one drawer and the pistol in another. . . . After this, he went back to bed and commenced writing. At nights now he was on the boat, mostly, although on some nights he was in upper Michigan where he had lived as a boy. This was the first time when he had been really awake in the night and still unable to leave the dream. . . . He knew he had been out of his mind but he did not care as long as he could write in the daytime. Whatever happened to him now he did not care as long as he could write in the daytime. Whatever happened to him now he considered of no importance as long as he could write. He wrote well that day. . . . [21]

NOTES

Introduction | Wars and Their Omnipresence

1. Paul Fussell, *The Great War and Modern Memory*, ix.

2. Patrick Hemingway, foreword to *HOW*, xi.

3. Kirk Curnutt, quoted in James H. Meredith, *Understanding the Literature of World War I*, 2.

4. Frederick J. Hoffman, *The Twenties*, 76.

5. Wendy Steiner, "The Diversity of American Fiction," 849–50.

6. Elaine Scarry, *The Body in Pain*, 64.

7. Eric J. Leed, *No Man's Land: Combat and Identity in World War I*, 189.

8. Carlos Baker, *Ernest Hemingway: A Life Story*, 14–24; Michael S. Reynolds, *The Young Hemingway*, 6.

9. Denis Brian, *The True Gen: An Intimate Portrait of Ernest Hemingway by Those Who Knew Him*, 14; Marcelline Hemingway Sanford, *At the Hemingways: With Fifty Years of Correspondence between Ernest and Marcelline Hemingway*, 150. According to Marcelline, several times Clarahan and Ernest hiked the three hundred miles from the Chicago boat drop in Lower Michigan to the family cottage on Walloon Lake, camping and cooking along the way.

10. Lillian Ross, "How Do You Like It Now, Gentlemen?" 24.

11. Ibid., 23.

12. Michael Reynolds's 1976 book *Hemingway's First War: The Making of "A Farewell to Arms"* shows this conglomerate method to perfection. Hemingway illustrated his abilities to collect and then shape a different whole even in those early years, as he progressed toward the writing of his 1929 novel.

13. Introduced to the bullfight by Gertrude Stein and Alice B. Toklas, who were among the few Americans who had ever traveled to the Spanish bullfights, Hemingway quickly saw himself as an American expert—another marker of his intense rivalry with Stein (see Wagner-Martin, *"Favored Strangers": Gertrude Stein and Her Family*, 170–80.) In 1923 Hemingway wrote to Bill Horne that the bullfight "isn't just brutal like they always told us. It's a great tragedy—and the most beautiful thing I've ever

seen and takes more guts and skill and guts again than anything possibly could. It's just like having a ringside seat at the war with nothing going to happen to you" (*SL* 88).

14. Information about the books Hemingway borrowed and owned comes from the Sylvia Beach Papers at the Firestone Library, Princeton University, and from compendiums of his books in various locations by James Brasch, Joseph Sigman, and Michael Reynolds, as well as from his correspondence with Maxwell Perkins.

15. Baker, *A Life Story*, 161.

16. Because Crane had never been to war, Hemingway noted, his creation of Henry Fleming and his physical and emotional struggles in war had come entirely from stories about battle, writings about war (Tolstoy's *War and Peace* was a great influence), and his own understanding of fear and courage. Hemingway also credited the Mathew Brady photographs of Civil War experiences with influencing Crane (*MAW* 10). Whether or not Hemingway was reading Crane's war fiction, he recommended to young writers what he thought were Crane's best stories, "The Open Boat" and "The Blue Hotel" (see Arnold Samuelson, *With Hemingway: A Year in Key West and Cuba*).

17. Ernest Hemingway, preface to *The Great Crusade*, ix.

18. Ibid., viii.

19. Ernest Hemingway, preface to *All the Brave, Paintings by Luis Quintanilla*, 7.

20. Ibid.

21. Ibid., 11.

22. Ernest Hemingway, foreword to *Treasury for the Free World*, xiii.

23. Ibid.

24. Kurt Vonnegut, "Kurt Vonnegut on Ernest Hemingway," 21; Charles Whiting, *Papa Goes to War: Ernest Hemingway in Europe, 1944–45*, xi; Thomas Strychacz, "Seeing through Fractures: *In Our Time, For Whom the Bell Tolls*, and Picasso's *Guernica*," 77–78.

25. Sean Hemingway, introduction to *HOW*, xx.

26. Ella Winter to Carlos Baker, February 10, 1962, unpublished, Carlos Baker Papers, Firestone Library, Princeton University.

27. Adrienne Monnier, *The Very Rich Hours of Adrienne Monnier*, 45–46.

28. Margaret Anderson, *My Thirty Years' War*, 258–59.

29. Archibald MacLeish, *Published and Perished*, 103–5.

Chapter One | The Writer Writes

1. This passage moves next to record the death of ambulance driver Passini, one of whose legs is completely gone "and the other was held by tendons and part of the trouser and the stump twitched and jerked as though it were not connected." Then the narrator returns to his own devastation, and the passage ends with his realization, when he puts his hand to his knee, that the "knee wasn't there. My hand went in and my knee was down on my shin. . . . I looked at my leg and was very afraid" (*FTA* 56). The effectiveness of the scene grows as the character's recognition of physical damage is described.

2. Michael S. Reynolds, *Hemingway: An Annotated Chronology*, 23–25.

3. She was seven years older than he. Agnes's diary and the reminiscences of Henry Villard—who befriended both Agnes and Hemingway while he, too, was convalescing at the Milan hospital—were published in 1989 as *Hemingway in Love and War.* The film produced then was drawn largely from that text, written by Villard and critic James Nagel. Agnes's diary recounts as well her worries about Hemingway's reliance on drinking.

4. See chapter 9, n. 3, for further discussion of this loss.

5. Anderson used this term prominently in the introduction to his *Winesburg, Ohio* (New York: Huebsch, 1919); the full title of this book was originally *Winesburg, Ohio: A Group of Tales of Ohio Small Town Life.* The diffidence Anderson's use of the term shows reflects the importance for American writers of providing something "new"—in the sense of Ezra Pound's phrase "Make it new"—so as to distinguish *American* writing from British. Hemingway had been looking for the new in fiction through reading Ivan Turgenev's *A Sportsman's Sketches*, where the narrator is also continuing, linking together the disparate characters of his narrative just as George Willard, the young journalist, does in the Anderson volume. Critic Paul Smith points to an even closer model, that of E. W. Howe's "An Anthology of Another Town," published in the *Saturday Evening Post* (Smith, *A Reader's Guide to the Short Stories of Ernest Hemingway*, xxi). In Hemingway's case, deciding upon a continuing narrator to appear throughout his early writing—in fact, throughout much of his oeuvre of short fiction—gave the reading world his Nick Adams, a relatively tough, no-frills, and strongly masculine young midwesterner. The fact that Nick was also the first of Hemingway's severely wounded war veterans shows his pervasive concern with World War I and its often-ignored, and isolated, trauma victims.

6. Baker, *A Life Story*, 102.

7. Peter Griffin, *Along with Youth: Hemingway, the Early Years*, 125.

8. Ibid., 125–26.

9. Ibid., 124.

10. Ibid., 127.

11. Jennifer Haytock, *At Home, at War*, 58.

12. Ernest Hemingway, *Three Stories and Ten Poems*, 54.

13. Ernest Hemingway, *Ernest Hemingway: 88 Poems*, 47.

14. Ibid., 35. To critic Philip Young's often-discussed theorizing that Hemingway became the writer he was because of that 1918 wounding, this poem and manuscript material from Hemingway's early career lend support.

15. Jeffrey Meyers, *Hemingway: A Biography*, 50.

16. After "Up in Michigan" appeared as the lead-off story in the 1923 *Three Stories and Ten Poems*, it was considered too impolite, in both punning title and content, to be published by United States houses.

17. Smith, *A Reader's Guide*, xxviii.

18. Charles A. Fenton, *The Apprenticeship of Ernest Hemingway: The Early Years*, 46.

19. Ibid., 75.

20. Scott Donaldson, "Hemingway of *The Star*," 89.

21. Robert O. Stephens, *Hemingway's Nonfiction: The Public Voice*, 57.

22. Quoted in Max Westbrook, "Grace under Pressure: Hemingway and the Summer of 1920," 21.

23. Ibid., 22–23. None of the quoted letters mention Hemingway's drinking, but beer and alcohol were plentiful in the Michigan woods; the Hemingways as a family, however, prohibited imbibing long before Prohibition became the law of the United States.

24. Scarry, *Body in Pain*, 65.

25. Evelyn Jaffe Schreiber, *Race, Trauma, and Home in the Novels of Toni Morrison*, 2.

26. Judith Herman, *Trauma and Recovery: The Aftermath of Violence—from Domestic Abuse to Political Terror*, 238–39.

27. Ibid., 51, 193.

28. Cathy Caruth, *Unclaimed Experience: Trauma, Narrative, and History*, 1, 61.

29. Kali Tal, *Worlds of Hurt: Reading the Literatures of Trauma*, 6.

30. Paul Hendrickson, *Hemingway's Boat: Everything He Loved in Life, and Lost, 1934–1961*, 16, 291. In a 1950 letter, Hemingway contrasted his sons' teenage years with his own, saying that most of his rebellion had been against the "harsh" discipline within his family (*SL* 703).

31. Alice Miller, *The Drama of the Gifted Child*, 57. See also Alice Miller, *For Your Own Good*; Kay Redfield Jamison, *Touched with Fire: Manic-Depressive Illness and the Artistic Temperament*; and Laura Vickroy, *Reading Trauma Narratives*.

32. Tal, *Worlds of Hurt*, 15, 18.

33. Herman, *Trauma and Recovery*, 133, 194; Herman's brackets.

34. Caruth, *Unclaimed Experience*, 138.

35. At least some of Hadley's letters to Hemingway have survived and are in the Hemingway Collection at the John F. Kennedy Presidential Library and Museum, Boston, MA. (See my *Ernest Hemingway: A Literary Life* and Bernice Kert's *Hemingway Women* for more information about the correspondence.)

36. John Peale Bishop, *The Collected Essays of John Peale Bishop*, 44.

37. Hemingway's March 26, 1923, letter to his father was typical. He wrote that he was "en route for Germany by cabled request of The Star to do a series of 12 articles on the French and the Germans. . . . I've been 38 hours on the train and am awfully tired. I've traveled nearly 10,000 miles by R. R. this past year. Been to Italy 3 times. Back and forth Switzerland-Paris 6 times. Constantinople-Germany-Burgundy-The Vendee. Sure have a belly full of travelling" (*SL* 81).

38. Gertrude Stein, *The Autobiography of Alice B. Toklas*, 216–17.

39. Henri Bergson, *Introduction to Metaphysics*, 27–28; my italics.

40. There are scattered revealing comments in Hemingway's letters to Stein, as when he said, on February 18, 1923, "I've been working hard and have two things done. I've thought a lot about the things you said about working and am starting that way at the beginning. . . . Am working hard about creating and keep my mind going about it all the time. Mind seems to be working better" (*SL* 79).

41. P. D. Ouspensky famously listed four dimensions, with the fourth leading to the mystical. In books published in 1920 and 1922, Ouspensky discussed progressions in thought congruent with the fakir, the monk, and the yogi, and then the less explicit

"fourth way." All the work here is inner; one continues to live the same life as before. For Hemingway to move beyond this fourth dimension and to suggest there can be a *fifth* is a radical statement. Ouspensky, *Tertium Organum, The Third Canon of Thought, A Key to the Enigmas of the World*.

Chapter Two | in our time, *In Our Time* and Dimensionality

1. Edmund Wilson, "Mr. Hemingway's Dry-Points," 340–41.

2. Milton A. Cohen, *Hemingway's Laboratory, The Paris "in our time,"* x–xi.

3. John Dos Passos, *The Best Times: An Informal Memoir*, 44.

4. John W. Aldridge, "Afterthoughts on the Twenties and *The Sun Also Rises*," 115–16.

5. Alex Vernon, ed., *Teaching Hemingway and War*, 5.

6. In 2015, A. E. Hotchner published *Hemingway in Love: His Own Story: A Memoir*, his fictionalized account of the early Paris years, which, according to Hotchner, his friend Hemingway had given him in conversation toward the end of the writer's life, and he replicated Hemingway's language from his notes taken in the early 1960s. About his great love for Hadley, for example, Hemingway told his friend, "Hadley was the only woman who mattered in my life, her full body and full breasts. . . . I adored her looks and the feel of her in bed" (30).

7. Joe Fassler, "'Why Novel-Writing Is Like Spelunking': An Interview with Chang-rae Lee."

8. Pound referred to Hemingway as an "Imagist," "applying the stricture against superfluous words to his prose, polishing, repolishing, and eliminating, as can be seen in the clean hard paragraphs of the first brief *In Our Time*" ("Small Magazines," 700).

9. Ernest Hemingway, "An Interview with Ernest Hemingway," 33.

10. Ibid., 35.

11. Smith, *A Reader's Guide*, 25–101.

12. Alix Du Poy Daniel, "The Stimulating Life with Gertrude & Co.," 17; Samuel Barlow, "Ave Dione, A Tribute." Hemingway wrote to Stein while he and Hadley were back in Toronto for the baby's birth, saying that he was giving up journalism ("You ruined me as a journalist last winter. Have been no good since. Like a bull, or a noville, rather, well stuck but taking a long while to go down"). He closed that November 9, 1923, letter by saying, "I'm quitting on January 1. I have some good stories to write—will try not to be turgid" (*SL* 102). (Evidently, that word was one Stein had used about his earlier prose.)

13. Marsden Hartley, *Adventures in the Arts*, 195.

14. *Three Soldiers* was John Dos Passos's second novel about World War I. The first, to which Hemingway referred later, was *One Man's Initiation—1917*.

15. Alex Vernon, "War: World War I," 391, 393.

16. David Seed, *Cinematic Fictions*, 71.

17. Frederic J. Svoboda, "The Great Themes in Hemingway: Love, War, Wilderness and Loss," 156.

18. See John Raeburn, *Fame Became of Him: Hemingway as a Public Writer*, Leonard J. Leff, *Hemingway and His Conspirators: Hollywood, Scribners, and the Making of*

American Celebrity Culture; and Loren Glass, *Authors, Inc.: Literary Celebrity in the Modern United States, 1880–1980.*

19. Hemingway seems to have forgotten that lesson as he wrote his second novel, *The Torrents of Spring* (*The Sun Also Rises* was his first novel, but it was still in draft form when he wrote the takeoff of Sherwood Anderson's *Dark Laughter* and other fictions). Subtitled *A Romantic Novel in Honor of the Passing of a Great Race* and using a quotation from Henry Fielding to the effect that comedy stems from "affectation," *The Torrents of Spring* ridicules most of life's happenings, including war.

20. Meredith, *Understanding the Literature of World War I*, 3; see also Pamela Boker, *The Grief Taboo in American Literature: Loss and Prolonged Adolescence in Twain, Melville, and Hemingway*, and David Wyatt, *Hemingway, Style, and the Art of Emotion.*

21. Ulrich Baer, "Modernism and Trauma," 316.

22. Malcolm Cowley, "Nightmare and Ritual in Hemingway," 51, 49.

23. Typical of Hemingway's notes in the Kennedy Library archive is this deleted paragraph from "Big Two-Hearted River," in which the author laments the loss of his boyhood friends: "When he married he lost Bill Smith, Odgar, the Ghee, all the old gang. He lost them because he admitted by marrying that something was more important than the fishing. They were all married to fishing. He'd been married to it before he married Helen, really married to it. It wasn't any joke. So he lost them all. Helen thought it was because they didn't like her" (manuscript #277, Ernest Hemingway Collection, John F. Kennedy Library).

Chapter Three | When the *Sun* Rose

1. Brian, *True Gen*, 55. The Pamplona trip on which the novel was based occurred in 1925. In 1923, Hemingway went to the bullfights with Bill Bird and Robert McAlmon, including Hadley for only the Pamplona segment; in 1924 the Hemingways joined a party of Sally and Bill Bird, McAlmon, Donald Ogden Stewart, George O'Neil, John Dos Passos, and Chink Dorman-Smith (some from that group fished the Irati River). In 1925 the Hemingways' group included Harold Loeb, Stewart, Duff Twysden and Pat Guthrie, and their Michigan friend Bill Smith. It was on this trip that Hemingway began writing the novel and continued working on it night after night. The great irony of Hadley Hemingway's vivid memory is that she did not appear at all in *The Sun Also Rises*.

2. Hemingway, "An Interview with Ernest Hemingway," 32.

3. Frederic J. Svoboda, *Hemingway and "The Sun Also Rises": The Crafting of a Style*, 45-50, 115-16.

4. The famous discarded opening focuses on Brett: "This is a novel about a lady. Her name is Lady Ashley and when the story begins she is living in Paris and it is Spring. That should be a good setting for a romantic but highly moral story. As every one knows, Paris is a very romantic place. Spring in Paris is a very happy and romantic time. Autumn in Paris, although very beautiful, might give a note of sadness or melancholy that we shall try to keep out of this story" (manuscript #200, Ernest Hemingway Collection, John F. Kennedy Library).

5. Miriam Marty Clark, "Hemingway's Early Illness Narratives and the Lyric Dimensions of 'Now I Lay Me,'" 7, 9.

6. Debra Moddelmog leads readers to see the possible divergences in apparent heterosexuality in her 1999 book *Reading Desire: In Pursuit of Ernest Hemingway*, using the rubric "contradictory bodies" to show the otherness in the sexuality presented by Hemingway. See also Mark Spilka, *Hemingway's Quarrel with Androgyny*; Carl P. Eby, *Hemingway's Fetishism: Psychoanalysis and the Mirror of Manhood*; and Nancy R. Comley and Robert Scholes, *Hemingway's Genders: Rereading the Hemingway Text*.

7. John Raeburn, *Fame Became of Him*, 41.

8. Carlos Baker, *Hemingway: The Writer as Artist*, 82–83.

9. Scott Donaldson, "Humor in *The Sun Also Rises*," 37; see also James Hinkle, "What's Funny in *The Sun Also Rises*," 133-49.

10. Zvonimir Radeljkovic, "Initial Europe: 1918 as a Shaping Element in Hemingway's Weltanschauung," 133.

11. John Aldridge, "Afterthoughts," 117.

12. This phrasing came late to Hemingway. In the manuscript version, he had written, "It's nice as hell to think so" (manuscript #200, Hemingway Collection, Kennedy Library).

13. Aldridge, "Afterthoughts," 128. Aldridge provides this classic explanation, calling the novel's movement the result of "a series of alternating scenes of conflict and recuperation from the conflict. The fishing interlude in Burguete and Jake's holiday in San Sebastian both represent rest and curative periods following stressful experiences, first of Paris, then of Pamplona. In both, emotional decorum is almost fanatically maintained. . . . In Burguete there are only men without women and in San Sebastian only one man alone in the good company of himself."

14. The vignette of Maera's dying leads directly to part 1 of Hemingway's "Big Two-Hearted River," his masterful story of willed convalescence. A reader could surmise that Nick's wounding has left him in a similar state of unconsciousness. His recovery, then, as he fishes alone, is even more heartening.

15. John Killinger, *Hemingway and the Dead Gods*, 22-23.

16. Ivan Kashkeen's summary seems apt: "The theme of violence and death is seldom absent from Hemingway's work. That may be because Hemingway took part in two world wars and two smaller wars. . . . War made Hemingway see death without disguise or heroic allusions. . . . It was at the front that Hemingway got to know the harsh world that wants to solve all conflicts by war, a world of wolves where everyone wars on everyone else" ("Alive in the Midst of Death: Ernest Hemingway," 163).

17. David F. Richter, "'At Five in the Afternoon': Toward a Poetics of *Duende* in Bataille and Hemingway," 113–14.

18. Mark Cirino, "That Supreme Moment of Complete Knowledge: Hemingway's Theory of the Vision of the Dying," 242.

19. Killinger, *Hemingway and the Dead Gods*, 18.

20. Richard Ruland and Malcolm Bradbury, *From Puritanism to Postmodernism: A History of American Literature*, 304.

21. Also see Linda Wagner-Martin, "'I Like You Less and Less': The Stein Subtext in *Death in the Afternoon*."

22. Such a characterization of the medical doctor might also have related to Hemingway's vexed feelings about his own father—and his family's disappointment that Hemingway had not gone to college in order to become an educated man.

23. Earlier in this letter Hemingway described his having been in bed with "broncho pneumonia." Without realizing how ill he was, he had steered across from Havana and, "sweating from fighting a big marlin, got caught in rainsquall was what got me sick" (*SL* 361).

Chapter Four | To the War

1. Smith, *Guide to the Short Stories*, 172.

2. Ross, "How Do You Like It Now, Gentlemen?" 36.

3. That Hemingway had perfected this technique shows clearly in the opening he created for *A Farewell to Arms*, a poem itself of such sonority that it is often quoted: "In the late summer of that year we lived in a house in a village that looked across the river and the plain to the mountains. In the bed of the river there were pebbles and boulders, dry and white in the sun, and the water was clear and swiftly moving and blue in the channels. Troops went by the house and down the road and the dust they raised powdered the leaves of the trees. The trunks of the trees too were dusty and the leaves fell early that year" (*FTA* 3).

4. Clark, "Hemingway's Early Illness Narratives," 9. Biographer Jeffrey Meyers points out that much of the description of war wounding might have come from Rudyard Kipling's war fiction. He aligns this Hemingway story with, for example, Kipling's "At the End of the Passage," where the veteran goes to bed with a hunting spur to prevent his going to sleep—and thus having horrifying nightmares. Meyers, *Hemingway*, 115.

5. Hemingway's July 1923 letter to Bill Horne suggests that the silkworm situation, which kept the nerve-wracked veteran from sleeping, was Horne's story (*SL* 85–86).

6. Clark, "Hemingway's Early Illness Narratives," 9.

7. Ellen Andrews Knodt, "Toward a Better Understanding of Nicholas Adams in Hemingway's 'A Way You'll Never Be,'" 77. Knodt's 2016 essay provides material for a stronger comparison between the several kinds of physical damage. She points out that the brain is often damaged "even if no visible wound results."

8. Herman, *Trauma and Recovery*, 35, 37.

9. Caruth, *Unclaimed Experience*, 4.

10. Much of what the emergent male had learned had to do with war. It also had to do with love. The tone of Nick's learning was consistently serious, even somber: that learning was punctuated with the despairingly bleak recognition Hemingway drew in "Soldier's Home," "The Killers," and "A Clean, Well-Lighted Place."

11. Alex Vernon, "War, Gender, and Ernest Hemingway," 110.

12. Ibid., 111.

13. Ray B. West Jr., "The Biological Trap," 139.

14. Fraser Drew, "April 8, 1955 Conversation with Hemingway: Unedited Notes on a Visit to Finca Vigia," 113. Drew recorded that Hemingway called *The Sun Also Rises* "the most moral book" he had ever written.

15. Michael S. Reynolds, foreword to *At the Hemingways: With Fifty Years of Correspondence between Ernest and Marcelline Hemingway*, by Marcelline Hemingway Sanford, x–xi; Reynolds's brackets.

16. Earlier in this letter, he described being injured when the skylight in the toilet broke and his head was badly cut: "We stopped the hemmorage [*sic*] with 30 thicknesses of toilet paper . . . and a tourniquet of kitchen towel and a stick of kindling wood. . . . We went out to Neuilly to Am[erican] Hospital where they fixed it up, tying the arteries, putting in three stitches underneath and six to close it . . . a damned nuisance" (*SL* 272).

17. Hemingway admitted much later, in a letter to Malcolm Cowley, that "he was really badly spooked back in those days [after World War I]." He was afraid that if critics began "messing around with that business" it might come back, "that he might get it again." Recounted by Philip Young in Brian, *True Gen*, 212.

18. Hemingway to Owen Wister, in *The Letters of Ernest Hemingway*, vol. 3, 537–38.

19. Robert A. Martin, "Hemingway and the Ambulance Drivers in *A Farewell to Arms*," 195.

20. See Reynolds's *Hemingway's First War* (154–58, 112), as well as Haytock, *At Home, at War*; Bernard Oldsey, *Ernest Hemingway: The Papers of a Writer*; and Griffin, *Along with Youth*. Reynolds points out that the name Frederic Henry was probably drawn from *Henri* Beyle, *Frederic* Stendhal's real name—hence the spelling of Frederic. Reynolds says of the blending between fact and imagination, "These several points where the novel and historical circumstances coincide . . . show that Hemingway had a total grasp of the military, social and political situation" (112). Hemingway included excerpts from two of his novels in his *Men at War* collection; the retreat is one of those excerpts.

21. Robert Penn Warren, "Ernest Hemingway," 75–76; Svoboda, "Great Themes in Hemingway," 171, 169.

22. Griffin explains in detail why this choice was inexplicable; after all, Caporetto occurred eight months before Hemingway arrived in Italy. It was seen as a "national disgrace" (*Along with Youth*, 66–67). Reynolds wonders why it was crucial to Hemingway to accumulate such extensive material rather than using his firsthand knowledge for the book—"he avoided the terrain that he knew personally, just as he avoided using the victory at Vittorio Veneto" (*Hemingway's First War*, 104–28).

23. Mark Cirino, "The Nasty Mess: Hemingway, Italian Fascism, and the *New Review* Controversy of 1932," 31.

24. Diane Price Herndl, "Invalid Masculinity: Silence, Hospitals, and Anesthesia in *A Farewell to Arms*," 21.

25. Ibid., 32.

26. Trevor Dodman, "'Going All to Pieces': *A Farewell to Arms* as Trauma Narrative," 98.

27. Ibid., 96.

28. Jeffrey Hart, *The Living Moment: Modernism in a Broken World*, 86, 81. Amid all the controversy about Catherine Barkley's role in the novel, as a comfort or as a counselor for Frederic Henry, Delbert Wylder's 1969 commentary has stood firm. Using Henry's shooting of the runaway sergeant as an example of Henry's "inhuman" response to war, Wylder names Catherine the "hero": "Frederic Henry helps to destroy himself, and helps to destroy Catherine." See Wylder, *Hemingway's Heroes*, 78, 87–88.

29. William Dow, "*A Farewell to Arms* and Hemingway's Protest Stance: To Tell the Truth without Screaming," 51.

30. Jackson J. Benson, *Hemingway: The Writer's Art of Self-Defense*, 191.

Chapter Five | Politics and Celebrity

1. Charles Scribner Jr., preface to *The Complete Short Stories of Ernest Hemingway*, xvi.

2. Charles Scribner Jr., foreword to *DLT*, xvi–xvii.

3. Smith, *Guide to the Short Stories*, 193.

4. Stephen Cooper, *The Politics of Ernest Hemingway*, 8.

5. Peter L. Hays, "Hemingway as Social and Political Writer," 111.

6. Ibid.

7. Hemingway ran into the same kind of problem with uninformed readers when he tried to place "Homage to Switzerland." That story focuses on three European politicians, with narratives handled repetitively and ironically; but if readers did not know the significance of the men portrayed, the story would seem ineffective. In a letter Hemingway wrote to a collector on August 15, 1932, he said nothing about politics but pointed instead to the fact that he had created "a new form" so that "the fact that the three parts all open the same way—or practically the same is intentional and is supposed to represent Switzerland metaphysically" (*SL* 367).

8. Cooper, *Politics of Ernest Hemingway*, 134.

9. Stephens, *Hemingway's Nonfiction*, 100.

10. Frederic J. Svoboda, "Houses and Museums," 130. Svoboda assesses Hemingway's continuous need for domestic comfort. He saw the writer's complex persona—which had "a domestic as well as adventurous side"—dominated by his need to live "a rather conventional, middle-class life."

11. Kert, *The Hemingway Women*, 227. John Raeburn notes that *Vanity Fair* nominated Hemingway and Pauline as "America's Favorite Gypsy Couple," replacing movie stars Douglas Fairbanks and Mary Pickford (*Fame Became of Him*, 49).

12. Kert, *The Hemingway Women*, 229.

13. Michael Reynolds, *Hemingway: The 1930s*, 54.

14. Reynolds is the most candid of Hemingway's biographers. He states that Hemingway "was never comfortable with his own children until they were old enough to fish and hunt. Then he was their instructor, showing them the way water changes color over the reef, teaching them to clean their kill, instructing them. . . . Hemingway was not good at communicating this love when they were small, nor did he let them interfere with either of his two driving interests: the outdoor life and writing" (*The 1930s*, 189).

15. See Robert W. Trogdon, "'I Am Constructing a Legend': Ernest Hemingway in Guy Hickok's *Brooklyn Daily Eagle* Articles," on the closeness of the men's friendship.

16. Without quoting the lists and descriptions about the Cuban and Gulf fish, one can easily believe that Hemingway thought of himself as a student—not only of the country but of its plants, fish, animals, and weather. The same was true of other places. In an essay about Hemingway's fascination with the French bicycle races, for example, William Boelhower makes the point that not only did Hadley, Pauline, and Ernest all have bicycles that they rode vigorously in Paris and other locations (Hemingway dressed in "a striped jumper like a contestant on the Tour de France") but when Dos Passos went with Hemingway to the six-day bicycle races, Dos Passos remarked that his friend "knew all the statistics and the names and lives of the riders" (William Boelhower, "Hemingway, the Figure of the Bicycle, and the Avant-Garde Paris," 55). Hemingway warned Dos Passos *not* to write about the races because they were "his domain" (Dos Passos, *Best Times*, 145).

17. Kert, *The Hemingway Women*, 246; see Brian, *True Gen*, 90.

18. Baker, *A Life Story*, 222, 244; Kert, *The Hemingway Women*, 27–72. Although there may have been a sexual affair, Baker notes that Jane Mason's instability (one time wrecking her car while Jack and Patrick rode in the backseat) would have cooled Hemingway's professed ardor. He supposedly wrote his war-trauma story "A Way You'll Never Be" for her. After she fell or jumped from a second-story height and broke her back, she spent months at Doctor's Hospital in New York. During her stay in New York, she made some of her letters from Hemingway available to her psychiatrist, Lawrence Kubie—an act that infuriated Hemingway.

19. Raeburn, *Fame Became of Him*, 46.

20. Ibid., 49.

21. Ibid., 84.

22. Marilyn Elkins, "The Fashion of Machismo," 102. Elkins references a 1934 *Vanity Fair* article that included paper dolls, in appropriate costumes, designed as Hemingway in various kinds of dress: "Ernie, the Neanderthal Man," "Ernie as Isaac Walton," "Ernie as Don Jose, the Toreador," and "Ernie the Unknown Soldier," among others. Each choice reaffirmed Hemingway's masculinity, his hard-won struggle to avoid an effete profile.

23. His April 1936 letter, "On the Blue Water: A Gulf Stream Letter," gave readers Santiago's story in miniature, later to be told in *The Old Man and the Sea*. In a June 1935 essay for *Outdoor Life*, Hemingway provided the narrative of voracious sharks ("Beating Sharks to a Marlin").

24. Quoted in Reynolds, *The 1930s*, 212.

25. James H. Meredith, "Hemingway's Key West Band of Brothers, the World War I Veterans in 'Who Murdered the Vets?' and *To Have and Have Not*," 242–43.

26. Ernest Hemingway, "Who Murdered the Vets?" 9.

27. Ibid. Hemingway's descriptions were intentionally graphic: "There were bodies floating in the ferry slip. The railroad embankment was gone and the men who had cowered behind it and finally, when the water came, clung to the rails, were all gone with it. You could find them face down and face up in the mangroves. They hung on

there, in shelter, until the wind and the rising water carried them away. They didn't all let go at once but only when they could hold on no longer. Then further on you found them high in the trees where the wind swept them. You found men everywhere and in the sun all of them were beginning to be too big for their blue jeans and jackets that they could never fill when they were on the bum and hungry" (ibid.).

Chapter Six | Hemingway's Epics

1. Michael S. Reynolds, *Hemingway: The Final Years*, 129.

2. John J. Teunissen, "*For Whom the Bell Tolls* as Mythic Narrative," 224.

3. Alex Vernon warns against tying *For Whom the Bell Tolls* too directly to the Spanish Civil War. He asks that the novel "be read less as a historical gesture than as a contemporaneous call for resolve by all those opposed to fascism, not just Spain's defeated antifascists" (*Teaching Hemingway and War*, 4).

4. Smith, *Guide to the Short Stories*, xvi.

5. Baker, *A Life Story*, 245.

6. On his return from the safari, Hemingway bought his diesel-powered thirty-eight-foot boat with an advance from Gingrich for *Esquire* letters. Named the *Pilar* (for the Zaragoza shrine as well as for Pauline), the $7,500 boat made possible his trips to Bimini to go fishing. Baker says that Hemingway was "in a state of rapture" when the boat was delivered in the spring of 1934 (*A Life Story*, 245).

7. In December 1940, Hemingway wrote that his tax rate had climbed to 62 percent (*SL* 521); the following year he explained to Pauline about the $500 a month he agreed to pay her after their divorce, "I pay over $15,000 tax on the $6000 you get tax free" (*SL* 525).

8. Anthony E. Rebollo, "The Taxation of Ernest Hemingway," 413–30.

9. Because Hemingway lived at least partly on Hadley Richardson's inheritance during their marriage and then on the finances that Pauline Pfeiffer brought to their marriage, it could be that taxes were less of an issue during those years. But once he had married Martha Gellhorn, who earned her living as a journalist, and then subsequently during his last marriage, to Mary Welsh, who did not earn income at that time, the constant payment of federal and state taxes became only *his* burden, necessarily increasing his frustration and anxiety.

10. Kashkeen, "Alive in the Midst of Death," 168; Wylder, *Hemingway's Heroes*, 124.

11. Svoboda, "Great Themes in Hemingway," 160. It is somewhat more dramatically presented in the novel, when Harry talks to the captain as he is being rescued: "'Like trying to pass cars on the top of hills. On that road in Cuba. On any road. Anywhere. Just like that. I mean how things are. The way that they been going. . . . A man,' Harry Morgan said. . . . 'One man alone ain't got. No man alone now.' He stopped. 'No matter how a man alone ain't got no bloody fucking chance.' He shut his eyes. It had taken him a long time to get it out and it had taken him all of his life to learn it" (*THAHN* 225).

12. Toni Morrison, *Playing in the Dark: Whiteness and the Literary Imagination*, 71, 76.

13. When Hemingway earlier wrote to Perkins about *To Have and Have Not*, it sounded much richer. The book was to contrast Key West with Cuba, and it "also contains what I know about the mechanics of revolution and what it does to the people engaged in it. There are two themes in it—the decline of the individual—The Man Harry—who shows up first in 'One Trip Across'—and then his re-emergence as Key West goes down around him—and the story of a shipment of dynamite. . . . Also have the hurricane and the vets in it" (*SL* 448). See James Meredith's "Hemingway's Key West Band of Brothers" for important information about Hemingway's use of the veterans in this novel. Meredith also argues that what Hemingway learned in writing *To Have and Have Not* gave him important practice in handling the multiple narratives of *For Whom the Bell Tolls*.

14. Alex Vernon views Frederic Henry, as he leaves the hospital and "in the rain" continues his despairing walk, as intending to commit suicide—giving real force to the idea of surrogacy; his great loss compounds "the problem of his general war trauma and his malaise and self-disregard. He has no purpose, no reason for being in the Italian army nor, one suspects, for being at all" (*Hemingway's Second War*, 202–5).

15. Hemingway chose to include the section of the novel about Sordo in his *Men at War* anthology, obviously proud of the way Sordo tricks the forces that outnumber him and his remaining four men.

16. Hoffman, *The Twenties*, 97.

17. That he seems to have written both African stories in a kind of secrecy feeds into this autobiographical suggestion. In his 2015 fictionalized account, Hotchner draws the scene of Hemingway's telling Fitzgerald that he had been right about Pauline. "No matter what they tell you about reliving the past, it's not a bridge, and you can't go back over it. . . . Her money corrupted both of us." Later the Hemingway figure adds, "Being together was boring" (Hotchner, *Hemingway in Love*, 144; see Kert, *The Hemingway Women*; Caroline Moorehead, *Gellhorn: A Twentieth-Century Life*; Ruth A. Hawkins, *Unbelievable Happiness and Final Sorrow: The Hemingway-Pfeiffer Marriage*; Verna Kale, *Ernest Hemingway: A Critical Life*; and Baker, *A Life Story*). That the fictional characters had been married for eleven years took Hemingway's chronology back to his earliest days of friendship with Pauline Pfeiffer.

18. Rose Marie Burwell, *Hemingway: The Postwar Years and the Posthumous Novels*, 141.

19. James Plath, "Barking at Death: Hemingway, Africa, and the Stages of Dying," 311. Plath points out that the fifth "memory" section, the ascent to the mountaintop, is—unexpectedly—*not* italicized; Hemingway wanted the reader to be confused, or to see that the line between life and death blurs. Of interest too is the observation Mark Spilka makes about the elaborate description of the pilot for the rescue aircraft: "old Compton" is a British pilot from Kipling's imaginary world of male camaraderie. In leaving with this vestige of the male bonding that Hemingway had so longed for, Harry denies Helen any role in his death. See Spilka, "Abusive and Nonabusive Dying in Hemingway's Fiction," 216.

20. Hays, "Hemingway as Social and Political Writer," 115.

21. Morrison, *Playing in the Dark*, 58.

22. Ernest Hemingway, preface to *The First Forty-Nine [Stories]*, 3–4.

23. In Hemingway's publisher's note to the first printing of the play, he explained usefully that "the title refers to the Spanish rebel statement in the fall of 1936 that they had four columns advancing on Madrid and a Fifth Column of sympathizers inside the city to attack the defenders of the city from the rear." The four columns advancing on Madrid shot their prisoners. When members of the Fifth Column were captured inside the city in the early days of the war, they were also shot. Hemingway was torn between telling truths and protecting the rebel side; he continued, "Later they were to be tried and given prison or labor camp sentences or sentences to execution depending upon the crimes they had committed against the Republic. But in the early days they were shot. They deserved to be, under the rules of war, and they expected to be" (*FC* iv–v).

24. Jose Luis Castillo-Puche, *Hemingway in Spain*, 13.

25. Vernon, *Hemingway's Second War*, 164–65.

26. Amanda Vaill, *Hotel Florida: Truth, Love, and Death in the Spanish Civil War*, xxiii, 102, 113.

27. Ibid., 149.

28. "Fascism Is a Lie," 4. Quoted in Kert, *The Hemingway Women*, 304. Kert also quotes a pro-Loyalist address by Gellhorn, delivered the next day before the American Writers Congress. Gellhorn pointed out, "The writers who are now in Spain . . . were just brave, intelligent people doing an essential job in war . . . completely unaware of *themselves*. . . . A man who has given a year of his life, without heroics or boastfulness, to the war in Spain, or who, in the same way, has given a year of his life to steel strikes, or to the unemployed, or to the problems of racial prejudice, has not lost or wasted time. He is a man who has known where he belonged" (304).

29. Among the fallout from Hemingway's involvement in the Spanish Civil War was his seeming lack of concern for the fate of José Robles, a good friend and translator of John Dos Passos's. Robles was also Vladimir Gorev's aide. Vaill speculates that Robles (perhaps) knew too much about Russia's plans for Spain. Whatever the reasons, Robles was killed, and it took years for Dos Passos's friendship with Hemingway to resume. See Vaill, *Hotel Florida*, 175, 359.

30. Gregory H. Hemingway, *Papa: A Personal Memoir*, 6, 23; Gregory Hemingway's italics.

31. Scribner also worried about Hemingway's use of Andre Marty's real name toward the end of the novel, to which concern Hemingway wrote, "Andre Marty is the name of a real person. . . . He really had the people shot and is in no position to sue. Also he is a fugitive from justice" (*SL* 510).

32. Ernest Hemingway, preface to *The Great Crusade*, xi; my italics.

33. Hemingway did not forgive Agustin's bloodthirsty responses; in fact, Jordan says to himself, with very little self-satisfaction, "You have liked to kill as all who are soldiers by choice have enjoyed it at some time whether they lie about it or not" (*FWBT* 286).

34. In his study of the manuscript versions of this novel, critic Thomas Gould points out that "revision" of the book meant that Hemingway *expanded* sections that made the case against war. It was, in Gould's words, as if Hemingway's "message" to his readers

was that "war is a violent and tragic assault on the bodies and emotions of all those involved, so do not enter into it lightly or with any misconceptions" ("'Anti-War Correspondence,' Reshaping Death in *For Whom the Bell Tolls*," 248).

35. A few hours before this scene, Jordan had mused, "How little we know of what there is to know. I wish that I were going to live a long time instead of going to die today because I have learned much about life in these four days; more, I think, than in all the other time. I'd like to be an old man and to really know" (*FWBT* 380).

36. In the midst of relentless action, this moment of stillness is an example of what Charles Molesworth describes as "the emotional balance or mediation" required to maintain "the core of the moral vision in the novel." Spoken most explicitly by Anselmo, this vision is "most artistically complex and interesting when the pressures are greatest" ("Hemingway's Code: The Spanish Civil War and the World Power," 84–85).

37. Teunissen, "*For Whom the Bell Tolls* as Mythic Narrative," 234.

38. Allen Josephs, *"For Whom the Bell Tolls": Ernest Hemingway's Undiscovered Country*, 81, 84.

39. H. R. Stoneback, "'The Priest Did Not Answer': Hemingway, the Church, the Party, and *For Whom the Bell Tolls*," 101–2. Stoneback's essay provides a hagiography of the Catholic saints—Andres (Saint Andrew), Sordo (Santiago, or Saint James), Anselmo (Saint Anselm), and Pablo (Saint Paul); he also makes interesting points about the relationship between Pablo and the priest during the extermination of the fascist villagers.

40. Lawrence R. Broer, "Bulls and Bells: Their Toll on Robert Jordan," 201–02, citing *FWBT* 370.

41. Donald F. Bouchard, *Hemingway, So Far from Simple*, 98. Bouchard defines as "epic" the way Hemingway structured all "relationships to time, and, in broad terms, Hemingway's African adventure explores the effects of time and its use and abuse."

42. Gerry Brenner, who early claimed an epic categorization for the novel, compares the description of Jordan's last act to that of Roland's rearguard martyrdom in the eighth century, reminding readers of the lengthy tradition of epic heroes who choose to die (*Concealments in Hemingway's Works*, 5).

Chapter Seven | To the War Once Again

1. Baker, *A Life Story*, 363. According to Baker, the prize was going to go to Hemingway, but then the Pulitzer judges' vote was overridden by Nicholas Murray Butler, the president of Columbia University (the site of the governance for all Pulitzer prizes). He declared the book unsuitable. The fact that the novel had earlier sold many copies because it was a major Book-of-the-Month Club selection did not lessen Hemingway's disappointment.

2. Moorehead, *Gellhorn*, 173.

3. James H. Meredith, "War: World War II," 406.

4. Martha Gellhorn, *Travels with Myself and Another*, 20–22.

5. Peter Moreira, *Hemingway on the China Front: His WWII Spy Mission with Martha Gellhorn*, xv–xvi, 56.

6. Travel conditions remained difficult. As Hemingway wrote to Perkins about the return flight from Rangoon, "The last leg of the trip from Kunming to here was pretty bad and when we got over Hongkong the static was so bad the telefunken would not work and with a 200 foot ceiling we circled for nearly an hour before we could get down through. Have flown 18,000 some miles since I saw you last and have about 12,000 more to fly before see you again" (*SL* 522).

7. Reynolds, *Annotated Chronology*, 98.

8. Moreira, *Hemingway on the China Front*, 204.

9. Patrick Hemingway, foreword to *HOW*, xii.

10. Doug Underwood, *Chronicling Trauma: Journalists and Writers on Violence and Loss*, 152.

11. Meredith, "War: World War II," 402.

12. Brian, *True Gen*, 91–92, 98. Peter Moreira, too, sees evidence of what he terms Hemingway's "deterioration" during the early forties: "The unpleasant side of his character became more prominent, his boasts became lies, his bluster became bullying, and his insensitivity to his wives became abusive" (*Hemingway on the China Front*, 199).

13. Susan F. Beegel, "Hemingway and Hemochromatosis," 375–76.

14. Hendrickson, *Hemingway's Boat*, 252.

15. Vernon, "War: World War I," 392.

16. Moorehead, *Gellhorn*, 187, 198.

17. Patrick Hemingway, foreword to *HOW*, xiii.

18. Terry Mort, *The Hemingway Patrols*, 129, 142–43, 153, 226.

19. Moorehead, *Gellhorn*, 198; Kert, *The Hemingway Women*, 291; and see Baker, *A Life Story*, 376–80. According to Moorehead and Kert, Gellhorn could not sympathize with these "missions" and saw her spouse and his often derelict cronies as men playing soldier, drinking day and night, and living a fantasy life that was an insult to the real military activity in Europe.

20. Quoted in Burwell, *Hemingway*, 43–44. He often took his two younger sons to this location with him. As Mort wonders, if Hemingway really believed in the possibility of his U-boat hunting finding something, would he expose his children to that risk? Mort, *Hemingway Patrols*, 153–54.

21. Baker, *A Life Story*, 380; Moorehead, *Gellhorn*, 135–36.

22. Moorehead, *Gellhorn*, 198; Baker, *A Life Story*, 380.

23. Burwell, *Hemingway*, 44. Burwell's account of Hemingway's FBI file (the existence of which, later in Hemingway's life, caused him much anguish) stresses that J. Edgar Hoover did not want to offend American Ambassador to Cuba Spruille Braden, who admired Hemingway and was supporting the sub-hunting operation. That effort cost Braden more than twice what the State Department had authorized (it included salaries for the crew and gas for the *Pilar*). Hoover feared both Hemingway's writing (he was supposedly working on a novel about his anti-German activities) and Gellhorn's friendship with President and Mrs. Roosevelt.

24. Moorehead, *Gellhorn*, 216–17; Reynolds, *Annotated Chronology*, 103.

25. Baker, *A Life Story*, 392.

26. Brian, *True Gen*, 150.

27. Ibid., 150, 154.

28. Ibid., 212.

29. John Groth, *Studio: Europe*, 11. Groth's observation echoes what Edwin Rolfe said about Hemingway during the Spanish Civil War: "Among the American visitors, the outstanding one, and the one best-loved by the Lincoln boys . . . was Ernest Hemingway. The presence of this huge, bull-shouldered man with the questioning eyes and the full-hearted interest in everything Spain was fighting for instilled in the tired Americans [of the Lincoln Brigade] some of his own strength and quiet unostentatious courage" (*The Lincoln Battalion*, 70).

30. Baker, *A Life Story*, 397.

31. Ibid., 399.

32. Brian, *True Gen*, 151.

33. Baker, *A Life Story*, 403.

34. Brian, *True Gen*, 159; and see Leicester Hemingway, *My Brother, Ernest Hemingway*.

35. Robert Fuller, "Hemingway at Rambouillet," 68. Robert Stephens made the point in 1968 that security during war likely curtails journalists' ability to cover the fighting. He explained that "the *Collier's* series was uneven. . . . Hemingway's intrusive personality accounted, in part at least, for the highs and lows. In 'London Fights the Robots' he was hobbled by security measures in his attempts to tell either about German rocket performances or those of British interceptors. In place of facts he attempted to substitute manner and the result was an unhappy failure to convey the interceptor pilots' lyric feeling for their planes" (*Hemingway's Nonfiction*, 337).

36. See the transcript in appendix A of Denis Brian's *True Gen* (323–31) and in the National Archives in College Park, Maryland. See also Reynolds, *The Final Years*, 105.

37. The rough-and-tumble Hemingway also made an appearance in this letter. He described for his son that he had "lost my Burberry raincoat . . . have a battle jacket with the zipper broken held together by safety pins. Wear same two shirts worn last two months, both at once, have head cold, chest cold, trouble on both flanks, shelling the Bejesus behind, shelling the ditto ahead . . . and never felt happier."

38. Brian, *True Gen*, 169.

39. Vonnegut, "Kurt Vonnegut on Ernest Hemingway," 23.

40. Mort, *Hemingway Patrols*, 130.

41. Meredith, "War: World War II," 407.

42. Susan F. Beegel, "The Monster of Cojimar: A Meditation on Hemingway, Sharks, and War," 12; Meyers, *Hemingway*, 411; and see William Walton, "The Battle of Huertgen Forest"; Whiting, *Papa Goes to War;* and Meredith, "War: World War II."

43. Meredith, "War: World War II," 408. Shrouded in secrecy, as all dimensions of the United States correspondents' role of necessity were, and complicated in this case by Hemingway's visible celebrity, the standard journalistic proof of the facts of Hemingway's participation does not exist—particularly after Hemingway's interrogation at Nancy that October.

44. Ibid.

Chapter Eight | After the War

1. As early as October 8, 1944, when Hemingway was in Nancy being interrogated, he wrote to Lanham, "Buck I miss you very much. I feel like a swine here while you fight." He continued, "Have some luck and if anything ever happens to us we will all have a fine time with the better element in hell" (*SL* 573–74).

2. Stephens, *Hemingway's Nonfiction*, 84–85.

3. Stanley Cooperman, "Old Age Ideally Brings Humility and True Pride to Man," 76, 78. Earlier in this essay, Cooperman summarizes the themes within Hemingway's writing, that his "overriding fear is not loss of life . . . but loss of will: the failure of manhood itself. And it was the divinity of manhood—a *mystique* defined by the sacred trinity of willed sacrifice, pride, and endurance—which Hemingway worshipped (and worried) throughout his life."

4. Beegel, "The Monster of Cojimar," 10–12; and see Reynolds, *The Final Years*, 117–25.

5. Hemingway, "An Interview with Ernest Hemingway," 30.

6. Beegel, "The Monster of Cojimar," 13.

7. Reynolds, *The Final Years*, 105.

8. Ibid., 113, 125. Carlos Baker tells a variant of this story, but this time Pelkey was driving a motorcycle and Robert Capa was the third man. The Germans were firing from the ground, not the air. But Hemingway's keen hearing remained the point of the story. See Baker, *A Life Story*, 405.

9. Hendrickson, *Hemingway's Boat*, 336–37.

10. Baker, *A Life Story*, 443–44.

11. Underwood, *Chronicling Trauma*, 18–19.

12. Miller, *Drama of the Gifted Child*, 38–40.

13. Baker, *A Life Story*, 442–43.

14. Burwell, *Hemingway*, 48; Michael S. Reynolds, "Hemingway as American Icon," 7.

15. In the manuscript of *Islands in the Stream*, begun during that postwar year, Hemingway expressed a similar sentiment through the mind of the character Roger: "He had replaced everything except the boys with work and the steady hard-working life he had built on the island. That is, he thought he had. I would rather love a good house and the sea and my work than a woman, he thought. He knew it could never be true. But he could almost make it" (*IIS* 7).

16. Quoted in Burwell, *Hemingway*, 95.

17. Ibid., 50.

18. Joseph Warren Beach, "How Do You Like It Now, Gentlemen?" 232.

19. Ernest Hemingway, "Talk with Mr. Hemingway," 14. Digressing into a discussion of what ideal literary criticism should be, Hemingway explained to Breit, "Many times critics do not understand a work when a writer tries for something he has not attempted before." See also Ernest Hemingway, "Success, It's Wonderful!" 58.

20. Hemingway, "Success," 58.

21. Thomas Strychacz attributes the difference between Hemingway's earlier writing about war and his accomplishment in *For Whom the Bell Tolls* to the author's

shifting attitudes: "His experience in the Spanish Civil War and his awareness of the rise of Fascism reshaped his opinions of what war was *for*. . . . *For Whom the Bell Tolls* seems to argue that war is a horror that must be endured if Fascism is to be defeated" (Strychacz, "Seeing through Fractures," 78).

22. Benson, *Hemingway*, 88.

23. Meyers, *Hemingway*, 470–71.

24. Michael Seefeldt, "Reconsidering the Travesty of Himself," 254–55.

25. Brian, *True Gen*, 226.

26. Brenner, *Concealments in Hemingway's Works*, 5.

27. Seefeldt, "Reconsidering the Travesty of Himself," 253.

28. Baker, *A Life Story*, 477.

29. Robert E. Gajdusek, *Hemingway in His Own Country*, 373.

30. Mark P. Ott, "Tanks, Butterflies, Realists, Idealists: Hemingway, Dos Passos, and the Imperfect Ending in Spain of 1937–1938," 157, 160.

31. Adam R. Long, "Artifice and Reality: The Blending of Venice and America in *Across the River and Into the Trees*," 185–86 in manuscript.

32. Criticism about gender since the 1990s has benefited from the work of Nancy Comley and Robert Scholes, Carl Eby, Debra Moddelmog, and others. Jennifer Haytock perhaps expresses the author's difficulties in this novel when she says, "Hemingway recognized the complexity of both masculinity and femininity as well as the dependent relationship between these concepts. . . . His war writings provide an opportunity to explore what happens to masculinity when *femininity* changes" (*At Home, at War*, 80).

33. Giacomo Ivancich, "Address to the Hemingway Society Congress—June 22, 2014," 18–19 in manuscript.

34. Hemingway to Adriana Ivancich, April 10 and 15 and June 16, 1950, Ernest Hemingway Collection, John F. Kennedy Library.

35. Philip Young, *Ernest Hemingway: A Reconsideration*, 118–19.

36. Sarah Wood Anderson, *Readings of Trauma, Madness, and the Body*, 23, 28.

Chapter Nine | *The Old Man and the Sea*

1. Harvey Breit, *The Writer Observed*, 171.

2. Hemingway, "A Letter from Ernest Hemingway," 122.

3. James H. Meredith, "Hemingway's Spain in Flames, 1937," 146. To those cataclysmic events, Marc Seals adds the loss of Hemingway's first cache of good writing. Given that Hemingway found his true emotional center in his work of writing, Hadley's seemingly careless handling of the suitcase that contained all his fiction could be figured as a betrayal of his art (or, broadly interpreted, of his life). Seals discusses Hemingway's writing about the loss in his fiction. (See Seals, "Trauma Theory and Hemingway's Lost Paris Manuscripts," 78–83, and Ronald E. McFarland, *Appropriating Hemingway*.) Hemingway spent a good proportion of his preface to Lee Samuels's *A Hemingway Check List* telling the story again of "the loss of everything the husband had written and not yet published (original manuscript, typewritten copy and carbons, each in its separate folder) through having a suitcase stolen in the Gare de Lyons in

1922 . . . while she [his wife] went out to buy herself a bottle of Vittel water" (n.p.).
Peter Hays discusses adding to any list of possible traumatic experiences Hemingway's
many head and brain injuries, as well as such happenings as the author created or
remembered in "Indian Camp" ("Hemingway, PTSD, and Clinical Depression," 141).

    4. Mark Cirino, *Ernest Hemingway: Thought in Action*, 43–51.

    5. Bouchard, *Hemingway*, 150.

    6. Beegel, "The Monster of Cojimar," 26–27.

    7. Hemingway used this figure, 122 killed, frequently, although there is no evidence
at all that he killed any Germans. His son Jack questioned the statement, saying, "I
think that's what he probably wished he had done. I suspect he killed some. His contacts with the OSS came up during the breakthrough to Paris and then anything was
likely to have happened" (Brian, *True Gen*, 161).

    8. Several years after the novella was published, on September 24, 1954, Heming-
way wrote candidly to Bernard Berenson, "I have an exaggerated confidence in the Old
Man book. Each day I wrote I marveled at how wonderfully it was going and I hoped
that on the next day I would be able to invent truly as I had done the day before. When
I had finished, there were only 3 or 4 corrections to be made and I thought there must
be something wrong, but each time I read it, it made the same effect on me as a reader,
not as one who had written it, that it made before. I still can't read it without emotion"
(*SL* 836).

    9. William Faulkner said this in his review of the novella for *Shenandoah*: "His best.
Time may show it to be the best single piece of any of us, I mean his and my contemporaries. This time, he discovered God, a Creator. Until now, his men and women
had made themselves, shaped themselves out of their own clay; their victories and
defeats were at the hands of each other. . . . But this time, he wrote about pity: about
something somewhere that made them all. . . . It's all right. Praise God that whatever
made and loves and pities Hemingway and me kept him from touching it any further"
("Review of *The Old Man and the Sea*," 273).

    10. Charles Scribner Jr. died suddenly on February 11, 1952, of a heart attack; from
that time on, Wallace Meyer was Hemingway's editor at Scribner's.

    11. Reynolds, *The Final Years*, 297.

    12. In H. R. Stoneback's detailed discussion of Santiago's origins—contrary to his
being assumed to be from Cuba—he makes several key points. One is that in the
Canary Islands, three of Hemingway's favorite places fused—Spain, Africa, and Cuba.
The blue-eyed protagonist is, according to the Islands' belief system, not only "strange"
and "mystical" but, probably, deeply religious, and his effort to find and kill the marlin
could be seen as a pilgrimage. Stoneback, "'You Know the Name Is No Accident':
Hemingway and the Matter of Santiago," 168–69.

    13. Leo Marx, *The Machine in the Garden: Technology and the Pastoral Ideal in Ameri-
ca*, 362–63; Susan F. Beegel, "Thor Heyerdahl's *Kon-Tiki* and Hemingway's Return to
Primitivism in *The Old Man and the Sea*," 546.

    14. Seefeldt, "Reconsidering the Travesty of Himself," 262.

    15. Reynolds, *The Final Years*, 211.

    16. Debra Moddelmog, "Queer Families in Hemingway's Fiction," 174.

    17. Carlos Baker, "The Boy and the Lions," 306.

18. "I'll never tell them anything again. If they kill him Juma will drink his share of the ivory or just buy himself another god-damned wife. . . . Never, never tell them. Try and remember that. Never tell anyone anything ever. Never tell anyone anything again" (*CSS* 550).

19. Cooperman, "Old Age," 81–82.

20. Bouchard, *Hemingway*, 169.

21. Ibid., 163.

22. Ibid., 164.

23. H. R. Stoneback, "Pilgrimage Variations, Hemingway's Sacred Landscapes," 460–61. Stoneback attributes what he calls the "deep structure" of the 1926 novel to Jake's pilgrimage "on the road of Santiago—from Paris to Bayonne to Roncevaux to Pamplona," concluding that both Jake Barnes and Hemingway "knew the moral and spiritual anguish and joy of the true pilgrim" (461). See also F. I. Carpenter, "Hemingway Achieves the Fifth Dimension," and Joseph J. Waldmeir, "*Confiteor Hominem*: Ernest Hemingway's Religion of Man."

24. Stoneback, "'You Know the Name Is No Accident,'" 169.

25. Stoneback, "Pilgrimage Variations," 462.

26. Ibid., 464.

27. Ibid. With some acerbity, Stoneback reminds his readers, and Hemingway's, that "Santiago is *not* a Christ figure; he is a *Santiago* figure. . . . Santiago may not be 'religious,' as he protests, but he is devout." The critic continues, "He is a celebration and a celebrant in the communion of all being, all nature, and an emblem of the dignity of all people, working people, poor people, and of all who suffer and endure with courage, pride, humility, and compassion" ("'You Know the Name Is No Accident,'" 168–74, 177).

28. Bouchard, *Hemingway*, 157.

Chapter Ten | The Late Years

1. Michael R. Federspiel remarks that Petoskey, Michigan, near where the Hemingways had a cottage, in the fall was very different than in summer: "It was quiet: the wind cutting and the water a cold, icy gray. [Hemingway] wandered the streets, hanging out at the local barbershop, the train station, and the new Carnegie Library." When he wrote, he used Bill Smith's typewriter, which he had borrowed. *Picturing Hemingway's Michigan*, 172.

2. Susan F. Beegel, "The Environment," 240–41.

3. Years later, Hemingway repeated this sentiment about living in Cuba: "I always had good luck writing in Cuba. It is close to the water front; it is out of town and on a hill so that it is cool at night. It is a good place to work and live and keep in shape to write as well as I can. . . . You find me a place in Ohio where I can live on the top of a hill and be fifteen minutes away from the Gulf Stream and have my own fruit and vegetables the year round . . . and I'll go live in Ohio" ("Letter from Ernest Hemingway," 122–23).

4. Hemingway's letter to Flanner mentioned as well that one reason for going to Africa was so that he would "get very tired too with nothing connected with my head

and see the animals without them seeing you" (*SL* 387). From his Paris days on, every-one who knew Hemingway understood his recurrent insomnia.

5. Selden Rodman, "Ernest Hemingway," 55.

6. Mary Welsh Hemingway, *How It Was*, 102–03, 166, 168; Kert, *The Hemingway Women*, 414–16.

7. *Look* magazine sponsored much of the safari, planning to publish a feature story based on Theisen's photographs. But Theisen left October 1. The good hunting he had witnessed deteriorated through the fall, and by December the happy mood of the safari had turned grim.

8. Baker, *A Life Story*, 514. The following description of the safari is also from this work.

9. Ibid., 521; Reynolds, *The Final Years*, 274; Frederick Voss, *Picturing Hemingway: A Writer in His Time*, 42.

10. Quoted in Hendrickson, *Hemingway's Boat*, 426.

11. Meredith, "Hemingway's Spain in Flames," 146.

12. Brian, *True Gen*, 238. Mary Hemingway countered this assumption in inter-views with Brian. For instance, she said, "That year he had hepatitis, Ernest didn't drink anything for fourteen months. Before and after that we usually had two martinis before lunch and two or three martinis before dinner together and at least a bottle of wine, and depending on the number of guests more bottles of wine. Ernest never took anything after dinner, or only on the rarest occasions. He would go to bed at ten-thirty or eleven and wake about daybreak without having had anything alcoholic since dinner."

13. Ibid.

14. Reynolds, *The Final Years*, 302.

15. Anders Österling, "Award Ceremony Speech," Nobel Prize in Literature 1954, Nobel Foundation, http://www.nobelprize.org/nobel_prizes/literature/laure-ates/1954/press.html.

16. Ernest Hemingway, "Nobel Prize in Literature Acceptance Speech"; reprinted in Baker, *A Life Story*, 528–29. In an earlier set of comments, Hemingway listed his regret that neither Mark Twain nor Henry James ever received the award—and he also listed Isak Dinesen, Bernard Berenson, and Carl Sandburg (*A Life Story*, 527).

17. Reynolds, *The 1930s*, 213.

18. Hemingway, introduction to *A Farewell to Arms*, ix.

19. Like much in his later life, starting to write first thing in the morning was a ritual for Hemingway. He explained to George Plimpton during the *Paris Review* conversation that he started work "as soon after first light as possible. . . . When you stop you are as empty, and at the same time never empty but filling" (Hemingway, "An Interview with Ernest Hemingway," 24–25).

20. In his perseverance in the face of approaching death, Cantwell was much like Hemingway, his creator. A few pages after this thought, Cantwell reminds himself, "Figuring things out has been your trade. Figuring things out when they were shoot-ing at you." And he continues that line of thought, "I have killed enough and I have shot as well or better than I can shoot" (*ARIT* 291–92).

21. Manuscript #260, Ernest Hemingway Collection, John F. Kennedy Library.

BIBLIOGRAPHY

Primary

Hemingway, Ernest. *Across the River and into the Trees*. New York: Scribner's, 1950.

———. *By-Line: Ernest Hemingway: Selected Articles and Dispatches of Four Decades*. Ed. William White. New York: Scribner's, 1967.

———. *Complete Poems*. Ed. Nicholas Gerogiannis. Lincoln: University of Nebraska Press, 1992.

———. *The Complete Short Stories of Ernest Hemingway: The Finca Vigia Edition*. New York: Scribner's, 1987.

———. *The Dangerous Summer*. New York: Scribner's, 1985.

———. *Death in the Afternoon*. New York: Scribner's, 1932.

———. "Dying, Well or Badly." *Ken*, April 21, 1938.

———. Ernest Hemingway Collection. John F. Kennedy Presidential Library and Museum, Boston, MA.

———. Ernest Hemingway Collection. Harry Ransom Humanities Research Center, University of Texas at Austin.

———. *Ernest Hemingway, Dateline: Toronto, The Complete "Toronto Star" Dispatches, 1920–1924*. Ed. William White. New York: Scribner's, 1985.

———. *Ernest Hemingway: 88 Poems*. Ed. Nicholas Gerogiannis. New York: Harcourt Brace, 1979.

———. Ernest Hemingway Papers. Lilly Library, Indiana University Bloomington.

———. *Ernest Hemingway: The Selected Letters, 1917–1961*. Ed. Carlos Baker. New York: Scribner's, 1981.

———. "Ernest Hemingway Talks of Work and War." In *Writers and Writing*, by Robert Van Gelder, 95-98. New York: Scribner's, 1946.

———. *A Farewell to Arms*. New York: Scribner's, 1929.

———. *A Farewell to Arms*. Hemingway Library Edition. Ed. Sean Hemingway. New York: Scribner's, 2012.

———. "Fascism Is a Lie." *New Masses*, June 22, 1937, 4.

———. *"The Fifth Column" and Four Stories of the Spanish Civil War*. New York: Scribner's, 1968.

————. Foreword to *A Fly-Fisher's Life*, by Charles Ritz, 7. Trans. Humphrey Hare. London: Max Reinhardt, 1957.

————. Foreword to *Man and Beast in Africa*, by Francois Sommer, 5–7. Trans. Edward Fitzgerald. London: Herbert Jenkins, 1953.

————. Foreword to *Man in the Ranks: The Story of Twelve Americans in Spain*, by Joseph North, n.p. New York: Friends of the Abraham Lincoln Brigade, 1939.

————. Foreword to *Treasury for the Free World*, ed. Ben Raeburn, xiii–xv. New York: Arco, 1946.

————. *For Whom the Bell Tolls*. New York: Scribner's, 1940.

————. *The Garden of Eden*. New York: Scribner's, 1986.

————. *Green Hills of Africa*. New York: Scribner's, 1935.

————. *Hemingway and the Mechanism of Fame: Statements, Public Letters, Introductions, Forewords, Prefaces, Blurbs, Reviews, and Endorsements*. Ed. Matthew J. Bruccoli. Columbia: University of South Carolina Press, 2006.

————. *Hemingway on War*. Ed. and with an introduction by Sean Hemingway. With a foreword by Patrick Hemingway. New York: Scribner's, 2003.

————. *in our time*. Paris: Three Mountains, 1924.

————. *In Our Time*. Rev. ed. New York: Scribner's, 1930.

————. "An Interview with Ernest Hemingway." By George Plimpton. *Paris Review*, Spring 1958. Reprinted in *Ernest Hemingway: Five Decades of Criticism*, ed. Linda Welshimer Wagner, 21–38. East Lansing: Michigan State University Press, 1974.

————. Introduction to *A Farewell to Arms*, 1948 ed., vii–x. New York: Scribner's, 1948.

————. Introduction to *In Sicily*, by Elio Vittorini, n.p. Trans. Wilfrid David. New York: New Directions, 1949.

————. Introduction to *Studio: Europe*, by John Groth, n.p. New York: Vanguard, 1945.

————. *Islands in the Stream*. New York: Scribner's, 1970.

————. "A Key West Girl." In *Key West Hemingway: A Reassessment*, ed. Kirk Curnutt and Gail D. Sinclair, 25–26. Gainesville: University Press of Florida, 2009.

————. "A Letter from Ernest Hemingway" [to Earl Wilson]. *New York Post*, August 31, 1952, 121-22.

————. *The Letters of Ernest Hemingway*. Vol. 1, *1907–1922*. Ed. Sandra Spanier and Robert W. Trogdon. New York: Cambridge University Press, 2011.

————. *The Letters of Ernest Hemingway*. Vol. 2, *1923–1925*. Ed. Sandra Spanier, Albert J. DeFazio III, and Robert W. Trogdon. New York: Cambridge University Press, 2013.

————. *The Letters of Ernest Hemingway*. Vol. 3, *1926–1929*. Ed. Rena Sanderson, Sandra Spanier, and Robert W. Trogdon. New York: Cambridge University Press, 2015.

————, ed. *Men at War*. New York: Crown, 1942.

————. *Men Without Women*. New York: Scribner's, 1928.

————. *A Moveable Feast*. New York: Scribner's, 1964.

———. *A Moveable Feast*. Restored ed. Ed. Sean Hemingway. With a foreword by Patrick Hemingway. New York: Scribner's, 2009.

———. "Nobel Prize in Literature Acceptance Speech." http://www.nobelprize.org/nobel_prizes/literature/laureates/1954/hemingway-speech.html.

———. *The Old Man and the Sea*. New York: Scribner's, 1952.

———. "On the American Dead in Spain." *New Masses*, February 14, 1939, 3.

———. "On Cathedrals." Item 630, Hemingway Collection, John F. Kennedy Presidential Library and Museum, Boston, MA.

———. Preface to *A Hemingway Check List*, by Lee Samuels. New York: Scribner's, 1951.

———. Preface to *All the Brave, Paintings by Luis Quintanilla*, ed. Elliot Paul and Jay Allen, 7–11. New York: Modern Age Books, 1939.

———. Preface to *The First Forty-Nine [Stories]*. In *The Complete Short Stories of Ernest Hemingway*. New York: Scribner's, 1987.

———. Preface to *The Great Crusade*, by Gustav Regler, vii–xi. New York: Longmans, Green, 1940.

———. Preface to *Salt Water Fishing*, by Van Campen Heilner, vii–viii. New York: Knopf, 1953.

———. Publisher's note to *"The Fifth Column" and the First Forty-nine Stories*. New York: Scribner's, 1938: v–vi.

———. *The Spanish Earth*. Cleveland, OH: J. B. Savage, 1938.

———, narr. *The Spanish Earth*. Dir. Joris Ivens. Photo. John Ferno. Music arrang. Marc Blitzstein and Virgil Thomson. Contemporary Historians, 1937. Film.

———. "Success, It's Wonderful!" Interview by Harvey Breit. *New York Times Book Review*, December 3, 1950, 58.

———. *The Sun Also Rises*. New York: Scribner's, 1926.

———. "Talk with Mr. Hemingway." Interview by Harvey Breit. *New York Times Book Review*, September 17, 1950, 14.

———. *Three Stories and Ten Poems*. Paris: Contact, 1923.

———. *To Have and Have Not*. New York: Scribner's, 1937.

———. *The Torrents of Spring*. New York: Scribner's, 1926.

———. *Under Kilimanjaro*. Ed. Robert W. Lewis and Robert E. Fleming. Kent, OH: Kent State University Press, 2005.

——— "Who Murdered the Vets?" *New Masses*, September 17, 1935, 9–10.

———. *Winner Take Nothing*. New York: Scribner's, 1933.

———. "The Writer and War." In *The Writer in a Changing World*, ed. Henry Hart, 69–73. New York: Equinox Cooperative Press, 1937.

Secondary

Aldridge, John W. "Afterthoughts on the Twenties and *The Sun Also Rises*." In *New Essays on "The Sun Also Rises,"* ed. Linda Wagner-Martin, 109–29. New York: Cambridge University Press, 1987.

American Psychiatric Association. *Diagnostic and Statistical Manual of Mental Disorders*. 4th ed. Washington, DC: American Psychiatric Association, 2000.

Ammary, Silvia. *The Influence of the European Culture on Hemingway's Fiction*. Lanham, MD: Lexington, 2015.

Anderson, Margaret. *My Thirty Years' War*. Westport, CT: Greenwood, 1929.

Anderson, Sarah Wood. *Readings of Trauma, Madness, and the Body*. New York: Palgrave Macmillan, 2012.

Baer, Ulrich. "Modernism and Trauma." In *Modernism*, ed. Astradur Eysteinsson and Vivian Liska, 1:307–18. Amsterdam: John Benjamins, 2007.

Baker, Carlos. "The Boy and the Lions." In *Ernest Hemingway: Five Decades of Criticism*, ed. Linda Welshimer Wagner, 306–19. East Lansing: Michigan State University Press, 1974.

———. *Ernest Hemingway: A Life Story*. New York: Scribner's, 1969.

———, ed. *Hemingway and His Critics*. New York: Hill & Wang, 1961.

———. *Hemingway: The Writer as Artist*. 1952. Reprint, Princeton, NJ: Princeton University Press, 1972.

Barlow, Samuel L. M., Jr. "Ave Dione, A Tribute." Lake Collection. Harry Ransom Humanities Research Center, University of Texas at Austin.

Barnes, Julian. "Homage to Hemingway." *New Yorker*, July 4, 2011, 60–66.

Beach, Joseph Warren. "How Do You Like It Now, Gentlemen?" In *Hemingway and His Critics*, ed. Carlos Baker, 227–44. New York: Hill & Wang, 1961.

Beach, Sylvia. Borrowing records for Ernest Hemingway, 1925–1929, from Shakespeare and Company. Sylvia Beach Papers, Firestone Library, Princeton University.

———. Borrowing records for Gertrude Stein, 1920, from Shakespeare and Company. Sylvia Beach Papers, Firestone Library, Princeton University.

Beegel, Susan F. "The Environment." In *Ernest Hemingway in Context*, ed. Debra A. Moddelmog and Suzanne del Gizzo, 237–46. New York: Cambridge University Press, 2013.

———. "Hemingway and Hemochromatosis." In *Ernest Hemingway: Seven Decades of Criticism*, ed. Linda Wagner-Martin, 375–88. East Lansing: Michigan State University Press, 1998.

———. "The Monster of Cojimar: A Meditation on Hemingway, Sharks, and War." *The Hemingway Review* 34, no. 2 (2015): 9–35.

———. "Thor Heyerdahl's *Kon-Tiki* and Hemingway's Return to Primitivism in *The Old Man and the Sea*." In *Hemingway: Eight Decades of Criticism*, ed. Linda Wagner-Martin, 513–52. East Lansing: Michigan State University Press, 2009.

Benson, Jackson J. *Hemingway: The Writer's Art of Self-Defense*. Minneapolis: University of Minnesota Press, 1969.

Benstock, Shari. *Women of the Left Bank: Paris, 1900–1940*. Austin: University of Texas Press, 1986.

Bergson, Henri. *Introduction to Metaphysics*. Trans. T. E. Hulme. 1912. Reprint, Indianapolis, IN: Liberal Arts Press, 1955.

———. *Mind-Energy: Lectures and Essays*. Trans. H. Wildon Carr. New York: Henry Holt, 1920.

Bishop, John Peale. *The Collected Essays of John Peale Bishop*. New York: Scribner's, 1948.

Blume, Lesley M. M. *Everybody Behaves Badly: The True Story behind Hemingway's Masterpiece*. New York: Eamon Dolan/Houghton Mifflin Harcourt, 2016.

Boelhower, William. "Hemingway, the Figure of the Bicycle, and the Avant-Garde Paris." *The Hemingway Review* 34, no. 2 (2015): 52–71.

Boker, Pamela. *The Grief Taboo in American Literature: Loss and Prolonged Adolescence in Twain, Melville, and Hemingway*. New York: New York University Press, 1996.

Boreth, Craig. *The Hemingway Cookbook*. Chicago: Chicago Review Press, 1998.

Bouchard, Donald F. *Hemingway, So Far from Simple*. Amherst, NY: Prometheus, 2010.

Bradbury, Ray. "The Kilimanjaro Machine." *Life*, January 22, 1965, 71–72, 74–76, 79.

Brasch, James D., and Joseph T. Sigman. *Hemingway's Library: A Composite Record*. New York: Garland, 1981.

Breit, Harvey. *The Writer Observed*. New York: Collier, 1961.

Brenner, Gerry. *Concealments in Hemingway's Works*. Columbus: Ohio State University Press, 1983.

Brian, Denis. *The True Gen: An Intimate Portrait of Ernest Hemingway by Those Who Knew Him*. New York: Grove Press, 1988.

Broer, Lawrence R. "Bulls and Bells: Their Toll on Robert Jordan." In *Hemingway's Spain: Imagining the Spanish World*, ed. Carl P. Eby and Mark Cirino, 192–213. Kent, OH: Kent State University Press, 2016.

———. *Hemingway's Spanish Tragedy*. Tuscaloosa: University of Alabama Press, 1973.

Brumback, Theodore. "With Hemingway before *A Farewell to Arms*." *Kansas City Star*, December 6, 1936, 1C, 2C. Reprinted in *Ernest Hemingway, Cub Reporter*, ed. Matthew J. Bruccoli, 3–11. Pittsburgh, PA: University of Pittsburgh Press, 1970.

Burwell, Rose Marie. *Hemingway: The Postwar Years and the Posthumous Novels*. New York: Cambridge University Press, 1996.

Carpenter, F. I. "Hemingway Achieves the Fifth Dimension." In *Ernest Hemingway: Five Decades of Criticism*, ed. Linda Welshimer Wagner, 279–87. East Lansing: Michigan State University Press, 1974.

Caruth, Cathy. *Unclaimed Experience: Trauma, Narrative, and History*. Baltimore, MD: Johns Hopkins University Press, 1996.

Castillo-Puche, Jose Luis. *Hemingway in Spain*. Trans. Helen R. Lane. Garden City, NY: Doubleday, 1974.

Caswell, Claude. "City of Brothelly Love: The Influence of Paris and Prostitution on Hemingway's Fiction." In *French Connections: Hemingway and Fitzgerald Abroad*, ed. J. Gerald Kennedy and Jackson R. Bryer, 75–100. New York: St. Martin's Press, 1998.

Chamberlin, Brewster S. *The Hemingway Log: A Chronology of His Life and Times*. Lawrence: University Press of Kansas, 2015.

Cirino, Mark. *Ernest Hemingway: Thought in Action*. Madison: University of Wisconsin Press, 2012.

———. "The Nasty Mess: Hemingway, Italian Fascism, and the *New Review* Controversy of 1932." *The Hemingway Review* 33, no. 2 (2014): 30–47.

———. *Reading Hemingway's "Across the River and Into the Trees."* Kent, OH: Kent State University Press, 2016.

———. "That Supreme Moment of Complete Knowledge: Hemingway's Theory of the Vision of the Dying." In *War + Ink: New Perspectives on Ernest Hemingway's Early Life and Writings*, ed. Steve Paul, Gail Sinclair, and Steven Trout, 242–59. Kent, OH: Kent State University Press, 2014.

Clark, Miriam Marty. "Hemingway's Early Illness Narratives and the Lyric Dimensions of 'Now I Lay Me.'" In *Hemingway: Eight Decades of Criticism*, ed. Linda Wagner-Martin, 3–18. East Lansing: Michigan State University Press, 2009.

Cohen, Milton A. *Hemingway's Laboratory, The Paris "in our time."* Tuscaloosa: University of Alabama Press, 2005.

Coleman, Charles A., Jr. *PTSD and Hemingway's "A Way You'll Never Be": The Mark of Confidence*. Chapel Hill, NC: PTSD Press, 2014.

Comley, Nancy R., and Robert Scholes. *Hemingway's Genders: Rereading the Hemingway Text*. New Haven, CT: Yale University Press, 1994.

Cooper, Stephen. *The Politics of Ernest Hemingway*. Ann Arbor, MI: UMI Research Press, 1987.

Cooperman, Stanley. "Old Age Ideally Brings Humility and True Pride to Man." In *Death in Ernest Hemingway's "The Old Man and the Sea,"* ed. Dedria Bryfonski, 75–84. Farmington Hills, MI: Greenhaven Press, 2014.

———. *World War I and the American Novel*. Baltimore, MD: Johns Hopkins University Press, 1967.

Cote, William E. "Correspondent or Warrior? Hemingway's Murky World War II 'Combat' Experience." *The Hemingway Review* 22, no. 1 (2002): 88–104.

Cowley, Malcolm. "Nightmare and Ritual in Hemingway." In *Hemingway: A Collection of Critical Essays*, ed. Robert P. Weeks, 40–51. Englewood Cliffs, NJ: Prentice-Hall, 1962.

Curnutt, Kirk. *Ernest Hemingway and the Expatriate Modernist Movement*. Vol. 2. Farmington Hills, MI: Gale, 2000.

Daiker, Donald A. "What to Make of Hemingway's 'Summer People'?" *The Hemingway Review* 34, no. 2 (2015): 36–51.

Daniel, Alix Du Poy. "The Stimulating Life with Gertrude & Co." *Lost Generation Journal* 6 (Summer 1979): 16–18.

DeFazio, Albert J., III, ed. *Dear Papa, Dear Hotch: The Correspondence of Ernest Hemingway and A. E. Hotchner*. Columbia: University of Missouri Press, 2005.

Deibler, William E. "Date-Line: D-Day: Ernest Hemingway Reported on Ernest Hemingway, Martha Gellhorn Reported on the War, Both Were Searching for the Truth." *North Dakota Quarterly* 68, nos. 2/3 (2001): 295–302.

del Gizzo, Suzanne. "Going Home: Hemingway, Primitivism, and Identity." In *Hemingway: Eight Decades of Criticism*, ed. Linda Wagner-Martin, 479–512. East Lansing: Michigan State University Press, 2009.

———, and Frederic J. Svoboda, eds. *Hemingway's "The Garden of Eden": Twenty-Five Years of Criticism.* Kent, OH: Kent State University Press, 2012.

Dimbleby, Jonathan. *The Battle of the Atlantic.* New York: Oxford University Press, 2016.

Djos, Matts. "Alcoholism in Ernest Hemingway's *The Sun Also Rises*: A Wine and Roses Perspective on the Lost Generation." In *Ernest Hemingway's "The Sun Also Rises": A Casebook,* ed. Linda Wagner-Martin, 139–53. New York: Oxford University Press, 2002.

Dodman, Trevor. "'Going All to Pieces': *A Farewell to Arms* as Trauma Narrative." In *War in Ernest Hemingway's "A Farewell to Arms,"* ed. David Haugen and Susan Musser, 94–125. Farmington Hills, MI: Greenhaven Press, 2014.

Donaldson, Scott. *By Force of Will: The Life and Art of Ernest Hemingway.* New York: Viking, 1977.

———. *Fitzgerald & Hemingway: Works and Days.* New York: Columbia University Press, 2009.

———. "Hemingway of *The Star.*" In *Ernest Hemingway: The Papers of a Writer,* ed. Bernard Oldsey, 89–107. New York: Garland, 1981.

———. "Humor in *The Sun Also Rises.*" In *New Essays on "The Sun Also Rises,"* ed. Linda Wagner-Martin, 19–42. New York: Cambridge University Press, 1987.

Donnell, David. *Hemingway in Toronto, A Post-modern Tribute.* Windsor, ON: Black Moss Press, 1982.

Dos Passos, John. *The Best Times: An Informal Memoir.* New York: New American Library, 1966.

Dow, William. "*A Farewell to Arms* and Hemingway's Protest Stance: To Tell the Truth without Screaming." In *War in Ernest Hemingway's "A Farewell to Arms,"* ed. David Haugen and Susan Musser, 49–68. Farmington Hills, MI: Greenhaven Press, 2014.

Drew, Fraser. "April 8, 1955 Conversation with Hemingway: Unedited Notes on a Visit to Finca Vigia." *Fitzgerald-Hemingway Annual* (1970): 113.

Dudley, Marc. *Hemingway, Race, and Art: Bloodlines and the Color Line.* Kent, OH: Kent State University Press, 2012.

Eby, Carl P. *Hemingway's Fetishism: Psychoanalysis and the Mirror of Manhood.* Albany: State University of New York Press, 1999.

Elkins, Marilyn. "The Fashion of Machismo." In *A Historical Guide to Ernest Hemingway,* ed. Linda Wagner-Martin, 93–115. New York: Oxford University Press, 2000.

Ellis, Havelock. *The Dance of Life.* Boston: Houghton Mifflin, 1923.

Evans, Oliver. "'The Snows of Kilimanjaro': A Revaluation." In *Hemingway's African Stories: The Stories, Their Sources, Their Critics,* ed. John M. Howell, 150–57. New York: Scribner's, 1969.

Farah, Andrew. *Hemingway's Brain.* Columbia: University of South Carolina Press, 2017.

Fassler, Joe. "'Why Novel-Writing Is Like Spelunking': An Interview with Chang-rae Lee." *Atlantic,* July 11, 2011.

Faulkner, William. "Review of *The Old Man and the Sea*." In *Ernest Hemingway: Six Decades of Criticism*, ed. Linda W. Wagner. East Lansing: Michigan State University Press, 1987.

Federspiel, Michael R. *Picturing Hemingway's Michigan*. Detroit, MI: Wayne State University Press, 2010.

Fenstermaker, John J. "Ernest Hemingway, 1917–1918: First Work, First War." In *War + Ink: New Perspectives on Ernest Hemingway's Early Life and Writings*, ed. Steve Paul, Gail Sinclair, and Steven Trout, 14–35. Kent, OH: Kent State University Press, 2014.

Fenton, Charles A. *The Apprenticeship of Ernest Hemingway: The Early Years*. New York: Viking, 1962.

Fleming, Robert E. "Politics." In *Ernest Hemingway in Context*, ed. Debra A. Moddelmog and Suzanne del Gizzo, 287–96. New York: Cambridge University Press, 2013.

Flora, Joseph. *Reading Hemingway's "Men Without Women."* Kent, OH: Kent State University Press, 2008.

Florezyk, Steven. *Hemingway, the Red Cross, and the Great War*. Kent, OH: Kent State University Press, 2014.

Ford, Ford Madox. Introduction to *A Farewell to Arms*, by Ernest Hemingway. New York: Modern Library, 1932.

Frank, Arthur. *The Wounded Storyteller*. Chicago: University of Chicago Press, 1995.

Frederking, Laurette Conklin, ed. *Hemingway in Politics and Rebellion*. New York: Routledge, 2010.

Fuller, Robert. "Hemingway at Rambouillet." *The Hemingway Review* 33, no. 2 (2014): 66–80.

Fussell, Paul. *The Great War and Modern Memory*. New York: Oxford University Press, 1975.

Gajdusek, Robert E. *Hemingway in His Own Country*. Notre Dame, IN: University of Notre Dame Press, 2002.

Gellhorn, Martha. *Travels with Myself and Another*. London: Allen Lane, 1978.

Gladstein, Mimi Riesel. *The Indestructible Woman in Faulkner, Hemingway, and Steinbeck*. Ann Arbor, MI: UMI Research Press, 1986.

———. "Mr. Novelist Goes to War: Hemingway and Steinbeck as Front-Line Correspondents." *War, Literature, and the Arts* 15, nos. 1/2 (2003): 258–66.

Glass, Loren. *Authors, Inc.: Literary Celebrity in the Modern United States, 1880–1980*. Albany: New York University Press, 2004.

Gould, Thomas. "'Anti-War Correspondence,' Reshaping Death in *For Whom the Bell Tolls*." In *Hemingway: Up in Michigan Perspectives*, ed. Frederic J. Svoboda and Joseph J. Waldmeir, 241–48. East Lansing: Michigan State University Press, 1995.

Griffin, Peter. *Along with Youth: Hemingway, the Early Years*. New York: Oxford University Press, 1985.

———. *Less than a Treason: Hemingway in Paris*. New York: Oxford University Press, 1990.

Grimes, Larry. "Hemingway's Religious Odyssey: The Afro-Cuban Connection in Two Stories and *The Old Man and the Sea*." In *Hemingway, Cuba, and the Cuban Works*, ed. Larry Grimes and Bickford Sylvester, 150–64. Kent, OH: Kent State University Press, 2014.

———. Introduction to "The State of Things in Cuba: A Letter to Hemingway," by Richard Armstrong. In *Hemingway, Cuba, and the Cuban Works*, ed. Larry Grimes and Bickford Sylvester, 75–83. Kent, OH: Kent State University Press, 2014.

Groth, John. *Studio: Europe*. New York: Vanguard, 1945.

Guill, Stacey. "The Interpretation of a New Warscape in *The Spanish Earth*, Picasso's *Guernica*, and Hemingway's *For Whom the Bell Tolls*." *Hemingway Review* 34, no. 1 (2014): 13–29.

———. "War: Spanish Civil War." In *Ernest Hemingway in Context*, ed. Debra A. Moddelmog and Suzanne del Gizzo, 395–401. New York: Cambridge University Press, 2013.

Hart, Jeffrey. *The Living Moment: Modernism in a Broken World*. Evanston, IL: Northeastern University Press, 2012.

Hartley, Marsden. *Adventures in the Arts*. New York: Boni & Liveright, 1921.

Hawkins, Ruth A. *Unbelievable Happiness and Final Sorrow: The Hemingway-Pfeiffer Marriage*. Fayetteville: University of Arkansas Press, 2012.

Hays, Peter L. "Ailments, Accidents, and Suicide." In *Ernest Hemingway in Context*, ed. Debra A. Moddelmog and Suzanne del Gizzo, 207–16. New York: Cambridge University Press, 2013.

———. "Hemingway as Social and Political Writer." *The Hemingway Review* 34, no. 2 (2015): 111–17.

———. "Hemingway, PTSD, and Clinical Depression." In *Teaching Hemingway and War*, ed. Alex Vernon, 133–42. Kent, OH: Kent State University Press, 2016.

Haytock, Jennifer. *At Home, at War*. Columbus: Ohio State University Press, 2003.

Hemingway, Carol. "907 Whitehead Street." *The Hemingway Review* 23, no. 1 (2003): 8–23.

Hemingway, Gregory H. *Papa: A Personal Memoir*. Boston: Houghton, 1976.

Hemingway, Hilary. *Hemingway in Cuba*. New York: Rugged Land, 2003.

Hemingway, Leicester. *My Brother, Ernest Hemingway*. Sarasota, FL: Pineapple Press, 1996.

Hemingway, Mary Welsh. *How It Was*. New York: Knopf, 1976.

Hemingway, Patrick. Foreword to *Hemingway on War*, by Ernest Hemingway, xi–xv. New York: Scribner's, 2003.

———. "Remarks." Key West Literary Festival Conference on Hemingway, January 1984.

Hemingway, Sean. Introduction to *A Farewell to Arms* (Hemingway Library Edition), by Ernest Hemingway, xiii–xix. New York: Scribner's, 2012.

———. Introduction to *Hemingway on War*, by Ernest Hemingway. New York: Scribner, 2003.

Hemingway, Valerie. "At Hemingway's Table: Food for the Five Senses." *The Hemingway Review* 33, no. 1 (2013): 93–99.

————. "Hemingway's Cuba, Cuba's Hemingway." *Smithsonian*, August 2007, 66–76.

————. *Running with the Bulls: My Years with the Hemingways.* New York: Ballantine, 2004.

Hendrickson, Paul. *Hemingway's Boat: Everything He Loved in Life, and Lost, 1934–1961.* New York: Knopf, 2011.

Herlihy, Jeffrey. *In Paris or Paname: Hemingway's Expatriate Nationalism.* Costerus 191. Amsterdam: Rodopi, 2012.

Herman, Judith. "Complex PTSD: A Syndrome in Survivors of Prolonged and Repeated Trauma." *Journal of Traumatic Stress* 5, no. 3 (1992): 377–91.

————. *Trauma and Recovery: The Aftermath of Violence—from Domestic Abuse to Political Terror.* New York: Basic, 1997.

Herndl, Diane Price. "Invalid Masculinity: Silence, Hospitals, and Anesthesia in *A Farewell to Arms.*" In *Hemingway: Eight Decades of Criticism*, ed. Linda Wagner-Martin, 19–35. East Lansing: Michigan State University Press, 2009.

Hinkle, James. "What's Funny in *The Sun Also Rises.*" In *Ernest Hemingway's "The Sun Also Rises,"* ed. Harold Bloom, 133–49. New York: Chelsea House, 1987.

Hoffman, Frederick J. *The Twenties.* Exp. ed. New York: Free Press, 1965.

Hotchner, A. E. *Hemingway in Love: His Own Story: A Memoir.* New York: St. Martin's Press, 2015.

Hutchisson, James M. *Ernest Hemingway: A New Life.* State College: Pennsylvania State University Press, 2016.

Irmscher, Christoph. "Naked Hemingway." *Lilly Library News & Notes*, February 8, 2016.

Ivancich, Giacomo. "Address to the Hemingway Society Congress—June 22, 2014." In *Hemingway and Italy: Twenty-First Century Perspectives*, ed. Mark Cirino and Mark P. Ott, 13–30 (manuscript version). Gainesville: University Press of Florida, 2017.

James, William. *A Pluralistic Universe: Writings 1902–1910.* New York: Library of America, 1987.

Jamison, Kay Redfield. *Touched with Fire: Manic-Depressive Illness and the Artistic Temperament.* New York: Free Press, 1994.

Josephs, Allen. *"For Whom the Bell Tolls": Ernest Hemingway's Undiscovered Country.* New York: Twayne, 1994.

————. "Hemingway's Out of Body Experience." *The Hemingway Review* 2, no. 2 (1983): 11–17.

Justice, Hilary K. *The Bones of the Others: The Hemingway Text from the Lost Manuscripts to the Posthumous Novels.* Kent, OH: Kent State University Press, 2006.

Kale, Verna. *Ernest Hemingway: A Critical Life.* London: Reaktion Books, 2016.

Kashkeen, Ivan. "Alive in the Midst of Death: Ernest Hemingway." In *Hemingway and His Critics*, ed. Carlos Baker, 162–79. New York: Hill & Wang, 1961.

Kert, Bernice. *The Hemingway Women.* New York: Norton, 1983.

Killinger, John. *Hemingway and the Dead Gods.* Lexington: University of Kentucky Press, 1960.

Kinnamon, Keneth. "Hemingway and Politics." In *The Cambridge Companion to Hemingway*, ed. Scott Donaldson, 149–69. New York: Cambridge University Press, 1996.

Knodt, Ellen Andrews. "Toward a Better Understanding of Nicholas Adams in Hemingway's 'A Way You'll Never Be.'" *The Hemingway Review* 35, no. 2 (2016): 70–86.

Lamb, Robert Paul. *Art Matters: Hemingway, Craft and the Creation of the Modern Short Story*. Baton Rouge: Louisiana State University Press, 2010.

Larson, Kelli A. *Ernest Hemingway: A Reference Guide, 1974–1989*. Boston: Hall, 1991. See also each issue of *The Hemingway Review* for ongoing bibliographies.

Leed, Eric J. *No Man's Land: Combat and Identity in World War I*. New York: Cambridge University Press, 1979.

Leff, Leonard J. *Hemingway and His Conspirators: Hollywood, Scribners, and the Making of American Celebrity Culture*. Lanham, MD: Rowman & Littlefield, 1997.

Lewis, Robert W. *Hemingway on Love*. New York: Haskell House, 1973.

Long, Adam R. "Artifice and Reality: The Blending of Venice and America in *Across the River and Into the Trees*." In *Hemingway and Italy: Twenty-First Century Perspectives*, ed. Mark Cirino and Mark P. Ott, 178–94 (manuscript version). Gainesville: University Press of Florida, 2017.

Macdonald, Dwight. "Hemingway's Baby Talk." In *Readings on "A Farewell to Arms,"* ed. Gary Wiener, 142–46. San Diego, CA: Greenhaven Press, 2000.

MacLeish, Archibald. *Published and Perished*. Boston: David R. Godine, 2002.

Mandel, Miriam B., and Jeremiah M. Kitunda. "Hemingway's Reading in Natural History, Hunting, Fishing, and Africa." In *Hemingway and Africa*, ed. Miriam B. Mandel, 41–84. Rochester, NY: Camden House, 2011.

Martin, Robert A. "Hemingway and the Ambulance Drivers in *A Farewell to Arms*." In *Ernest Hemingway: Six Decades of Criticism*, ed. Linda W. Wagner, 195–204. East Lansing: Michigan State University Press, 1987.

Marx, Leo. *The Machine in the Garden: Technology and the Pastoral Ideal in America*. New York: Oxford University Press, 1964.

Mazzeno, Laurence W. *The Critics and Hemingway, 1924–2014*. Rochester, NY: Camden House, 2016.

McFarland, Ronald E. *Appropriating Hemingway*. Jefferson, NC: McFarland, 2015.

Melling, Philip. "Cultural Imperialism, Afro-Cuban Religion, and Santiago's Failure in *The Old Man and the Sea*." *The Hemingway Review* 26, no. 1 (2006): 6–24.

Mellow, James R. *Hemingway: A Life without Consequences*. Boston: Houghton Mifflin, 1992.

Meredith, James H. "Hemingway's Key West Band of Brothers, the World War I Veterans in 'Who Murdered the Vets?' and *To Have and Have Not*." In *Key West Hemingway: A Reassessment*, ed. Kirk Curnutt and Gail D. Sinclair, 241–66. Gainesville: University Press of Florida, 2009.

———. "Hemingway's Spain in Flames, 1937." In *Hemingway's Spain: Imagining the Spanish World*, ed. Carl P. Eby and Mark Cirino, 146–51. Kent, OH: Kent State University Press, 2016.

————. *Understanding the Literature of World War I*. Westport, CT: Greenwood Press, 2004.

————. *Understanding the Literature of World War II*. Westport, CT: Greenwood Press, 1999.

————. "War: World War II." In *Ernest Hemingway in Context*, ed. Debra A. Moddelmog and Suzanne del Gizzo, 402–08. New York: Cambridge University Press, 2013.

Meyers, Jeffrey. *Hemingway: A Biography*. New York: Harper, 1985.

Miller, Alice. *The Drama of the Gifted Child*. Trans. Ruth Ward. New York: Basic Books, 1981.

————. *For Your Own Good*. Trans. Hildegarde Hannum and Hunter Hannum. New York: Farrar Straus, 1983.

Miller, Madelaine Hemingway. *Ernie: Hemingway's Sister "Sunny" Remembers*. New York: Crown, 1975.

Moddelmog, Debra A. "Queer Families in Hemingway's Fiction." In *Hemingway and Women: Female Critics and the Female Voice*, ed. Lawrence R. Broer and Gloria Holland, 173–89. Tuscaloosa: University of Alabama Press, 2002.

————. *Reading Desire: In Pursuit of Ernest Hemingway*. Ithaca, NY: Cornell University Press, 1999.

Molesworth, Charles. "Hemingway's Code: The Spanish Civil War and the World Power." In *Blowing the Bridge: Essays on Hemingway and "For Whom the Bell Tolls,"* ed. Rena Sanderson, 83–97. Westport, CT: Greenwood Press, 1992.

Monnier, Adrienne. *The Very Rich Hours of Adrienne Monnier*. Trans. Richard McDougall. New York: Scribner's, 1976.

Montgomery, Constance Cappel. *Hemingway in Michigan*. New York: Fleet, 1966.

Montgomery, Marion. "The Leopard and the Hyena: Symbol and Meaning in 'The Snows of Kilimanjaro.'" In *Hemingway's African Stories: The Stories, Their Sources, Their Critics*, ed. John M. Howell, 145–49. New York: Scribner's, 1969.

Moorehead, Caroline. *Gellhorn: A Twentieth-Century Life*. New York: Holt, 2003.

Moreira, Peter. *Hemingway on the China Front: His WWII Spy Mission with Martha Gellhorn*. Washington, DC: Potomac, 2006.

Moreland, Kim. "Bringing 'Italianicity' Home, Hemingway Returns to Oak Park." In *Hemingway's Italy: New Perspectives*, ed. Rena Sanderson, 51–61. Baton Rouge: Louisiana State University Press, 2006.

————. "Death by Drowning: Trauma Theory and *Islands in the Stream*." In *Hemingway, Cuba, and the Cuban Works*, ed. Larry Grimes and Bickford Sylvester, 213–28. Kent, OH: Kent State University Press, 2014.

————. "Hemingway and Women at the Front." In *War + Ink: New Perspectives on Ernest Hemingway's Early Life and Writings*, ed. Steve Paul, Gail Sinclair, Steven Trout, 286–323. Kent, OH: Kent State University Press, 2014.

Morrison, Toni. *Playing in the Dark: Whiteness and the Literary Imagination*. New York: Random House, 1992.

Mort, Terry. *Hemingway at War*. New York: Pegasus, 2016.

———. *The Hemingway Patrols*. New York: Scribner's, 2009.

Nickel, Matthew C. "Across the Canal and into Kansas City: Hemingway's West-ward Composition of Absolution in *Across the River and into the Trees*." In *War + Ink: New Perspectives on Ernest Hemingway's Early Life and Writings*, ed. Steve Paul, Gail Sinclair, Steven Trout, 324–49. Kent, OH: Kent State University Press, 2014.

———. *Hemingway's Dark Night: Catholic Influences and Intertextualities in the Work of Ernest Hemingway*. Wickford, RI: New Street Communications, 2013.

———. "Religion." In *Ernest Hemingway in Context*, ed. Debra A. Moddelmog and Suzanne del Gizzo, 347–56. New York: Cambridge University Press, 2013.

O'Connor, John. "Before the Fame, There Was the Fishing." *New York Times*, October 4, 2015, 10.

O'Hara, John. "The Author's Name Is Hemingway." *New York Times Book Review*, September 10, 1950, 1, 30.

Oldsey, Bernard, ed. *Ernest Hemingway: The Papers of a Writer*. New York: Garland, 1981.

Oliver, Charles M. *Ernest Hemingway A to Z: The Essential Reference to His Life and Works*. New York: Facts on File, 1999. Print. Expanded as *Critical Companion to Ernest Hemingway*. New York: Facts on File, 2007.

Ott, Mark P. *A Sea of Change: Ernest Hemingway and the Gulf Stream, A Contextual Biography*. Kent, OH: Kent State University Press, 2008.

———. "Tanks, Butterflies, Realists, Idealists: Hemingway, Dos Passos, and the Imperfect Ending in Spain of 1937–1938." In *Hemingway's Spain: Imagining the Spanish World*, ed. Carl P. Eby and Mark Cirino, 152–61. Kent, OH: Kent State University Press, 2016.

Ouspensky, P. D. *Tertium Organum, The Third Canon of Thought, A Key to the Enigmas of the World*. Trans. Nicholas Bessaraboff and Claude Bragdon. New York: Knopf, 1944.

Parker, Dorothy. "Profiles: The Artist's Reward." *New Yorker*, November 30, 1929, 28.

Plath, James. "Barking at Death: Hemingway, Africa, and the Stages of Dying." In *Hemingway and Africa*, ed. Miriam B. Mandel and Jeremiah M. Kitunda, 299–319. Rochester, NY: Camden House, 2011.

Pound, Ezra. "Small Magazines." *The English Journal* 19, no. 9 (November 1930): 700.

Radeljkovic, Zvonimir. "Initial Europe: 1918 as a Shaping Element in Hemingway's Weltanschauung." In *Ernest Hemingway: The Papers of a Writer*, ed. Bernard Oldsey, 133–38. New York: Garland, 1981.

Raeburn, John. *Fame Became of Him: Hemingway as a Public Writer*. Bloomington: Indiana University Press, 1984.

Rebollo, Anthony E. "The Taxation of Ernest Hemingway." In *Hemingway: Eight Decades of Criticism*, ed. Linda Wagner-Martin, 411–36. East Lansing: Michigan State University Press, 2009.

Reynolds, Michael S. *Hemingway: The American Homecoming*. Cambridge: Blackwell, 1992.

———. *Hemingway: An Annotated Chronology*. Detroit, MI: Omnigraphics, 1991.

———. "Hemingway as American Icon." In *Picturing Hemingway: A Writer in His Time*, ed. Frederick Voss, 1–9. Washington, DC: Smithsonian National Portrait Gallery, 1999.

———. *Hemingway: The Final Years*. New York: Norton, 1999.

———. *Hemingway: The 1930s*. New York: Norton, 1997.

———. *Hemingway: The Paris Years*. New York: Norton, 1989.

———. *Hemingway's First War: The Making of "A Farewell to Arms."* Princeton, NJ: Princeton University Press, 1976.

———. *Hemingway's Reading, 1910–1940: An Inventory*. Princeton, NJ: Princeton University Press, 1981.

———. "The *Sun* in Its Time: Recovering the Historical Context." In *New Essays on "The Sun Also Rises,"* ed. Linda Wagner-Martin, 43–64. New York: Cambridge University Press, 1987.

———. "A Supplement to Hemingway's Reading: 1910–1940." *Studies in American Fiction* 14, no. 1 (Spring 1986): 99–108.

———. *The Young Hemingway*. New York: Blackwell, 1986.

Richter, David F. "'At Five in the Afternoon': Toward a Poetics of *Duende* in Bataille and Hemingway." In *Hemingway's Spain: Imagining the Spanish World*, ed. Carl P. Eby and Mark Cirino, 113–27. Kent, OH: Kent State University Press, 2016.

Rodman, Selden. "Ernest Hemingway." In *Tongues of Fallen Angels*, 51–61. Norfolk, CT: New Directions, 1974.

Rolfe, Edwin. *The Lincoln Battalion*. New York: Random House, 1939.

Ross, Lillian. "How Do You Like It Now, Gentlemen?" In *Hemingway: A Collection of Critical Essays*, ed. Robert P. Weeks, 17–39. Englewood Cliffs, NJ: Prentice-Hall, 1962.

Rovit, Earl. *Ernest Hemingway*. New York: Twayne, 1963.

Ruland, Richard, and Malcolm Bradbury. *From Puritanism to Postmodernism: A History of American Literature*. New York: Penguin, 1991.

Samuelson, Arnold. *With Hemingway: A Year in Key West and Cuba*. New York: Random House, 1984.

Sanford, Marcelline Hemingway. *At the Hemingways: With Fifty Years of Correspondence between Ernest and Marcelline Hemingway*. With a foreword by Michael S. Reynolds. Moscow: University of Idaho Press, 1999.

Scarry, Elaine. *The Body in Pain*. New York: Oxford University Press, 1985.

Schreiber, Evelyn Jaffe. *Race, Trauma, and Home in the Novels of Toni Morrison*. Baton Rouge: Louisiana State University Press, 2010.

Scribner, Charles, Jr. Foreword to *Ernest Hemingway, Dateline: Toronto, The Complete "Toronto Star" Dispatches, 1920–1924*, by Ernest Hemingway, ed. William White, xxv–xxvii. New York: Scribner's, 1985.

———. Preface to *The Complete Short Stories of Ernest Hemingway: The Finca Vigia Edition*, xv–xviii. New York: Scribner's, 1987.

Seals, Marc. "Trauma Theory and Hemingway's Lost Paris Manuscripts." In *Hemingway: Eight Decades of Criticism*, ed. Linda Wagner-Martin, 75–87. East Lansing: Michigan State University Press, 2009.

Seed, David. *Cinematic Fictions*. Liverpool: Liverpool University Press, 2009.

Seefeldt, Michael. "Reconsidering the Travesty of Himself." In *Hemingway: Up in Michigan Perspectives*, ed. Frederic J. Svoboda and Joseph J. Waldmeir, 249–64. East Lansing: Michigan State University Press, 1995.

Sindelar, Nancy W. *Influencing Hemingway*. Lanham, MD: Rowman & Littlefield, 2014.

Smith, Paul. "Love and Death in Hemingway's Spanish Novel." In *Hemingway: Up in Michigan Perspectives*, ed. Frederic J. Svoboda and Joseph J. Waldmeir, 213–20. East Lansing: Michigan State University Press, 1995.

———. *A Reader's Guide to the Short Stories of Ernest Hemingway*. Boston: Hall, 1989.

Smith, Ronald. "Nick Adams and Post-Traumatic Stress Disorder." *War, Literature, and the Arts* 9, no. 1 (Spring–Summer 1997): 39–48.

Spilka, Mark. "Abusive and Nonabusive Dying in Hemingway's Fiction." In *Eight Lessons in Love: A Domestic Violence Reader*, 210–22. Columbia: University of Missouri Press, 1997.

———. *Hemingway's Quarrel with Androgyny*. Lincoln: University of Nebraska Press, 1990.

Stein, Gertrude. *The Autobiography of Alice B. Toklas*. New York: Harcourt Brace, 1933.

———. Stein Archive. Undated manuscripts. Beinecke Rare Book & Manuscript Library, Yale University.

———, and Leon Solomons. "Normal Motor Automatism." *Harvard Psychological Review*, September 1896, 495–512.

Steiner, Wendy. "The Diversity of American Fiction." In *Columbia Literary History of the United States*, ed. Emory Elliott, 845–72. New York: Columbia University Press, 1988.

Stephens, Robert O. *Hemingway's Nonfiction: The Public Voice*. Chapel Hill: University of North Carolina Press, 1968.

Stoneback, H. R. "Hemingway's Happiest Summer—'The Wildest, Most Beautiful, Wonderful Time Ever Ever': or, The Liberation of France and Hemingway." *North Dakota Quarterly* 64, no. 3 (1997): 184–220.

———. "Pilgrimage Variations, Hemingway's Sacred Landscapes." In *Hemingway: Eight Decades of Criticism*, ed. Linda Wagner-Martin, 457–76. East Lansing: Michigan State University Press, 2009.

———. "'The Priest Did Not Answer': Hemingway, the Church, the Party, and *For Whom the Bell Tolls*." In *Blowing the Bridge: Essays on Hemingway and "For Whom the Bell Tolls,"* ed. Rena Sanderson, 99–112. Westport, CT: Greenwood Press, 1992.

———. "'You Know the Name Is No Accident': Hemingway and the Matter of Santiago." In *Hemingway, Cuba, and the Cuban Works*, ed. Larry Grimes and Bickford Sylvester, 165–80. Kent, OH: Kent State University Press, 2014.

Strong, Amy L. *Race and Identity in Hemingway's Fiction*. New York: Palgrave Macmillan, 2008.

Strychacz, Thomas. "Seeing through Fractures: *In Our Time, For Whom the Bell Tolls,* and Picasso's *Guernica.*" In *Teaching Hemingway and War*, ed. Alex Vernon, 77–91. Kent, OH: Kent State University Press, 2016.

Svoboda, Frederic J. "The Great Themes in Hemingway: Love, War, Wilderness and Loss." In *A Historical Guide to Ernest Hemingway*, ed. Linda Wagner-Martin, 155–72. New York: Oxford University Press, 2000.

———. *Hemingway and "The Sun Also Rises": The Crafting of a Style.* Lawrence: University Press of Kansas, 1983.

———. "Houses and Museums." In *Ernest Hemingway in Context*, ed. Debra A. Moddelmog and Suzanne del Gizzo, 130–40. New York: Cambridge University Press, 2013.

Sylvester, Bickford. "The Cuban Context of *The Old Man and the Sea.*" In *The Cambridge Companion to Hemingway*, ed. Scott Donaldson, 243–68. Cambridge: Cambridge University Press, 1996.

Tal, Kali. *Worlds of Hurt: Reading the Literatures of Trauma.* Cambridge: Cambridge University Press, 1996.

Teunissen, John J. "*For Whom the Bell Tolls* as Mythic Narrative." In *Ernest Hemingway: Six Decades of Criticism*, ed. Linda W. Wagner, 221–37. East Lansing: Michigan State University Press, 1987.

Trogdon, Robert W. "'I Am Constructing a Legend': Ernest Hemingway in Guy Hickok's *Brooklyn Daily Eagle* Articles." *Resources for American Literary Study* 37 (2014): 181–207.

———. *The Lousy Racket: Hemingway, Scribners, and the Business of Literature.* Kent, OH: Kent State University Press, 2007.

———, ed. *Ernest Hemingway: A Literary Reference.* New York: Carroll & Graf, 1999.

Trout, Steven. *On the Battlefield of Memory: The First World War and American Remembrance, 1919–1941.* Tuscaloosa: University of Alabama Press, 2010.

Underwood, Doug. *Chronicling Trauma: Journalists and Writers on Violence and Loss.* Urbana: University of Illinois Press, 2011.

Vaill, Amanda. *Hotel Florida: Truth, Love, and Death in the Spanish Civil War.* New York: Farrar Straus, 2014.

Vernon, Alex. "Afterthoughts on *The Rites of War* and *The Sun Also Rises* Inspired by *For Whom the Bell Tolls.*" *The Hemingway Review* 35, no. 1 (2015).

———. *Hemingway's Second War: Bearing Witness to the Spanish Civil War.* Iowa City: University of Iowa Press, 2011.

———. *Soldiers Once and Still: Ernest Hemingway, James Salter, and Tim O'Brien.* Iowa City: University of Iowa Press, 2004.

———. "War, Gender, and Ernest Hemingway." In *Hemingway: Eight Decades of Criticism*, ed. Linda Wagner-Martin, 91–114. East Lansing: Michigan State University Press, 2009.

———. "War: World War I." In *Ernest Hemingway in Context*, ed. Debra A. Moddelmog and Suzanne del Gizzo, 388–94. New York: Cambridge University Press, 2013.

————, ed. *Teaching Hemingway and War*. Kent, OH: Kent State University Press, 2016.

Vickroy, Laura. *Reading Trauma Narratives*. Charlottesville: University of Virginia Press, 2015.

Villard, Henry S., and James Nagel, eds. *Hemingway in Love and War: The Lost Diary of Agnes von Kurowsky, Her Letters, and Correspondence of Ernest Hemingway*. Boston: Northeastern University Press, 1989.

Vonnegut, Kurt. "Kurt Vonnegut on Ernest Hemingway." In *Blowing the Bridge: Essays on Hemingway and "For Whom the Bell Tolls,"* ed. Rena Sanderson, 19–25. Westport, CT: Greenwood Press, 1992.

Voss, Frederick, ed. *Picturing Hemingway: A Writer in His Time*. Washington, DC: Smithsonian National Portrait Gallery, 1999.

Wagner, Linda W., ed. *Ernest Hemingway: Five Decades of Criticism*. East Lansing: Michigan State University Press, 1974.

————, ed. *Ernest Hemingway: Six Decades of Criticism*. East Lansing: Michigan State University Press, 1987.

————. "'Proud and Friendly and Gently': Women in Hemingway's Early Fiction." In *Ernest Hemingway: The Papers of a Writer*, ed. Bernard Oldsey, 63–72. New York: Garland, 1981.

————. "Tension and Technique: The Years of Greatness." In *American Modern: Essays in Fiction and Poetry*, 5–17. Port Washington, NY: Kennikat, 1980.

Wagner-Martin, Linda. "At the Heart of *A Farewell to Arms*." In *Hemingway's Italy: New Perspectives*, ed. Rena Sanderson, 158–66. Baton Rouge: Louisiana State University Press, 2006.

————. *Ernest Hemingway: A Literary Life*. New York: Palgrave Macmillan. 2007.

————. *Ernest Hemingway's "A Farewell to Arms."* Westport, CT: Greenwood Press, 2003.

————, ed. *Ernest Hemingway's "The Sun Also Rises": A Casebook*. New York: Oxford University Press, 2002.

————. *"Favored Strangers": Gertrude Stein and Her Family*. New Brunswick, NJ: Rutgers University Press, 1995.

————, ed. *Hemingway: Eight Decades of Criticism*. East Lansing: Michigan State University Press, 2009.

————, ed. *Hemingway: Seven Decades of Criticism*. East Lansing: Michigan State University Press, 1998.

————. "'I Like You Less and Less': The Stein Subtext in *Death in the Afternoon*." In *A Companion to Hemingway's "Death in the Afternoon,"* ed. Miriam B. Mandel, 59–77. Suffolk: Camden, 2004.

————, ed. *New Essays on "The Sun Also Rises."* New York: Cambridge University Press, 1987.

————. "The Romance of Desire in Hemingway's Fiction." In *Hemingway and Women: Female Critics and the Female Voice*, ed. Lawrence R. Broer and Gloria Holland, 54–69. Tuscaloosa: University of Alabama Press, 2002.

———. "The Secrecies of the Public Hemingway." In *Hemingway: Up in Michigan Perspectives*, ed. Frederic J. Svoboda and Joseph J. Waldmeir, 149–57. East Lansing: Michigan State University Press, 1995.

Waldhorn, Arthur. *A Reader's Guide to Ernest Hemingway*. New York: Farrar, 1972.

Waldmeir, Joseph J. "*Confiteor Hominem*: Ernest Hemingway's Religion of Man." In *Ernest Hemingway: Five Decades of Criticism*, ed. Linda Welshimer Wagner, 144–52. East Lansing: Michigan State University Press, 1974.

Walton, William. "The Battle of Huertgen Forest." *Life*, January 1, 1945, 33.

Warren, Robert Penn. "Ernest Hemingway." In *Ernest Hemingway: Five Decades of Criticism*, ed. Linda Welshimer Wagner, 75–102. East Lansing: Michigan State University Press, 1974.

Watson, William Braasch. "Hemingway's Attacks on the Soviets and the Communists in *For Whom the Bell Tolls*." *North Dakota Quarterly* 60, no. 2 (1992): 103–18.

———. "The Other Paris Years of Ernest Hemingway: 1937–1938." In *French Connections: Hemingway and Fitzgerald Abroad*, ed. J. Gerald Kennedy and Jackson R. Bryer, 141–60. New York: St. Martin's, 1998.

Werlock, Abby H. P. "Women in the Garden: Hemingway's 'Summer People' and 'The Last Good Country.'" In *Ernest Hemingway: The Oak Park Legacy*, ed. James Nagel, 124–44. Tuscaloosa: University of Alabama Press, 1996.

West, Ray B., Jr. "The Biological Trap." In *Hemingway: A Collection of Critical Essays*, ed. Robert P. Weeks, 139–59. Englewood Cliffs, NJ: Prentice-Hall, 1962.

Westbrook, Max. "Grace under Pressure: Hemingway and the Summer of 1920." In *Ernest Hemingway: Six Decades of Criticism*, ed. Linda W. Wagner, 19–40. East Lansing: Michigan State University Press, 1987.

White, William. "Father and Son: Comments on Hemingway's Psychology." *Dalhousie Review* 31 (Winter 1952): 276–84.

Whiting, Charles. *Papa Goes to War: Ernest Hemingway in Europe, 1944–45*. Wiltshire, UK: Crowood, 1990.

Wilson, Edmund. "Mr. Hemingway's Dry-Points." *The Dial* 77, no. 4 (October 1924): 340–41.

Wyatt, David. *Hemingway, Style, and the Art of Emotion*. New York: Cambridge University Press, 2015.

Wylder, Delbert E. *Hemingway's Heroes*. Albuquerque: University of New Mexico Press, 1969.

Yalom, Irvin D., and Marilyn Yalom. "Ernest Hemingway—A Psychiatric View." *Archives of General Psychiatry* 24 (June 1971): 485–94.

Young, Philip. *Ernest Hemingway*. Minneapolis: University of Minnesota Pamphlets on American Writers, no. 1 (1959).

———. *Ernest Hemingway: A Reconsideration*. New York: Harcourt, Brace & World, 1966.

INDEX